Community on Land

New Social Formations

Series Editors:
Charles Lemert, Wesleyan University
Judith Stacey, University of Southern California

Ethnicity: Racism, Class, and Culture
by Steve Fenton

Public Sociology: From Social Facts to Literary Acts
by Ben Agger

Community on Land: Community, Ecology, and the Public Interest
by Janel M. Curry and Steven McGuire

Forthcoming

The Promise Keepers: Postmodern Encounters with Men on the Religious Right
by Judith Newton

Gay and Lesbian Movements in the United States: The Politics of Identity and Diversity
by Steven Epstein

"White People Are Nosey": Talking about Race
by Anne Rawls

Hours to Lose: The Shorter Work Week and the Future of Labor
by Jonathan Cutler

Global Restructuring
by Wilma Dunaway

Who Is Responsible for the Poor? Poverty and the Politics of Social Morality
by Shana Cohen

Community on Land

Community, Ecology, and the Public Interest

JANEL M. CURRY AND STEVEN MCGUIRE

ROWMAN & LITTLEFIELD PUBLISHERS, INC.
Lanham • Boulder • New York • Oxford

ROWMAN & LITTLEFIELD PUBLISHERS, INC.

Published in the United States of America
by Rowman & Littlefield Publishers, Inc.
An Imprint of the Rowman & Littlefield Publishing Group
4720 Boston Way, Lanham, Maryland 20706
www.rowmanlittlefield.com

12 Hid's Copse Road, Cumnor Hill, Oxford OX2 9JJ, England

British Library Cataloguing in Publication Information Available

Library of Congress Cataloging-in-Publication Data

Curry, Janel M., 1956–
    Community on land : community, ecology, and the public interest / Janel M. Curry
and Steven McGuire.
        p. cm. — (New social formations)
    Includes bibliographical references and index.
    ISBN 0-7425-0160-4 (alk. paper) — ISBN 0-7425-0161-2 (pbk. : alk. paper)
        1. Human ecology—Philosophy. 2. Restoration ecology. 3. Community. 4.
Environmental ethics. I. McGuire, Steven. II. Title. III. Series.

GF80 .C87 2002
304.2'8—dc21

                                                                    2002016366

Printed in the United States of America

♾™ The paper used in this publication meets the minimum requirements of American
National Standard for Information Sciences—Permanence of Paper for Printed Library
Materials, ANSI/NISO Z39.48-1992.

Dedicated to our daughters,
Margaret and Kate McGuire and Marie and Karis Roper,
in the hope that throughout their lifetimes they will experience the richness of
community and deep connection to the land.

What, then, is the answer? The only other answer to the tragedy of the commons is the comedy of community. One is almost tempted to call it the Divine Comedy of community. Without some sort of sacredness, the comedy easily becomes black and obscene and returns once more to tragedy.

Kenneth E. Boulding in *Managing the Commons*,
edited by Garret Hardin and John Baden

CONTENTS

WILL THERE BE LAND FOR COMMUNITY?

CHARLES LEMERT

ONE OF MEXICO'S MOST ANCIENT TOWNS, Cholula, outside Puebla, was founded by the Toltecs sometime around 1500 B.C.E. For thirty-five centuries people have organized their lives in this town around common grounds, set aside for life's most important activities. For the Toltecs the common ground was a place of commerce, worship, and burial. When the Spanish came in the sixteenth century, Cholula had been thus settled for more than three thousand years. The conquistadors simply built their own sacred place on top of the Toltec one. Today both the Spanish Templo de la Virgen de los Remedios, a healing shrine that fused Christian and Mesoamerican sacred practices, and the underlying pyramids are in ruins. The town's common place is displaced, but not far. Cholula's zócalo is bordered by a church on one side, a park on another, cafés on the third, and closed by shops on the town's main commercial street.

To a remarkable extent, Cholula is not all that different from, say, Kyongju, the religious and administrative center during the height of Korea's ancient Silla Kingdom (668–935 C.E.). Kyongju is poised at the confluence of two small rivers that form a protective border around the commercial center. To the south a large open space of parkland limits the center. Beyond its natural river borders, Kyongju is embraced by the burial sites of the great Silla kings and, beyond them, the land is relatively open to farming and sparse settlement as it slopes up to the mountains to the East. Like the people of Cholula, the residents of Kyongju today work hard to satisfy the demands of foreign tourists, but take their leisure in the parks and along the rivers.

The story of local places in ancient Mexico and nearly as ancient Korea is the story of towns and cities everywhere. Malmesbury at the southern limit of the Cotswolds was settled in 924 C.E.; it is perhaps England's oldest town.

Malmesbury rests atop a prominent hill, around which the gentle spaces slide easily into active farm lands, small forests, and parkland. Today the village center is much more crowded than Cholula's. But it too is bordered by residences, the remains of a fourteenth-century abbey, shops, and the administrative center. The town square is very near the geographic top of the prominence. Through an occasional alleyway one can glimpse the land spreading in the surround.

Malmesbury, on a hill, is not all that different from Needham, Massachusetts, on the great plain west of the Charles River. There, in my wayward youth, I served a spell as minister of the town's First Parish (now Unitarian). The parish was organized in 1711 or so, still early in the colonial period. Its church library contains documents of the town's early government from a time when the economic, religious, and political spheres were all but indistinguishable. Needham's town commons, like hundreds of others in New England, is somewhat less crowded than Malmesbury's, though far less spacious than Cholula's. Still, the common ground is today bordered by the First Parish on one corner, a major bank on another, the town hall at the opposite end, and a series of shops (increasingly franchises of national drug and food chains) in the remaining borders.

That such different people, over such a long stretch of time, in so far-flung parts of the world should want to live in a respectful relation to common ground makes one wonder just how important the land is to community. It is all too easy to take the functionalist answer—that we require land for the resources we need for food, shelter, work, and play. This is true of course, but it would seem there is something far more mysterious, if that is the word, about the lure of common ground. There is a growing body of judgment among archaeologists that the human being, as we know her today, did not emerge from her long prehistory among the apes until between 40,000 and 50,000 years ago. Why then? Some say that was when in various parts of the globe, Turkey among others, *homo sapiens* had lost its natural enemies. As a result the humanoids grew in number, and with increasing population density they were forced, so to speak, to identify themselves as distinct from each other. Hence, the beginnings of consciousness of self—the primordial sign of human behavior and the single most necessary condition for human community.

Is it possible, thus, that the very nature of human life lies in our species being as social critters who must crowd together? And, if this, does it not follow that once our progenitors came down from the trees or out from the caves, they made communion with each other by honoring the land they settled? And were not these common grounds of theirs, like those of ours, the social places they were forced to revere, care for, and gather about *because* life itself depended on how they expressed their consciousness of self, hence their most precious human nature—which expression requires, it now seems obvious, some safe and appealing place for gathering?

Of all the insidious self-deceptions by which this youthful species of ours made itself modern, none has proven more arbitrary and destructive of the *common* good than that of private property. In the long view of human time, the idea that common land should be owned at all, much less become the private property of individuals, seems to be, to put it kindly, peculiar, if not absurd. Peoples, like the animals, struggle as a matter of course to possess territories. But always they have understood, or so one would think, that however long one possesses this or that plain or riverbed or hilltop, some damned enemy of Toltec, Silla, or Anglo pride will take it over. The common grounds of Cholula, Kyongju, and Malmesbury—however long they were settled by one group— over the centuries were the special places of any number of different human communities, each of which saw the value of the commons and wanted it for themselves. In like manner, the small and beautiful common places of small towns and neighborhoods in the so-called modern world are being overrun by a vast and powerful army of real estate agents, who make their millions on the bizarre idea that ownership of the lands is a natural right.

It could be said that modern social science was established in the nineteenth century in a still-unresolved argument over the community's right to keep its common ground apart from the individual's right to ownership. Was not Marx's first and continuing point of difference with the political economists just this: that social and class warfare began when possession of the land was turned over to the right to ownership of the land from which comes the means of production? In any case, the surprising thing is that the right of private ownership of the land settled so unequivocally into the modern conscience such that, since the nineteenth century, the question of who owns the land has been at best a marginal consideration.

But this has been slowly changing. Human geographers, British social theorists, a remarkable number of feminists, and a long, long list of literary nonfiction writers have increasingly returned to the land as their muse. This is for a very evident and urgent reason. While, strictly speaking, the land is not running out, the more terrifying fact is that the ravages of private, corporate interests—too long unbridled in their ownerly greed—are rapidly effacing the very ground of human community. The spoilage of rivers, atmosphere, and forests is enough already. But even worse is the way our common ground is divided and quartered by public controversies in which the ever-sacred growth of the economy is pitted against the public interest in protecting the natural state of things. So extreme are the contesting ideologies that it is seldom reflected upon that the most human economy is one that, whatever its industry, is rooted in a locale amid the gathered peoples who consume, as well as produce, the product. The ancient rule of respect for common spaces, whatever its functional necessities, returns ever again to the fact that humans must distinguish themselves amid the common life and this they do only when the issues of their enterprising labors are marked as worthy by the common market of human needs and desires.

Likewise, at the other extreme of the controversy, we forget, if we ever knew, that the land very likely never enjoyed a natural state apart from animal and human settlement. The European Diaspora illusion of the Americas as free and unsettled is countered by current evidence that, in all of the Americas, the congestion that may have led to the beginning of the human some 50,000 years ago was ever more well advanced by the time Europe discovered them. Cortez found Cholula just one of many well- and long-settled towns and cities on Mesoamerica, just as Columbus encountered the Taenos in the Caribbean and the later British settlers found the Pequots and other native communities in the Northeast. Some say that at the time of first contact with white people, North America was populated by as many as 100,000,000 people. Neither in the Americas, nor anywhere else, does it make sense to talk of the land apart from its settlement. This is why we talk today of space as always a social thing *in potentia*—space as the social ideals out of which local social places are created. Land is no abstraction. As such it is always settled.

So long as we humanoids revere either the dream of unbridled economic growth or the nostalgia for a pure past that never was, we will not come to terms with the most basic question of all. Will there be, in some distant or near future, land sufficient for community? To ask this question is to inquire into the nature of the human itself. To fail to ask it today is to refuse to face up to the apocalypse to come when common ground has run out and we humans have no gathered and revered place where we come to say and see who we are.

Community on Land: Community, Ecology, and the Public Interest by Janel M. Curry and Steven McGuire is one of the best books I have seen on the several converging issues announced by its subtitle. Many write on the ecology of local places. Wendell Berry and Gary Snyder come first to mind. Others write stirringly on the spiritual qualities of small community rooted in the open land. Kathleen Norris is one of these. Others write on the history of social spaces. William Cronin for example. There are others who propose political models for the restoration of the land. Bill McKibben is one of them. But very few of even the most distinguished and rightly celebrated authors who work this terrain write at one and the same time on the history, law, social policy, and political alternatives as do the authors of this book. This they do while keeping faith with the obviously real and vibrant passion of the human spirit that motivates the work and tightens the logic of its arguments.

There are sections in *Community on Land* that readers will treasure for their original thinking and provocative organizing of the facts. For me, the first section on the history of corporate personality and its codifications in the modern era was that section. But that is just mine (sparked I think from never really having understood Otto von Gierke when I was compelled to read him some forty years ago). Others will find other of the book's chapters as I found these. But all, I should say, would be well advised to read the whole, as I have— to meditate upon its teachings, and to allow the wisdom and learning these authors pack into their lively book to sink in enough to change heart and mind.

PREFACE

THIS BOOK IS THE PRODUCT of the Calvin Center for Christian Scholarship, which was established at Calvin College in 1976 to bring together scholars who wish to address pressing issues of theory and practice in the light of the Christian faith. The Center is based on the twin convictions that the resources of the Christian tradition have much to offer scholarly reflection, and that the fruits of scholarship have much to offer to communities of faith. The Center has also aimed to bridge some familiar gaps in the modern academy: between individual scholars, faith and reason, experts and laity, diagnosis and prescription.

The present volume meets these aims admirably. Janel Curry and Steve McGuire bring to their study a deep concern with the social and ecological quandaries in which "advanced" nations find themselves today, identify the common fault which lies behind these, and root that, in turn, in some basic premises of modern thought. Moreover, they draw off the traditions of faith as well as various examples of public policy to demonstrate that we are not stuck in these damaging ways but can find, and so help forge, a new way out of the morass.

The Calvin Center is grateful to the authors for their dedication in seeing this project through, and is pleased to present their case to a public that needs—and, we can hope, wants—to hear it.

James D. Bratt, Director
Calvin Center for Christian Scholarship

ACKNOWLEDGMENTS

WE WOULD LIKE TO THANK the Calvin Center for Christian Scholarship for its support of this project. This book would not exist without the vision of its founders to support collaborative, interdisciplinary research such as this. We would especially like to thank the staff of the CCCS, Donna Romanowski and Amy Bergsma, who were invaluable in their provision of enthusiasm, encouragement, skills, and knowledge in moving a manuscript to publication.

In addition to the support we received from the CCCS, Dean Birkenkamp, our Rowman & Littlefield editor, provided much energy for the completion of this book just by his quick understanding of the breadth of what we hoped to accomplish and support for maintaining that original conception.

Finally we would like to thank our colleagues who enrich our lives and thought through intense discussions that stretch our understanding of what it means to be human and to care for each other and the earth.

INTRODUCTION

History is perhaps better renamed "historiography": the writing of history and the consciousness of it as a thing made by human activity, and in the end the making of history and the suffering of it as the consequences of human actions and the processes they have set in motion and cannot always control. Law, I think, can very often be seen in the same way: as the making of judgements, coupled with the attempt to determine how far we can live with the judgements we have made in the past.[1]

J. G. A. Pocock

IN OUR PRESENT TIME, the health of the land suffers at the hand of humanity. Daily we hear about everything from the most recent research confirming the reality of global warming to news of the collapse of ocean fisheries. Creation is steadily being demeaned. Humankind increasingly and dangerously mistreats its land. At the same time, public figures decry our loss of community and sense of belonging while social scientists track its demise.[2] Community is becoming slowly but dangerously undone. While at first glance these two issues may seem unrelated, the argument of this book is that they are deeply intertwined both with each other and with various other social ills.

In this book we provide a historical analysis of community and land and how their diminishing health has been historically intertwined. But the story does not stop there. We also identify contemporary schools of thought, movements, and natural resource management structures that give hope for change. To us, speaking seriously means not just giving the facts and our interpretations of them, but being advocates for what we see as good and whole. Our advocacy stems from the same commitment that we have to scholarship.[3] For us, scholarship should be able to say what has gone wrong and what can go right. Thus, we provide an analysis of community and land as well as advocacy.

Our goal is to present a broad portrait of how to understand current problems of community and land. Our particular explanation for what has gone wrong with community and land will amount to an excursion into the depths of individualism. By individualism we mean the ways in which community has visibly receded. We propound that community and land have suffered together. Current environmental policies will fail to bring about the changes needed to restore health to nature and the human community because they favor the individual and/or the state at the expense of the community and ecological niche.

Environmental policy analysis requires an understanding of legal frameworks. Our particular legal framework embodies certain misleading presumptions about individuals, about communal groupings, and about the central state, as well as about the interrelations of these entities. The dominant legal discourse largely protects and favors the individual, fearing group tyranny over individual rights. Perceiving a world of self-interested individuals, such discourse in turn presumes the necessity of a purportedly neutral government, the state, to regulate self-interest. Societal notions of the individual and the state legitimate one another. Environmental policy analysis has long mirrored these twin preoccupations and continues to do so. The communal aspect of reality suffers as a result. The language used to talk about sociality becomes a self-fulfilling prophecy, leading to the decline of actual communities.

The concept of commons is fundamental to this understanding of the demise of community and land. We use the concept of commons several ways in the story that follows. Traditionally, the commons has referred to that part of the environment that was outside an individual's possession but to which they had some rights of usage, or usufruct rights. Pasture commons are still found in places as diverse as the Andes Mountains and Canada. The story of this book is of the demise of common lands; however, the concept of commons represents more than just a type of property ownership. The commons represents a way of being in community. Thus, the story of the rendering of the commons is also a story of the eroding of a sense both of the communal and of community rights. This more abstract definition of commons takes on a broader meaning, including communal concerns over everything from soils to children to the right to live and thrive in a particular place. As the sense of ownership of the environment became more individualized, so also did legal rights, which led to the demise of mediating structures that stand between the individual and the state. In addition, enlightened thought came to presume the autonomous individual as the basic building block of society. The traditional sense of embeddedness in family and community was lost and along with it a sense of connection with nature and commitment to a place.

Entities exist in the social space between the individual and the state. These include communal groups as well as ecological niches, both of which can transcend various jurisdictions. These entities are sometimes referenced in legal discourse and environmental policy analysis but remain without power and authority. Instead, policy discussions quickly move on to a kind of managerial model of democracy that assumes the individual and the state. This assumption and resulting policy structures further reduce the capabilities of local communal groupings to address environmental matters in democratic ways. Individualist presumptions about individual and state have arisen at the expense of communal groupings.

Social science has long valorized collective entities "mediating" between individual and state, as can be seen in discussions around such notions as social capital and voluntary associations. But an inquiry framed most fundamentally by reference to the individual and the state runs directly into the prominence of another institution in between individual and state: the corporation. The key to understanding our diminishing understanding of the commons is the historic rise of the corporation. First conceived of as an entity that could operate beyond the limitations of the individual or small group, it originally was restricted by its obligation to serve the public good. Over time it became legally defined as an "individual" and its social obligations were reduced. Though not obvious at the time, this rise of the corporation as a legal person led at the same time to the disempowerment of institutions that had stood between the state and the individual, such as the collective entities of community, guild, or church. Only the individual, including the corporate "person" and the state, remained legally empowered and sociologically conceived. Due to their natures and the workings of the economy, the imbalance between the corporate person and the individual human increased.

Today the business corporation wields enormous power and abrades loyalty to community and family. The rise of the business corporation is interwoven with the rise of individualism. To an appreciable extent, the individualism we face today is a corporate individualism. This rise of individualism embodied in European legal discourse over the past millenium readied the stage for corporate ascension at the expense of local community autonomy. The same corporate ascension played a crucial role in the faltering of local autonomy. Four hundred years ago the corporate form enabled Europe to expand. The colonialism of the European expansion turns out to be corporate colonialism. That expansion increasingly tied geographically separate locales into a common economy. The decline of community is about individualism, but it is also about local place increasingly subordinated to distant economic power. Environmental damage is about self-interested individualism, but it is also about land-use decisions being removed from local populations. Corporate ascension played an important role in both, irrevocably distending and altering human scale.[4]

The rise in individualism involved a shift away from humans as beings born into families and embedded within local collectivities. Human nature came to be envisaged as the lone *homo economicus* responding to market conditions. The imagery of disencumbered adult males engaging in relations governed by contract eclipsed that of humans situated within family and collectivity. In turn, these changes had implications regarding science and the kind of knowledge needed for a healthy landed community. We find important parallels between the European philosophy of the day and the colonial accession of land on the periphery at the same time, though those two developments are usually spoken of as if disconnected.

Along with the rise of the corporation and the disempowering of groups came the detachment of land from community. Before, the natural environment was considered outside the possession of any one person, but the individual had rights of usage tied to membership in a community. Subsequent economic and cultural developments that emphasized the existence of the individual over the communal eroded this relationship form. The loosening of social obligations moved landed resources into the realm of commodities that were abstracted from social context and traded on the open market. This detachment allowed for the exploitation of colonial lands by both corporation and state.

The development of sociological and philosophical concepts of the person paralleled legal societal concepts. Political and economic theory increasingly hinged on an individualistic imagination and concept of human nature. Such individualistic concepts of society were deeply intertwined with the growing prominence of individual property rights. Both had their impact on community and the land in the West and in the colonial lands. The Enlightenment's reflection of this new worldview found expression on the cultural landscape of the United States with its rationalized, grid-patterned survey system and isolated farmsteads. This landscape was the outcome of the Enlightenment-influenced Jeffersonian ideal of independent, self-sufficient farmers, which in turn built on private ownership of land.

Corporate ascension brought the rise of industrialization along with its system of individual laborers as well as resulting environmental degradation. The disempowerment of noncorporate structures, mediating between individual and state, as well as the legal prominence of the individual, made it increasingly difficult to counter the growing power of the corporate person and the state. Within the legal framework and societal worldview, natural resource management strategies that replaced the "commons" remained locked between the option of private ownership and state control.

The directions portrayed in the first part of this book need not be inevitable. Within the larger story of the demise of the commons and the rise of the corporate individual are positive alternatives and countervailing efforts. These more optimal ways of thinking and acting are presented in the latter part of the book. Some of these new ways of thinking arise from our encounters with the Third World. Just as these peoples were at the receiving end of the Colonizer Enlightenment, they now point the way for the previous colonizers to relearn the ability to be in community and to live within the limits of their resources. Other positive models come from within the West. Tired and frustrated with the status quo and desiring to build a deeper understanding of "being native to a place," local groups are trying new and creative ways of managing natural resources and empowering community. These initiatives range from the development of community forests to local planning of watersheds. When faced with the limitations of nature, those who inhabit particular places have had to turn to community-based strategies to survive and thrive. Communal stewardship of the land has forced many to seek an optimal scale for both policy and individual health. The planetary optimum thus entails local health.

Many before us have sought to maintain a form of life conforming to a human scale and hence local embeddedness throughout this entire history. We join this long line of advocates for initiatives that build on local health and involve local accountability, conflict resolution, and radical democracy. Such initiatives are counter, in theory as well as practice, to the dominant Enlightenment worldview that has exalted the universalizing theory and individualistic concepts of human nature.

We draw examples of these growing alternatives from the rural community context where the interaction among community and land are most clearly illustrated. Along Washington's Pacific Coast, Willapa Bay exemplifies local consensus and community management, rather than centralized state management and universalized science. Rangeland issues in eastern Oregon provide a similar dynamic. Forestry management in Tanzania similarly illustrates an instance of local consensus building with bottom-up management instead of decision-making by far-off agencies or corporations. The Quincy Library Group of Quincy, California, furnishes a U.S. example of locally based knowledge collection and monitoring, as well as the potential for local decision-making. On a larger scale, Canadian forestry has embodied local dialogue and thus reduced power disparities for participants. Though less than optimal, these cases and others make for an important contrast with current timber, fisheries, and rangelands management theory and practice. The contrasts in land management in turn reflect differences in how we understand our own nature and how we answer the important questions on how we might best live. Canadian and other variations on the commons present encouraging signs of communities that are attempting to recover and maintain a sense of what it means to be embedded in place and community.

We begin with the growth of individualism and the suffering of land and community.

Notes

1. G. A. Pocock, "Law, Sovereignty and History in a Divided Culture: The Case of New Zealand and the Treaty of Waitangi," *McGill Law Journal* 43, no. 3 (1998): 481-506, 483.

2. Robert D. Putnam, *Bowling Along: The Collapse and Revival of American Community* (New York: Simon and Schuster, 2000).

3. Alan F. Blum, *Theorizing* (London: Heineman, 1974); David Silverman, "Speaking Seriously Part One," *Theory and Society* 1, no. 1 (1974): 1-17.

4. Kirkpatrick Sale, *Human Scale* (New York: Putnam, 1980).

PART I

HISTORICAL OVERVIEW

CHAPTER 1

CORPORATE COLONIALISM

The classical bourgeois vision was not that of a society organically articulated into different groups, as in the medieval vision, but of a market order populated by discrete atoms. Political energy in the market order appeared to flow from such atomized wills or, marginally, from a neutral overarching state. A corporate charter could fit into such a scheme only as a temporary anomaly. . . . Between standardized individuals who were regarded as equal, and a state that was regarded as neutral, classical liberalism admitted no intermediate sources of political will.[1]

R. Jeffrey Lustig

Much of this latter task (of constructing an ecological conception of land in the eyes of the law) will require a communal act of remembering.[2]

Eric T. Freyfogle

IN ABOUT THE THIRD century A.D., a development took place in Europe that laid the groundwork for important changes a millennium and a half later with respect to community and its tie to the land. A new legal entity came into being over and above the individual. This entity—the corporation—assumed a place between the individual and the emperor. The latter began chartering its first incarnation, corporate families, in Rome at this time.

The eleventh and thirteenth centuries saw the distinct rise in this new legal body as European municipal areas were chartered into corporate bodies. Artisans and traders would organize together as groups within some city territories. They would procure rights such as those to make local laws, administer justice, and hold markets and fairs. In return they paid the lord a regular tax. Monarchs in effect delegated some of their governing powers to a subsidiary, creating a body politic with a degree of autonomy. Similarly, religious orders came to be treated as a corporate phenomenon beyond, not reducible to, their memberships. But when the original members of a monastery or guild died out, what was to happen to the ownership of the building or the

3

organization of the trade? The new invention embodied a communal good, with communal rights given over to a group entity.

In time, the corporation was accorded legal status as a (fictional) person of its own. Royal charters granted certain, often monopolistic, rights to collective groupings, and the corporate body took on a legal life in and of itself. Certain rights and responsibilities came to be located not just in individuals but in collective bodies and their corporate persons—"proto-corporations" in Christopher Stone's parlance.[3] In between the rights of the sovereign and those of the individual landowner, a new entity was appearing. Doubts about the personhood of the new entity that was less than the sovereign but more than a mere individual did exist but did not occasion controversies of great import.

The new entity was sometimes put to business use, but was primarily utilized for other, more cooperative ends exemplified by universities, guilds, and boroughs.[4] What if the corporation were to harm someone? Various wrongs could relatively easily be ascribed to individual human beings within these institutions.

> [I]t was to individuals that the law was properly addressed. The doctrine that corporations could do no wrong, though nascent in the law, had rarely much practical significance anyway. A law calculated to deal with individual human beings as actors, rather than as institutions, was not strongly at odds with the social facts, nor did it ordinarily work injustice.[5]

For the first few centuries, the chartered corporation made relatively little impact on those affected by it.

The new entity was not alone in residing in a conceptual space between the individual and the state. In Europe and elsewhere, the commons had long provided another important legal entity between individual and state, an alternate instance by which a social group was accorded legal rights. For example, a family farmed its own individual section of land but held rights to grazing areas and forest under the domain of the village. Members of the village shared resources. The needs of the individual and the larger collective were balanced.

Cooperation among people led to the sustenance of the relative health of the ecosystem. With a lack of mobility, villages functioned with a high degree of cooperation and with an eye to the health of the ecosystem. In Europe, the feudal understanding of property and landholding entailed certain responsibilities and privileges. "Property" was not available for pure exploitation; it implied responsibility for care, in service to the whole. Land use was also nonexclusive; it might be held in common or used by different persons at different times of the year. Land was not yet "movable property," readily amenable to buying and selling. But in the later feudal period the rising merchant class—bolstered by changes in the legal codes that in turn can be traced to a coalition of interest between the legal originators and the merchants—established different concepts of land and collectivity.

Ownership evolved into all-embracing legal power over an object such as land. Eventually, the right to property was characterized as a fundamental God-given tenet of "natural law," and hence not subject to challenge in the way that most legal tenets were. Such changes in thinking about the land and its users were not to take full force until the sixteenth century, and then very gradually. The end result was that:

> Human society is dissolved into isolated individuals, and the world of goods split up into discrete items. One can no longer speak of a duty to use property or behave toward others in a certain way: all such duties as may be imposed by law are *prima facie* derogations from the fundamental "right of property."[6]

The rise of the market economy initiated permanent changes in the way that humans related to each other and to their environment. Prior to the thirteenth century, land was held by the Crown and its use was granted to individuals only as long as a variety of social obligations to the Crown were kept. In addition, its control included not just land but communities of people. By the thirteenth century, land ownership began to loosen from its social obligations as it evolved into a *fee simple* form of ownership. This loosening of social obligations moved landed resources into the realm of commodities, abstracted from social context, and traded on the open market. England experienced enclosures of the commons and antienclosure riots in the late fifteenth century. Care for the land was increasingly moved away from being a community responsibility to being an individual concern. Short-term productivity increased; the land generated higher yields for increasingly widespread markets. Local subsistence gave way to external market production. By the 1600s, draining of the fens, mining operations, and the harvest of trees for shipbuilding caused troubling shortages and a "conservation consciousness," to use Carolyn Merchant's term.[7] Severe air pollution from coal and other sources wracked London by the latter half of the century. An increasing percentage of lands designated as commons became enclosed. At about the time that Thomas Hobbes was publishing the *Leviathan*, Gerrard Winstantley and the Diggers proposed a communal vision for the use of commons and opposed the power of the centralized state. They advocated and attempted to enact common ownership of land, but to no avail.[8]

The Columbian era inaugurated many changes in both the geographical and the conceptual landscape. The new worlds inhabited by exotic, savage "others" soon caught the European imagination. It was time to reach out and explore—to settle in. The Canary Islands had recently illustrated the value of that strategy—European plants and domesticated animals survived well there, and the native indigenous population could not successfully resist what turned out to be an invasion. The Canary ecosystem was transformed to produce sugar. The successful reception of sugar back home increased the market demand, as "the archipelago's forests gave way to cane fields, pasture, and bare slopes as the trees fell before the need for timber for the many new buildings and especially for the fuel to boil the fluid squeezed from the harvested cane."[9] The government on Tenerife unsuccessfully attempted to regulate forest use. Deforestation contributed to erosion, irregular stream flow, and reduced rainfall. Watercourses that were judged by Europeans at the beginning of the fifteenth century to be powerful enough to support mills became dry gullies, from then until now.

The Europeans of the heretofore backwater region sensed and relished their opportunity to expand. They were able to survive on lands at the edge of the known world. Indeed, they were successful at transplanting aspects of their own ecosystem, Europeanizing that which they had encountered. They could adjust readily to the climate, grow crops for the market back home, and overpower the inhabitants that they met.

The corporation was one institution particularly amenable to the needs of this expansion, becoming a legal entity that enabled new endeavors between individuals. Its existence allowed interested communities and groups to act on a new legal standing that was like an extension of the sovereign. The monarch delegated some of his/her rights and privileges to the local collective group, and as a corporate entity, the group in turn became an extension of the monarch's power. Based on the so-called collective good, such a group's charter might accord it powers of eminent domain in order to build a road or canal, but the "associative" elements of such corporations became "refined out."[10] Social bodies such as villages and church groups began, over the centuries, to find one form of the new entity—the business corporation—troublesome, then threatening, and, finally, dangerous to their health. The competition between the two sorts of corporate entities, the associative and the business, became increasingly uneven, for reasons elucidated by Marx. Such changes went hand in glove with shifts from community and landed resources embedded within community to individualism and a laissez-faire use of the land. The consequences of the laissez-faire shift in responsibility from corporate group to individual self-interest visibly eroded the land, albeit gradually.

Charters and Monopolies

Trade relationships and inequities formed the backdrop against which European powers explored beyond the known edge of the world. The state was ascending and was more effective at marshaling economic and political power than were smaller units. Wars and civil disturbances were endemic; rivalries proved lethal. Henry VII granted a "patent" or royal charter to John Cabot and sons for the purpose of discovery and acquisition of unknown lands to the west of England.[11] Charters, of which this was one of the first, stipulated clear sovereignty of the monarch with reference to her or his people, as well as clear *sine qua non* contingencies for the transaction to continue. The colonial charter was requisite for explorers to claim internationally (that is, European-recognized) valid legal title to soil. The same held for the authority needed to fund and govern settlements as they sought to establish new outposts.

Many charter recipients did receive monopoly privileges so that they were not accountable under common law regarding matters of trade. Explorer entrepreneurs required immunity from laws such as those forbidding Englishmen from leaving their country or from exporting particular commodities. All the early trading companies received special trading privileges comparable to the franchises of modern utility companies. The royally sanctioned capacity to exclude all others (European or alien) from commerce with the new settlement was also frequently negotiated. Many were also granted important powers of internal jurisdiction to the effect that the sovereign guaranteed the internal law of the corporation. Alternately, the sovereign delegated a subset of his lawmaking power to the corporate body.

Europeans became increasingly successful at establishing monopolies and at turning lands at the receding periphery into plantations. In this endeavor, the Dutch borrowed from an old Roman invention that the English had recently put to new use: the joint stock company. By 1602, the Dutch East India Company had consolidated massive capital investment and was granted the right to make war and treaties. The Company's apparent autonomy from the homeland was premised upon its strong identity of interests with those of the state, a state that was largely controlled by Dutch merchants and financiers. The Company mastered the seas for a time and monopolized the production conditions of the highly sought South Pacific spices. In time, the entire European spice trade was issued through its auspices. "Java was soon transformed into a 'mammoth state plantation' . . . for the production of coffee and sugar; a whole people . . . converted into a nation of . . . estate coolies, with their own natural aristocracy reduced to the position of foremen and superintendents."[12]

Clifford Geertz, in his book *Agricultural Involution*, describes how the superimposition of sugar production on the wet rice agricultural system of Java left the Javanese with no other choice than to drive their remaining subsistence agricultural resources harder and work them more carefully in order to feed the rising population. They were not allowed to become either part of the sugar-estate economy or to move into industrial production. In addition, what had been "waste lands" eventually filled up with coffee trees, forcing further intensification of the remaining subsistence pattern.[13] The Dutch system, then, pried agricultural products out of Java that were saleable on the world market without changing the fundamental structure of the indigenous economy. In this way, the Dutch corporate structure maintained its own institutions and control without fear of the growth of Javanese commercial institutions.

Bountiful revenues financed both Iberian empires. By this time, sugar had already been planted in Brazil and had been sent to Lisbon. A "settler colony" rather than an "exploitation colony" began in Brazil within a decade of the conquests. By 1570, sixty mills were producing sugar for an unrealized market back home.[14] Such revenues also enabled the region to purchase its manufactured goods from elsewhere in Europe, leading to further industrial development there as the colonies continued to provide raw materials and foodstuffs while transforming the land.

Many important changes took hold in this time of "guns and sails," or, to use Max Weber's term, "booty capitalism." Roughly half the Portuguese Crown's revenues in the 1500s came from New World imports or extracts.[15] Over seven million pounds of silver exported to Seville tripled the European supply of the metal. In 1600, nearly a quarter of the Spanish state's total revenue came from the American colonies.[16] Between 1503 and 1660, Europe's supply of precious metals had increased eightfold, initiating worldwide inflation. Wealth could now be measured by other means than land. Whereas nature's cycle of production, compounded by the problem of food spoilage over time, had limited the accumulation of wealth in the past, coin allowed for the transcendence of these limitations. Precious metals also facilitated worldwide trade.

The economies and ecologies of both the Europeans and the encountered native peoples of North and South America were transformed in absolutely fundamental and irrevocable ways. The fates of both regions became irrevocably intertwined to the extent that any later discourse portraying them as separate entities was misleading. Regions of the planet appearing at first glance to be quite remote from one another, with very little in common, turned out to be regions knitted together into one single, albeit slowly fusing, global economy.

Small villages attempting to sustain themselves with a long-established economy of place now experienced the impact of decisions made thousands of miles away. Foragers, horticulturists, and others living a relatively autonomous life that was anchored to the carrying capacity of a particular place found themselves making amends in order to adjust to the presence of visitors, sometimes invaders, who showed a peculiar single-mindedness. While such groups have always been at some risk of attack from their neighbors, and in some cases have long been dominated by or incorporated into the sphere of powerful neighbors, the level of European expansion and the longevity of its impact grew to new heights.

The scale of human society markedly changed in two senses. In a predominantly agrarian world, the population is widely dispersed over the land, and a relatively small proportion lives concentrated in city settlements. Slowly, at first, this world became one of large urban concentrations, each importing its food from the hinterlands. At the same time, the sphere of influence of the metropolitan cores extended farther and farther outward along their peripheries. If there had been a particular appropriateness to the human scale thus far, that scale now began to distend itself to its limits.

The singular institution that helped weave together the different continents and the chartered corporation was beginning to show promise in generating riches for its owners and managers. Some corporations, such as the Hudson's Bay Company, flourished. At one time the company owned and controlled a land base more extensive than all of western Europe, later evolving into the present-day retail giant.[17] Many corporations floundered, however. Either way, the transformations effected by their existence extended far beyond being merely economic.

Land use patterns underwent immediate changes. The Europeans continued to bring new species of plants and livestock to the region to take root, and in turn took back new species to the homeland. Many such plants as well as pigs, cows, and other animal species would find larger and more extensive niches in the new world than they had ever had in the old.[18]

Plants and animals that the colonists introduced began to spread by themselves. Each introduction subsequently generated a number of changes within the new host niche. Small changes within a fundamentally interrelated ecology led to complicated new interdependence. "In some cases, these changes were so widespread that it is difficult to assess what the natural environment was like in places such as New England before 1500."[19]

These new ecological additions fundamentally altered balances, introducing both viruses and predators into regions not always capable of counteracting their effects. Eric Wolf portrays the scope of these alterations in his term "the great dying."[20] On all counts, the European expansion very quickly introduced diseases in each of the new worlds. The invaders brought (albeit unintentionally) diseases for which the host populations had no protection. Such diseases proved lethal, decimating native communities; populations were halved within a generation's time. Nonhuman species, as well as the land itself, bore the consequences of comparable devastation.

When they arrived, the colonizers encountered a very tight community fabric. For example, prior to French colonization, the nomadic Taurig herders and Fallani farmers of the West African Sahel had worked out an intricate system of land use, interdependence, and regional trade that had allowed them to flourish within the drought-prone region. The French destroyed much of this system by creating an institutional structure that focused on peanut production and export at the expense of food crops, drought-resistant crops, and the symbiotic relationship between the Taurig and Fallani. In addition, the French rerouted trade via its ports along the Guinea coast, cutting off the trade routes across the Sahara Desert upon which the Tuarig had depended for the accumulation of high-value goods, which they needed to survive droughts. This colonial system ultimately undermined the delicate ecological and social balance of the western Sahel, destroying both the social and ecological processes by which the region survived its frequent droughts. The West African Sahel went from being the home of major African empires to a place that remains one of the remotest and poorest regions in the world.[21] The lesson is not that major alterations occurred or that all the changes were unfortunate, but rather that small, benignly intended changes unfolded in wide-reaching, unanticipated consequences, most of which undermined community and nature.

Corporate Conquest

At the dawn of the 1600s, rising state power had enabled England to subdue its Celtic periphery and new horizons beckoned. Francis Drake had recently returned from his pirating of Iberian ships, having accumulated remarkable riches. John Maynard Keynes would later comment that Drake's booty "may fairly be considered the fountain and origin of British foreign investments."[22] Walter Raleigh had been granted one of the monarch's patents for the purpose of discovering remote lands "not possessed of any Christian Prince, nor inhabited by any Christian people."[23] State-chartered monopolies had been dispatched to Turkey, the Middle East, and Asia, though Arab and Chinese lands presented challenges due to their military parity. In return for their special rights, the companies provided regular payments to the Crown.

James I found that his competitors were accruing significant economic advantages, and he wanted to develop two settlements on the North American coast, one to the north and one destined as Virginia. He needed a legal entity larger than the individual or ordinary partnership of individuals, an entity at a level more in keeping with that of the state itself and capable of generating as much capital as the sovereign. What was working for the Dutch was worth a try by James.

James helped establish an institution that would fundamentally alter the scale of human relations until that time. Up to that point, human and human-nature relations had remained on a scale where one could know those with whom one did business, traded, or had conflict. In the same way, direct connections could be made between a community or a landowner and the land upon which a community or individual depended. Kirkpatrick Sale has shown that optimal human relations are marked by this sense of "human scale."[24] This sense of scale, rooted as it is in locality of place, became increasingly distended by the new corporate entity.

The traditional, regulated company had acted as little more than a licensing agency, supervising, but not conducting, business itself. Individual profit and loss was of no concern to the company as a whole. The collectivity of members did not routinely act in toto:

> The joint-stock Company, on the other hand, was designed specifically to bring together larger funds than small groups could supply. Tremendous resources had to be assembled for Englishmen to embark on such costly and complicated ventures as trade with India. Entire fleets were needed, and they had to be supplied for voyages that could be fifteen times as long and as dangerous each way as the journey to Spain, the furthest afield that even the most ambitious merchants had traveled hitherto. On the way to Russia or the North-West passage the ships entered the Arctic circle, and in South America or the Far East they had to be prepared for the tropics. Completely novel circumstances had to be faced, and only by a pooling of effort and money could the enormous difficulties be overcome.[25]

Central management increased in import. Work took on hierarchical forms, later evolving into a form of social organization to be dubbed bureaucratic. Seamanship skills were no longer a requisite for subscribers, but capital became more of a requisite. Ventures no doubt caught the imagination of more than just the wealthiest of the gentry. Central management recruited nonmerchant aristocracy who stood ready to engage and profit from such endeavors. Over sixty-three hundred enthused individuals participated in ventures that the English initiated between 1575 and 1630. The corporation charged with Virginia included subscribers from nearly all the London City Companies, as well as about seven hundred private individuals from all ranks.[26]

Although many citizens distrusted monopoly powers, a great many were drawn to invest, while others feared the possibility of collapse or fraud. Thus, not just economic support was needed. The general citizenry required reassurance and the new corporate entity itself sought legitimacy. Some individuals were in a position, as members of Parliament, to provide both economic and policy support. Many such members invested, but in the long term, a smaller group was to furnish the legitimacy mantle. Several political philosophers, ones who gave form to the way European elites ever after would speak about human nature and matters of governance, took part in the founding of the new entity. These philosophers of the early or pre-Enlightenment would successfully define both human nature and the possibilities of community for the West. They were the ones from whom the culture would receive its influential guiding political ideas.

Thomas Hobbes was involved with the affairs of the Virginia Company. He also anticipated that corporations would generate difficulties, such as their ability to accumulate power. They could become a "worm in the body politic," or "chips off the block of sovereignty" that could misappropriate government power to themselves.[27] John Locke's patron, the Earl of Shaftesbury, held extensive financial interests in North America (e.g., the Hudson's Bay Company) and the West Indies. Shaftesbury was part owner of slave ships and was deeply involved in American projects. Locke was also secretary to the Lords Proprietors of Carolina and to the Council of Trade and Plantations to which he made important contributions in colonial policy. He additionally held investments in the slave-trading Royal Africa Company and assisted in writing the slave-sanctioning constitution of Carolina. This constitution outlined an aristocracy in which eight barons would own 40 percent of the colony's land, and only a baron could be governor. James Mill authored a history of British India,[28] and on the basis of that work was appointed assistant examiner and later examiner for the East India Company. John Stuart Mill entered the company's service in 1823 and succeeded to examinership. He remained in charge of India during the height of Brittania's appropriation of the region until the company was abolished in 1858.

Corporation-based colonization was alternately more and less benevolent than its later beneficiaries appear to be aware. Most of the early adventurers took possession of large swathes of land only symbolically. They made declarations, planted symbols, and moved on. Eventually, forts were constructed in certain strategic locations and reinforcements were sent. European states sponsored colonial wars against each other. Where the lands were already inhabited, it became difficult to assimilate territory beyond the edge of the settlement itself, except symbolically. A certain level of benevolence in relations with natives was prudent. Actual, and hence less benevolent, control was most available on a particular geographic form: islands. The British seized the Bermudas a year after encamping in Virginia. Soon they took over Barbados, Nevis, and St. Kitts in the Caribbean and produced first tobacco and then a more lucrative crop, sugar. For the same purposes they later seized the Bahamas and Jamaica from Spain.

The new social institution of the plantation produced sugar. Forerunner to the European factory, the plantation organized work in a new, larger-scaled, and more rationalized way. It was also labor intensive. The Carib Indians had died out too easily to fill the enslavement role assigned them, and so African slave dealers met the demand. By 1790, some 700,000 Africans had arrived on North America. Commonly accepted estimates of the slave trade put it at some ten million in total. The British Caribbean colonies alone imported an official estimate of 20,000 in the year 1709, though many would have then been rerouted to Spanish America. Sugar grew, and the slave trade peaked from 1750-1800, with 100,000 crossings a year. Peter Worsely estimates that another 36 million died in transit.[29]

Empire Exemplar

One example from this time period illustrates the many-faceted aspects of the forces that were at work. In 1661, the monarch chartered the British East India Company for exploration and annexation.[30] Bengal and Dacca were known as prosperous, promising regions for trade. They were trading cities equal to, if not more powerful than, London. The company's later records contained a number of agreements that could be classified as true international treaties. Having acquired Bombay from the Portuguese, Charles II needed a loan, which he procured from the company in exchange for Bombay. A post was set up. Interpersonal relations between cultures were rather amicable for a century, and political control held little interest for those arriving. The operation may not have satisfied all those back home with its levels of wealth creation, but it served as an agreeable enough enterprise. Those already inhabiting the region were treated less as an inferior race than as congenial neighbors with whom to trade.

In time, the company grew, carrying on commerce at more than one hundred and fifty trading stations. Economic imperatives and increased size gradually led from benevolence on the part of the corporation to control. With control, racist ideology greatly increased. In 1757, the company exploited a division between an Indian governor and local chiefs on one side and bankers on the other. It supported the latter. The company provoked the governor into military action at Plassey and then defeated him, afterward plundering the state treasury. The company in essence became the ruler.

Bengal was at the company's mercy. The company swiftly instituted a number of changes, setting up a monopoly over export and import trade and establishing prices to its own benefit. It ousted the local merchant class, extracted exorbitant profits, and soon became the official *diwan*, or official administration, in Bengal. It rationalized the tax system for increased revenue yield and the increased burden ruined many cultivators and artisans. Major famines hit the area in 1770 and 1773. The company utilized local capital, taxed India to pay for hiring Indians to serve in its army, and expanded its sphere of control. Military ascendancy soon subordinated a number of cities and their surrounding areas.

The company engaged in nominal "land reform," which enabled it to privatize land and redirect Indian agriculture toward the production of profitable commodities (such as sugar, cotton, and tobacco) for export. Land reform and a similarly executed "tax reform" marked the destruction of the local system of group and status rights and obligations, replacing it with individual rights to private property. In so doing, the company unraveled the local legal system based on status, supplanting it with the English one based on contract.

> Indian legal procedure considered that contesting parties to a dispute were not discrete individuals but were connected to others by complex and multiple social, political and ritual ties. It recognized the existence of socially, politically, and ritually unequal corporate lineages and castes, and understood cases of conflict as moments in ongoing relations among such groups. Now, however, members of corporate lineages were to be treated as individuals. English law insisted on defining plaintiffs and defendants as equal and individual partners to a contract, and on dealing only with the case before the judge, to the exclusion of the social matrix that had spawned the case. Indian practice had avoided final decisions and solutions, in favor of continuous negotiation. English legal procedure, in contrast, insisted on resolving a case brought before the court by a clear-cut decision.[31]

The import of many of the outgrowths showed itself to be substantial in the long term. The company continued to enlarge its sphere of control, geographically and economically, though neither the directors nor the home government wanted expansion. At the time of the American Revolution, the British Parliament intervened and established an English governor for the state of Bengal. The second governor, Wellesley, engaged in a series of treaties and wars, quadrupling the size of this corner of the empire. The company also established a monopoly in opium sales and production. The company secured an illegal market for opium in response to the emperor of China's possession of excess tea but lack of interest in trade.[32] In this way, China eventually was opened as a market for British manufactures. Later, Chinese rulers would try to stop the imports, but the British response was the initiation of the Opium Wars in 1839. The British proceeded to establish five trading ports. In 1848, they joined with French forces and invaded and opened the "stagnant Orient" to further trade. India's populace "mutinied" in 1857, which led to Great Britain's revocation of the company's charter. Although the British East India Company left, the empire stayed for almost another century.

To what does the extended example of the East India Company point? What is most telling regarding this new entity that lodged itself, as it were, between individuals and their state (back home), and between members of formerly close kinship networks? At its inception, the new entity exhibited a discomforting parity when the monarch beseeched it for a loan. That glint of political and economic power would escalate in ways that could not be imagined. Saved from bankruptcy by Parliament's tax dollars, the company changed its role from a trading company to a political sovereign. In other words, a group of London-based coinvestors would organize in such a way that legally they were no longer simply individuals. Their agents and employees would band together so effectively and lethally as to become southern India's sovereign. A single business corporation gradually invaded and took control of an area the size of half of Europe and held one-sixth of the world's population. At the same time, the company helped foster an identity of interests between itself and the British state. Like the Dutch East India Company, it exemplified the rewards for the aristocratic and merchant classes that could be achieved by a partnership between the state and the corporation. Business corporations were delegated state powers and in turn behaved like states. They were extensions of home states, supported by that centralized power, put to use for a monetary agenda. In turn they furthered the pecuniary needs of the home office. In doing so they shored up vulnerable, newly established centers of political power. They made an important contribution to, or modification of, the incipient rise of the European interstate system.

The company altered local economic arrangements and redirected them in accord with the agenda of the empire. Local autonomy decreased. Furnishing crops such as indigo and jute for the world market and cotton for British manufactures supplanted the subcontinent's self-sufficient practices of procuring food and clothing. Processing had been reserved for the home operation. India had turned its focus outward just as the Caribbean had gone from a self-provider of foods to an exporter of sugar for Europe while remaining heavily dependent on food importation. Both became vulnerable to the vagaries of the global market. English invader law supplanted collectivity with individualistic societal conceptions.

India had rivaled England in industrial development. Now colonials in India and throughout the new worlds persistently countered or destroyed indigenous industrialization in areas such as glass, shipbuilding, metal work, and paper. Through political and economic control, England flourished, at the expense of India, Ireland, Egypt, and others. Britain needed markets, and did not want competition for them. Other European powers acted similarly. The Dutch, for example, militated spice production in the Dutch East Indies and later the French directed the Sahel to produce cotton and peanuts for export. India, a once prosperous land, was on its way toward extreme impoverishment. Cities more than the equal of England's embarked on a path that would draw them inexorably toward extreme impoverishment. Subsequently, the region's poorest cities were the ones that experienced the longest British presence.[33]

As for the land, the empire's agenda dictated a system of agricultural monoculture that reduced methods for preserving the soil. They ploughed up fields of rice to make room for poppies. They privatized land. They undid stewardly indigenous food-growing practices because they violated the thinking of John Locke and other Europeans about efficient utilization of property. As more could be extracted from the land in the short term, they perceived previous practices as wasteful, often indicative of "vacant land."

In turn, the cash crops designated for Europe very often fit a pattern since referred to as the "Big Fix." Sugar, tea, coffee, opium, tobacco, and cocoa were among the most prominent export crops from settler states. Sugar particularly led to a huge change in Europeans' diets; one could argue that the entire package fit very efficaciously into the time and work experiences of those undergoing the industrial revolution.

Social arrangements in India and elsewhere were fundamentally redirected as well. Such alterations pervaded the colonial escapade. The increased use of coin meant that the women of Lhota Naga in India married at much younger ages and that a class of landless men experienced fundamental changes in the manner in which debts were handled. Roads were built into new lands to establish coffee monoculture in New Guinea in quantities large enough to service the global market, increasing mobility a hundredfold. Local community fabrics and social structures loosened as individuals left for harvest work.

The native peoples of British East Africa experienced a similar wrenching of people from land. Among many of the tribal peoples of the region, personhood could not be conceived of apart from family, and family could not be conceived apart from its land. Thus, land could not be sold in a way that did not establish an eternal bond. To do otherwise would be to cut oneself off from the past and the future. When the British colonized East Africa, they set apart lands in the Kenyan highlands for white-owned plantations while establishing reserves for the native population. They developed a state-imposed dualistic economy that did not allow native Africans to grow cash crops and thus not accumulate capital. However, a hut and poll tax were imposed on the native Africans in order to force them to migrate to white areas to work. Africans' ties to their own communities were so strong that plantation owners had to keep wages low in order to circumvent the tendency to return to their home areas immediately after they had earned enough money to pay the taxes. The system integrated East Africa into the world economy, but to the benefit of Europeans. The native Africans suffered not only from a loss of identity that came from migrating away from their communities and families but also from their lack of ability to benefit from this cash economy. The land suffered from agricultural intensification in the reserves as the population grew. Land and people suffered together.[34]

The entity created between the domain of the individual and that of the sovereign very quickly became an entity destructive to other middling (between individual and state) European corporate bodies along the order of guilds and parishes. Where it landed, it extracted individuals from their kinship networks and from their local place. In turn, home municipal states enacted protections so that their more local industries would not have to face free-market competition with industries from afar. In spite of this impact at home, home states continued to find a dovetailing of interests with the new corporate entity. The new practice of chartering a corporate body for business purposes fueled Europeans' desire for expansion. The conquest of one people by another had long existed but now took force on a greatly magnified scale. The corporate entity had existed for hundreds of years but had presumed to serve the common good, and enterprises such as the East India Company were given warrant for their special privileges on the grounds that they served the "public interest." Although chartered on narrow terms and for limited time frames, many began to take liberty with their more narrow charges, accruing power and control.

The most successful commercial corporations rose far above any individual. As for influence, they began to approach that of their accrediting sovereigns, demonstrating a remarkable propensity to develop size and influence. The Virginia Company sought early in the seventeenth century to "settle" its new colony. It, the Massachusetts Bay Company, the Bank of England, and the East India Company served almost as arms of the government, although some failed to last. The American "Crown Colonies" —the later states—were corporations chartered by the king. For the mother colonizer, they took responsibility for investment, production, taxes, property, labor, and markets. Yet, even with these changes, the monarch maintained some control. When Charles II appointed commissioners to inspect his charge and the settlers objected, the monarch asserted his sovereignty over their corporate body. Charters were revoked in other cases when their grantors—monarch or polity—were displeased with their creation.

Reluctance and Transformation

India's pitched battles and later "mutiny" made the less benign underbelly of corporate colonialism more evident. The institution that might have appeared to constitute mere trading was in reality being transformed into something else. The corporation granted a charter by the king became a Hobbesian adventurer-settler. It became an institution that invaded outward from Bengal and later stood behind the massacre of a thousand unarmed men, women, and children at Amritsar. The business entity that in its infancy captured competitor outposts, burned entire islands, and militarily turned Java into a mammoth state plantation, should not be thought of merely as an ingenious business-law invention enabling investment on a larger scale. India might be atypical in that certain castes provided its labor force rather than imported slaves, but would transatlantic enslavement have taken place on such a large scale *sans* corporation? The scale and severity of the slave trade is what changed in the latter half of the 1500s and a primary enabler was the new-scaled invention of the joint stock corporation.

The rebellion/mutiny in India paralleled lethal resistance from native conscriptees and nonnative slaves across the seven seas. Just as Maroon wars and slave rebellions began in 1519 in Espaniola and continued throughout colonial empires, indigenous attacks on the outposts demonstrated the less benign aspect of corporation colonialism again and again. Dozens of both sorts of actions could be enumerated.[35] Organized violence between colonists and slaves/ex-slaves finally eventuated in settlers' worst fears: a large-scale slave rebellion that succeeded. A mere two years after the French Revolution espousing liberty, fraternity, and equality, slaves revolted at the French colony of St. Dominique, on the island previously claimed by Columbus as Espaniola. Toussaint L'Overture's band repelled French, Spanish, and British forces and created the new state of Haiti at the dawn of 1804. The example seared the imagination everywhere, an early day domino theory come alive. Liberation struggles over the next fifteen years in Spanish America, combined with Napoleon's mastery of Spain, led to Bolivar's successes and the quick liberation of most of what are now designated as South and Central America. At this time there were anticolonial wars in the African Cape and in Burma; there would be many more throughout the remainder of the century.

Back in the motherlands, other corporate bodies such as guilds and churches began to find themselves at cross purposes with the new entity, just as colonized peoples had, albeit to a lesser and usually less lethal degree. The changes at home were paralleled by the emergence of a new individualistic societal and philosophical imagination that was to transform not only the legal standing of such corporate bodies, but also question their conceptual basis.

Notes

1. R. Jeffrey Lustig, *Corporate Liberalism* (Berkeley: University of California Press, 1982), 47-48.

2. Eric T. Freyfogle, "Ethics, Community and Private Land," *Ecology Law Quarterly* 23 (1996): 631-61, 650.

3. Christopher Stone, *Where the Law Ends: The Social Control of Corporate Behavior* (New York: Harper & Row, 1975), 13.

4. Edward S. Mason, "Corporation," in *The International Encyclopedia of the Social Sciences,* ed. David L. Sills (New York: Macmillan, 1968), 396-403.

5. Stone, *Where the Law Ends,* 13.

6. Michael E. Tigar, *Law and the Rise of Capitalism* (New York: Monthly Review Press, 1977), 197.

7. Carolyn Merchant, *The Death of Nature: Women, Ecology, and the Scientific Revolution* (San Francisco: Harper & Row, 1980).

8. Paul Theobald, *Teaching the Commons* (Boulder, Colo.: Westview, 1997), 65.

9. Alfred W. Crosby, *Ecological Imperialism* (New York: Cambridge University Press, 1986), 96.

10. Mason, "Corporation," 396-403.

11. George Lewis Beer, *The Origins of the British Colonial System, 1578-1660* (New York: Peter Smith Publishers, 1933).

12. Peter Worsely, "The Nation State, Colonial Expansion and the Contemporary World Order," in *Companion Encyclopedia of Anthropology,* ed. Tim Ingold (New York: Routledge, 1994), 1040-66, 1049, quoting Geertz and Panikkar.

13. Clifford Geertz, *Agricultural Involution: The Processes of Ecological Change in Indonesia* (Berkeley: University of California Press, 1963), 79-80.

14. Eric R. Wolf, *Europe and the People without History* (Berkeley: University of California Press, 1982), 150.

15. Worsely, "The Nation State," 1040-66.

16. Alan Thomas, *Third World Atlas* (London: Taylor and Francis, 1994), 32.

17. Jack Weatherford, *Indian Givers: How the Indians of the Americas Transformed the World* (New York: Fawcett Columbine, 1988), 33.

18. Crosby, *Ecological Imperialism*.

19. Brian R. Ferguson, "Tribal Warfare," *Scientific America* 226, no. 1 (1992): 108-13, 109.

20. Wolf, *Europe and the People*, 133.

21. Richard W. Franke and Barbarah H. Chasin, *Seeds of Famine: Ecological Destruction and the Development Dilemma in the West African Sahel* (Totowa, N.J.: Allanheld, Osmun Publishers, 1980).

22. Noam Chomsky, *Year 501* (Boston: South End, 1993), 6.

23. Arthur S. Keller and Oliver Lissitzyn, *Creation of Rights of Sovereignty through Symbolic Acts* (New York: Columbia University Press, 1983), 65.

24. Kirkpatrick Sale, *Human Scale* (New York: Putnam, 1980).

25. Theodore K. Rabb, *Enterprise and Empire* (Cambridge, Mass.: Harvard University Press, 1967), 29.

26. Rabb, *Enterprise and Empire*, 36.

27. Scott Buchanan, *The Corporation and the Republic* (New York: The Fund for the Republic, 1958).

28. Bhikhu Parekh, "Decolonializing Liberalism" in *The End of "ISMS?": Reflection on the Fate of Ideological Politics after Communism's Collapse*, ed. Aleksandras Shtromas (Cambridge, Mass.: Blackwell, 1994), 85-103, 89.

29. Worsely, "The Nation State," 1040-66.

30. Wolf, *Europe and the People*, 239-52.

31. Wolf, *Europe and the People*, 248.

32. Wolf, *Europe and the People*, 255.

33. Chomsky, *Year 501*, 151.

34. Arnold H. DeGraaff, Jean Olthuis, and Anne Tuininga, *Kenya: A Way of Life* (Toronto: Curriculum Development and Training Centre, 1981).

35. Thomas, *Third World Atlas*.

CHAPTER 2

COLONIZER ENLIGHTENMENT

When a society openly embraces political, economic, and education theory that hinges on an 'individualistic' and anthropo-centric conception of human nature, community disintegration is logical and predictable. . . . It doesn't require much thought to see how the Lockean emphasis on possessive individualism could mesh well with . . . Bacon and Descartes . . . and it requires very little additional analysis to see that the linking of these schools of thought was not a healthy prescription for the environment.[1]

Paul Theobald

There was a 'thingness' about Hobbesian and post-Hobbesian liberal thought that seems to have been both new and extraordinary in the history of political discourse . . . with a vocabulary of such materiality, liberal theory cannot be expected to give an adequate account of human interdependency, mutualism, cooperation, fellowship, fraternity, community, and citizenship.[2]

Benjamin Barber

WHILE EUROPE'S EXPLORER-ENTREPRENEURS were altering the geography and the conceptual imagery of the landscape beyond, its noted thinkers were working on resolving new problems. Travelers to America consistently shared their amazement about the personal political freedoms of the native peoples. They were also intrigued with the absence of a class system. Sir Thomas More's *Utopia* built on these new experiences and forever shaped the European imagination regarding sociopolitical possibilities. Soon the Baron de Lahontan revived the Greek-derived concept of anarchy to characterize the ruler-less Hurons. He found them orderly despite their lack of a formal state. Such notions caught on in literary circles and gained a wide currency, contributing to Rousseau's concept of the noble savage and Thomas Paine's concept of democracy.[3]

Conceptualizations of the relationship between humans and nature were changing as well. The Medieval Period was characterized by a split between the hands, the common laborer who worked with nature, and the head, the

21

intellectuals of the time. Intellectual work was directed toward understanding eternal and changeless things, resulting in the dominance of deductive science and an emphasis on the rationality of God. Because science and its applications were separated, any transformation of the landscape came very slowly. The relationship between humans and nature that arose out of this context was one where the universe was perceived to be ordered and structured—a frozen hierarchy. The human's role was to find one's proper place. The concept of progress was absent.

The age of exploration and the Reformation aided in bringing an end to this static worldview. The European encounter with the reality of a larger earth and unexplored lands expanded the imagination of the populace. In addition, the Reformation had several effects on human-land relations. It moved the emphasis from God's rationality to God's unreasonable love as revealed not only in the Bible but also in nature. Nature became something to observe and appreciate. Furthermore, it broke the Platonic influence that had separated hand and mind. Suddenly all callings were considered sacred and those who worked with nature were no longer relegated to lower status.

While the influence of the age of exploration and the Reformation were important for breaking the static worldview of the Medieval Period, the Enlightenment and the scientific revolution ultimately formulated the view of nature that was to dominate the West. The Reformation had emphasized nature as an expression of divine love, which turned human attention to its observation and led to the growth of inductive science. But soon, only those qualities that could be measured were considered the basis of truth and certainty. Descartes went so far as to claim that the only purpose that could be assigned to nature was that which was provided by a thinking mind. The basis for certainty became this reductionistic model of the world, abstracted from society, its context, and any aesthetic or spiritual meaning outside of its mathematical qualities. Francis Bacon went a step further. He equated this knowledge, gained from observation, with power and control. Gone was the harmonious whole with purpose and design. Gone was the world that illustrated the unreasonable love of God. The world became, in essence, a mechanistic system that had no meaning apart from human use and that exhibited no qualities apart from those that could be measured and quantified through the process of scientific reductionism.[4]

In Bacon's utopia, the man of science made important decisions based on his knowledge of nature's secrets. Such knowledge enabled the manipulation of organic life, thus creating artificial species and controlling the weather for human purposes. Because nature was unruly and in need of controlling, its close observation and dissection led to humanity's ability to place it under their domain. Nature *had* been formulated as a source of wisdom and embedded in sacred meaning. Bacon's new science fundamentally contributed to the move to think of nature as a passive mechanism in need of human oversight and management.

Men of reason and science were to do the judging of new knowledge claims. An absolute source of knowledge was available for the masters of its method. The rise of British imperialism coincided with the rise of the "reasonable man" of law.[5] In time, theory would gain a new criterion of truth: "we *know* an object insofar as we can *make* it."[6] Heidi Ballard has shown that Enlightenment notions of progress were coupled with a model of change that required and justified human dominion over nature and other societies.[7]

The Rise of Scientific Certainty

In 1636, soon after Bacon's utopian writings, René Descartes published his work on the achievement of certitude. Descartes' philosophy gave many subsequent philosophical writings an individualistic cast. He opted to become his own guide, and as Peter Hulme has pointed out, his was an age of discovery on geographic and conceptual fronts alike.[8] Mathematics gave Descartes his longed for certainty and uncovered the laws of nature. The human body functioned as a machine, as indeed did the entire cosmos. The individualism of the *cogito,* "I think therefore I am," sacrificed the notions of collective wisdom in favor of the concept of individual knowers. The individual, distrusting all but his own reasoning, ascended at the expense of the collective. Descartes reflected and contributed to a mechanical worldview, one harmonious only with his culture's increasingly centralized bureaucratic state structure.

Isaac Newton's 1686 articulation of the incipient science of mechanics established a new, more mechanistic cosmology over and against the extant religious one. Struck by its scientific successes, Renaissance Europe, even more than before, came to think of itself as the crown of creation. Newton's work cemented the mechanistic imagery by which his continent understood the world. It also established correlative assumptions about the production of knowledge about that world. Matter was presumed to be composed of small particles. Lawlike generalizations characterized the clocklike workings of the matters under study, which predicted the workings and, when successful, controlled them. Knowing was the result of the actions of a lone perceiving scientist interrogating nature. This process of gaining knowledge was seen as a secure foundation for knowledge claims. For empiricist epistemology, the trick was to stay close to sense data as given by such observations without straying too far into unsecured theory. Data could be received free of the contaminating influence of preconception and desire; its parts could be individually assessed.

In time the study of society would take on the same assumptions. The impact of such notions on the conceived nature of the individual was profound. Atomized thinking has come to be assumed across all discussions regarding problems related to community and the land.[9] This individual imagination is presumed to supplant earlier, more communal conceptions of society and view them as either embarrassingly utopian or nostalgic.

The Nature of Humans

Thomas Hobbes' writing in 1651 is commonly thought to have been more mindful of the impending English civil war than of the colonial settler states.[10] For some time, his culture had been moving toward the view that humans were fundamentally self-contained beings and were individually constituted rather than defined by community and family. The patently social humans increasingly understood themselves as an aggregation of autonomous individuals who were by nature selfish rather than essentially social. Social philosophers reflecting this new conception of human nature sought to build theoretical systems upon these human atoms.[11] The natural law theories of Hobbes, Locke, and others secularized the biblical concept of covenant into a contract. Even the church became merely a collection of individuals united by contractual agreement. An organic sense of unity and order disappeared.

Hobbes and many liberal expositors in his wake presumed a human nature that was inherently self-interested. Hobbes' notions of human motivation would have seemed odd to those of the past who had been tightly embedded in social structures. However, this notion has found acceptance in the modern world. Hobbes rejected the optimistic views of Aristotle and St. Thomas that people unite in society because of some natural sociability.[12] Even the commons was a thing of the past for a philosopher whose imagery of humanity resonated quite well with the burgeoning market economy.

Hobbes' *Leviathan* articulated a mechanical model of society composed of separate individual parts in competition with one another. The English civil war fueled Hobbes' belief that an all-powerful sovereign was needed to hold individual interests in check. Without such a sovereign, he thought humans' brutish nature would generate a war of all against all. The only way in which humans could transcend their state of nature was by entering into a social contract with each other—each in effect agreeing to clamp down on some of his or her selfish inclinations in return for the same. Hobbes provided no place for associations or groups at the intermediate level, such as the church, between his extremes of individual and commonwealth.[13] For Hobbes, no middle ground existed between the individual human and the absolute state.[14]

To escape this condition of nature, Hobbes thought that individuals had to submit to an absolute sovereign. The sovereign transcended and mediated the arbitrary self-interests of the dispersed individuals (or monads in later continental philosophy). No other way existed to manage competing self-interests or resolve conflicts based upon personal interest. He viewed the human mind as a calculating machine, with the sovereign holding the calculators in check. For Hobbes and many since, conflicting interests made the synthesis of communal consensus impossible.[15] Individual self-interests and individual values became arbitrary and untouchable by rational discussion. Under this scheme, societal attempts at transcending values and communally encompassing interests were futile. Hobbes completed the movement, initiated by Thomas More and by Niccolo Machiavelli, that removed political philosophy from ethics.[16] That is, whereas the political philosophy of Aristotle addressed the virtuous life and placed ethics center stage, Hobbes conceived of a scientifically grounded social philosophy. The translation of knowledge into practice became a technical problem, more a managerial adjustment to the social order than a continual assessment of its ethics. The regulation of social intercourse replaced the assessment of virtuous order. Bacon and Descartes paved the way as well. The laws of civil life could now be ascertained by scientific study.

This liberal notion of personhood restricted notions of justice to questions of distributing rights to individuals and regulating actions among self-defining individuals.[17] Joan Tronto says this conception of personhood created the boundary between morality and politics.[18] Morality began to be referred to as what one thinks is important to do and how one conducts one's relations with other people. Politics came to be restricted to the realm in which resources were allocated, public order maintained, and disputes about these activities were resolved.[19] The notion that politics and morality might have similar ends and means grew to be incomprehensible.[20] The state became seen as neutral, acting as an umpire.[21] Thus the traditional model of liberal and pluralistic society was one where law was supreme and the economic base determined everything else in society.[22] Individuals, each pursuing this own interest, especially their own economic interest, evaluated public institutions by how well they facilitated or contributed to their own advancement.[23]

Prior to Western Liberalism, justice was conceptualized as the virtue of society as a whole, evidenced by orderly social institutions. If a society fostered individual virtue and promoted happiness and harmony among its citizens, it was just. In contrast, liberal bourgeois societies abandoned these earlier ideas and sought to free individuals to define their own ends. Notions of justice under modern democracies became restricted to questions of distributing rights to individuals and regulating actions among self-defining individuals.[24] The state then had difficulty in conceiving of community rights or needs and could only have the role of mediating among individuals. Rights/needs of nature and community were thus outside conceptions of human nature.

Liberal discourse following Hobbes recurrently looked beyond interpersonal peacemaking and social control. Only the sovereign could authoritatively reconcile such matters.[25] No peace could be established without subjection. Men have "no pleasure . . . in keeping company where there is no power able to overawe them."[26] European regents were expanding their territories, leading the reorientation of the economy away from the manor and toward the farthest-reaching market. Hobbes' understanding of human nature in need of sovereign authority pointed in the same direction.[27]

The relationship between one individual and another became portrayed as a social contract. In return for the benefit of a sovereign, the individual renounced a certain freedom, thus subordinating himself to the regent. Hobbes felt that all rational humans would agree that more was to be gained than lost when all surrendered liberty to a proper sovereign. All would voluntarily assent to the need for the Leviathan. In this manner, Hobbes exemplified the demise of feudal law based upon status, supplanted by the age of discovery's concept of social contract. By the same stroke, justice evolved into respect for the validity of the contract. Hobbesian notions of the contract ("covenant") and its role in society were far broader than today, but after Hobbes, a narrower concept slowly took hold.

> Men thought their relationships with each other, and their relationship with the State, to be of a similar character. . . . [T]here was nothing very unreal in seeing a close relationship between "ordinary" contract and the "social" contract . . . the concept of contract was, in short, replacing custom as a source of law . . . and as the source of individual rights and duties.[28]

Contract entailed less a consensual choice and more a mutual agreement on rights and obligations. Much of the rhetorical power of the legal contract lay with its purported embodiment of legal equivalence. Contracting parties were portrayed as equals, beings characterized by freedom of choice in the individualist understanding of law at the time. Actual inequalities conceptually vanished under the auspices of the law and the political economy of the time. In turn, contractual standing became universalized as the prototypical metaphor for social relationship. Contracts were becoming a ubiquitous social mechanism purported to replace kinship and community-based systems of rights and obligations. They were the means of communication between these now "separate parcels."[29]

The increasingly atomized societal conception demanded an increasingly powerful sovereign. The world of individuals is a unidimensional world with everyone at the same level. Each is responsive to his own interests, which necessitates that the sovereign establish and maintain order. This social order presumes the sovereign's neutrality vis-à-vis its competing interests. The sovereign's existence alters the imagery from a one-dimensional humanity to a two-dimensional or bileveled one. The absolute sovereign stands above the multitudinous aggregates.

Hobbes may have been the first to introduce a contractual characterization of public law. Hobbes spoke for the new world of reason. He thus effected important early moves toward the subsequent liberal concept of civil society, in which the traditional ways, based on kinship, were replaced by the more reasoned universals of the civil realm. The civic, public realm evolved as a more rational domain than that which remained private and domestic. Loyalty to kinship, was thought to amount to loyalty based on relationship rather than merit. Thus, it missed objectivity by its personal attachment. But humans subordinated to a sovereign gained rationality and adherence to law. Humans subordinated to a sovereign freed themselves and entered the realm of reasoned public discourse.

These changes represented a narrowing of what encompassed human experience. Self-interest became increasingly powerful as a regulator of human activity because it required less of a rich social setting for individuals.[30] "Natural" virtue therefore began to gain its sustenance from two sources: from reason, that higher plane of human existence, and from sentiments, the grounding place of human existence, now rooted in the household.[31] Politics and morality were no longer seen as bound together. Women were associated with parochial and context-bound, moral sentiments that were considered at a lower level of moral discussions.[32] Relationships, care, and the communal in turn became tied to subordinate status in society.[33]

The contrast between universality and the particulars of context extended to the contrast between rule-making vs. moral decision-making. Social theory became an unchanging system of rules to be applied uniformly to all social phenomena, doctrines that constitute fixed and timeless systems of beliefs to be followed blindly. In contrast, earlier traditions of moral decision-making constituted a process whereby individuals and groups used an ethical framework grounded in deeply felt beliefs to construct meaningful everyday lives. The difference lay in distinguishing between theory as a dogma or closed system of ideas to be verified and tested, and theory as a story or narrative operating as an open system of ideas that can be retold and reformulated.[34]

The Enlightenment's universalism that informed our relationship to each other and to nature demanded the universality of distance and objectivity. The particular then was demoted to "emotion." Attentiveness, engrossment, the effective-receptive, as well as the local, were demoted with it. This is the problem of the *moral point of view* boundary according to Tronto. This boundary requires that moral judgements be made from a point of view that is distant and dis-interested, the requirements of reason.[35] Morality must then become part of a realm beyond the world of emotions and feelings since these show engrossment and attachment. Historian Martin Jay traces this increasingly dis-interested perspective through the images of "Lady Justice." Originally she had her eyes wide open as she weighed the issues of justice on her scales. Over time, the blindfold was added. Thus we moved from a view of morality that metaphorically included context and personal knowledge to one that would not be allowed to be shaped by local customs, or habits but rather should appear to be as universal as human reason.[36] Rationality began to be seen as a mental capacity of individuals rather than groups.[37] Groups were associated with the local community whose variations must be attributed to a lower order of moral thought. In contrast, moral philosophers were required to focus on the nature of moral thought, not on how to make certain that actors act morally.[38]

Carole Pateman has shown that the early social-contract theories of society and polity read as a "fraternal social contract."[39] Women and nonwhites were not included in the group who held equal rights. "All men are free" was meant to mean a universalized reading that all humans are free, but this philosophy could not be easily applied to women, who were deeply subordinate to their fathers/husbands in European law.[40] Similarly, "liberty, fraternity and equality" meshed more clearly with the reality of the day than did "liberty, community, and equality." Legally, the family unit was absorbed into one person, the male head of the house, just as Hobbes constituted the family as comprised of a man and his children and servants. Subsequent thinkers were able to treat the family, a collection or plurality, as one single "person" by presuming that it required hierarchical leadership, as did any other successful grouping.[41] In a deeply hierarchical world, even institutions on the scale of the family were thought to require a single leader. Women who married entered into "civil death." One of the earliest and most consistent uses of the term "contract" within the legal tradition was the reference to the contract of marriage.

The contract of Hobbes, Rousseau, Kant, and others provides our culture with its predominant imagery of political life and a particular assumption about human nature. Contract conjures up an idea of freely assenting individuals of supposed equal legal power. The prominent works on social contract treat humans as if they can live as separate individuals, not dependent upon society. In this imagery, individuals are prior to society, and they only come together to form it out of self interest. Unlike other creatures who flock from instinct, humanity joins with others rationally and reflectively, but each is autonomous and independent of community with no particular history. The universal individual of the social contract is a disembodied one.

A feminist and sociological understanding of humans sees them as fundamentally relational. Each individual is born to a woman and then, in a sense, passively accepts societal norms through socialization. Each new member enters unequally and involuntarily. Society dictates what each newcomer experiences and thinks. Sheldon Wolin states that it makes more sense to treat each human as embodying a birthright membership into society and its political institutions, than to treat them as disembodied individuals.[42] The notion of birthright avoids treating citizens as automatically equal. Birthright points to a crucial difference between two polarized understandings of human community, individualistic and social. In turn, birthright invites one to look at social relationships in terms of covenant rather than contract.

A belief that human beings are primarily relational contrasts with the Enlightenment view that humans are autonomous individuals, unattached and disconnected from social and environmental context.[43] Western philosophy typically begins with a supremely free consciousness and assumes an aloneness and emptiness at the heart of existence, identifying anguish as the basic human affect.[44] Virginia Held states that this notion of humanity is historically constrained: "To see contractual relations between self-interested or mutually disinterested individuals as constituting a paradigm of human relations is to take a certain historically specific conception of 'economic man' as representative of humanity."[45] She then asks us to imagine alternative ways of seeing the world: "What if we replaced the paradigm of economic man with the paradigm of mother and child as the primary social relation?"[46] Western liberal democratic thought has been built on the concept of the individual seen as a theoretically isolable entity that can assert interests, claim rights, and enter into contractual relations with other entities.[47]

Locke sought to move political thinking beyond the feudal model and conception of polity by which individuals were born into subordination. For Locke and his philosopher contemporaries the goal was to transcend the realm of tradition or custom, with its lack of a public sphere, and to move toward a realm of individual freedom and freely chosen loyalty to authority.

From Land Afar to Property within Reach

John Locke's writings, published in 1690, are important in several ways.[48] Locke's *Essay Concerning Human Understanding* helped found English empiricism. His apologias for property, the state, and the social contract deeply inform today's thinking on matters of community and democracy. The United States' Declaration of Independence and Constitution drew heavily on his work and Locke himself distinctly embodied the relationship between colonialism and liberalism, or empire and political philosophy.

Like Hobbes, Locke started with a state of nature, peopled by adult men unbeholden to others—a state of nature that God had furnished for humanity's use. God's gift entailed both the rights and the duty to fully develop the earth's resources. The *Second Treatise on Government* served to defend the principle of moving common land into private property.[49] For Locke, as for Bentham and others, the desire to acquire property was, and is, a natural feature of the human condition. Civil societies enabled each individual to surrender his or her right to protect his or her own property to the social contract. The government's role was to protect the property of individuals as the mediator of their self interest.

Lockean humans were assumed to be self-interested and rational. Reason was humanity's highest faculty, capable of generating a universally valid body of lawlike generalizations. The lack of reason among North American Indians was thought to result from their nomadic existence. Society as conceived by Locke was a collection of individual beings, and the foundation of society was the will of the individual. Locke concurred with Puritan concepts regarding both the general calling to faith and the more particular calling to occupation, but framed them in individualistic terms and ruptured the connection between the two. No longer was religion understood as being all encompassing. While the Puritans saw both callings as socially useful with the principal concern of their place within the economy of salvation, Locke saw the particular calling as involving labor for the gain of property.[50]

Locke thought that the fully rational society exemplified qualities such as industry, self-discipline, and control of passions. The laws of God became natural law, and for Locke the principles of natural law underwrote private property and the inequalities of wealth. Locke's *Second Treatise* held that humans had property in their own persons and in the labor of their hands and that the earth's resources could only fulfill their needs if it belonged to them apart from anything else. Ultimately, the individual pursued his or her interests apart from the larger whole, finding expression and fulfillment only in private ownership. The point of political association then was to protect the natural rights of property and liberty. Whereas the Hobbesian concept of human nature required the sovereign to oversee the conflicts resulting from self interest, the Lockean viewpoint was that people preserved themselves primarily by their labor, which was actualized by the utilization of property. People thus associated under a government that protected that which was most basic. For each, the point of political association was the protection of the individual.

The truly rational society was thought to be governed by a clearly defined, centralized political structure rather than traditional customs. The political order was now reduced to individuals' acting in their own interests to create institutions through contractual agreements with a consequently diminishing concept of the collective good. Bhikhu Parekh wrote about the varying ties between liberalism and the European colonial expansion personified by Locke and J. S. Mill.

> Locke said that since the indigenous North Americans did not enclose the land[,] they used it as one would use a common land, but they had no property in it. The land was therefore empty, vacant, wild, and could be taken over without their consent. . . . Even when Indians enclosed and cultivated land, they were not industrious and advanced enough to make the *best possible* use of it and produce as much as the English could, they were for all practical purposes guilty of wasting the land.[51]

Locke was familiar with the accounts of the North American territories. He had been fascinated by accounts of the Indians' peaceful, idyllic lives but would not interpret Indians' claims that their land was bounded, enclosed, put to best use, cultivated, or continually inhabited for generations, to mean that the Native Americans deserved their property. Against arguments that the Native Americans let the land lay fallow every three years for soil enrichment, Locke insisted that they did not make rational use of the land. Their practices amounted to "waste."

Locke thought that the commons best served humankind by being made available for individual private gain. On Locke's (mis)understanding of Scripture, God required each person to make as full a use of the land as possible. Such a requirement was thought to be a duty, a duty that gave rights of property. In this manner, humans could improve upon the laws of nature with their inventive ability to improve upon its productivity.[52] Nature was less a sacred, organic entity to adjust to than a domain subject to human improvement. In time, Locke's thought underwrote a remarkable accumulation of material goods on the part of his compatriots.

> The trouble with Indians (and the reason why they wasted the land) was that they had very few desires and were easily contented. Since they lacked the desire to accumulate wealth, engage in commerce, produce for an international market, and so on, they had no interest in exploiting the earth's potential to the fullest.[53]

For Locke, private accumulation of land was justifiable only if it eventually contributed to the public good. European appropriation of land in America led to public benefits, in that their use of the land would be far more efficient. On this colonial calculus, the public benefited, although that public was European.

As with later Enlightenment thought, Locke demarcated Europeans from those of other races and continents. Locke and others defined the English by what they were not, i.e., foraging and horticultural peoples who did not have a form of social control or political apparatus. Locke hoped that once the economy was based on a monetary system, English settlers would be able to buy up Native American lands and turn the erstwhile owners into their employees. He realized that the introduction of money would allow some people to transcend the natural limits of agricultural production and allow the accumulation of resources.

Locke saw the English political structure as the most important marker of comparison between themselves and Native Americans. Intellect itself, the superior reason that he saw enabling such formalized social control, was perhaps the most critical source of demarcation. Indians failed to measure up to the universal standard of progress. Thus their way of life had no moral claims on outsiders and could be dismantled. As Locke defined equality, only the civilized nations possessed it; noncivilized nations were placed outside the pale of international law and morality.

In actuality, Native Americans in New England exemplified complex relationships among people, natural resources, and property rights. A village held a right to the territory that it used during the various seasons of the year. People owned what they made with their own hands, and they held exclusive use of their fields. Beyond that, different groups of people could make different claims on the same tract of land depending on how they used it. Any village member, for instance, had the right to collect edible wild plants, cut birchbark or chestnut for canoes, or gather sedges for mats wherever these things could be found. Since village lands were usually organized along a single watershed, the same was true of rivers and the coast: Fish and shellfish could generally be taken anywhere, although things like the nets used to catch them, and the sites where they were installed, might be owned by an individual or kin group. At plentiful fishing sites, several villages might gather to share the wealth. Property rights, in other words, shifted with ecological use.[54] The way the Native Americans used the environment reflected intricate and complicated relationships among individuals and communities, negotiated over time and history. Resources were described in a way that reflected these same relations.

Locke and other Enlightenment thinkers universalized themselves as demarcated from the non-Europeans they encountered. That is, they took features that they ascribed to themselves, such as reason, and presumed comparisons between themselves and those who were apparently less advanced. Their own achievement was assumed to be a kind of endpoint along a dimension. Other peoples were then measured by their distance from white civilization. Europe came to see itself as not just another region but as the crown of a planetary process. All peoples then were competing on the same terms and were pointing toward the same goals, whether conscious of it or not.

Enlightenment worldview sought a science and a social science that searched for universal laws of behavior. Nonparliamentarian notions of consensus making were flattened into being characterized as pre-democratic societies. From then on, social science portrayed the study of a particular place as one that produced a deficient version of knowledge.

> With the creation of modern European identity in Enlightenment the world was reduced to European terms and those terms were equated with universality. . . . Those excluded from the domain of knowing, reason, equality and freedom by a buoyant British and French slavery or an expanding colonization are rendered in racist terms as qualitatively different. This was not simply a matter of excluding the enslaved from the realms of liberty and law . . . in the ubiquitous, all-defining gaze of the Enlightenment, the enslaved were purposively constructed as essentially different and strange. Through taking identity in opposition to this creation, Europeans become bound in their own being by the terms in which they oppress others.[55]

White civilization universalized what it took to be its assets, and invested self-understanding and self-congratulation in the differences. In doing so, it fundamentally tied its own particular raison d'être to the purported inferiority of those on the outside.

The project that universalizes itself and flattens its conception of others is a project that minimizes its own role by constituting difference as self-evident. "The beauty and necessity of this negative mode of forming identity is that the subject is not presented in limited terms that would contradict its equation with the universal. Even its seemingly limiting virtues of moderation and lawfulness correspond to transcendent harmony and order."[56] Those who held to an embodiment of reason viewed everything from a pinnacle. Their notion of the nature of democratic decision-making, for example, involved attempts to categorize others by universals rather than initiate dialogue.

The European contact with non-Europeans disordered them to a degree and with a permanence unmatched in the historical and ethnographic record. "The colonial situation provides another monumental instance of law initiating and sustaining pervasive disorder even in the pursuit of its pretense to secure order."[57] Peter Fitzpatrick and others point out that European-based law undermined the existing communal order. The tight web of small-scale[58] informal social control unraveled and was replaced by European formal social control. Communal mechanisms fell and gave way to an individualistic conception of society, a social contract model of the communal, and respondent growth in centralized state power.

Liberal Variation

Locke was not alone in his colonial interest. John Stuart Mill was one of the East India Company officers most responsible for India, joining the company well after Plassey and the consolidation of the empire. He joined at about the time it was exporting opium in order to finally open up an unyielding China for trade. His responsibility covered the later years of the company, through the mutiny of 1857 and the company's subsequent revocation of charter in 1858, when he took early retirement rather than work within a colonial bureaucracy that was accountable to elected officials.[59]

Mill, hailed throughout as an exemplar of liberalism and a progressive thinker, thought only autonomous and self-determining persons exemplified character and individuality. Mill granted that the resolutely autonomous individual, freed from the unthinking conformity to custom, was a rarity, and an endangered one. Too many people did not fit the bill and appeared to have little desire to change themselves in accordance with Mill's position on human improvement. Mill would invidiously agree with later apologists that conformity to custom was closer to human nature than was the autonomous individual. For him, individuality represented human destiny but went against human nature.[60]

"Education" took on iconlike importance as the institution capable of moving humanity forward, away from local custom. The learning process necessarily was unidirectional from civilizer to civilizee. As a conflict-resolution strategy, albeit not conceived in such terminology, education formed the primary route of conversion. Individuality, an autonomy willing to define itself in terms of its own carefully reasoned choices, was clearly for Mill a European capacity that was nonexistent elsewhere. The colonial gaze flattened and eliminated differences. Thus, no need existed for giving attention to local patterns of resource use or communal structures.

The liberalism of Mill's time depended on holding out material reward to those who had yet to rise to the top of the conceived universal norm of distance and rationality. Modernizing peoples needed to emulate the European polity in order to progress along the path to modernity. Successful development in the hinter regions was constituted by mimicking British lessons from political system to educational system to economic formula.

This worldview universalized itself. Ironically its values were exalted but not made to apply to the process of colonization itself. Colonizer enlightenment valued autonomy, choice, and detached rationality yet allowed little of the former. Classical liberalism focussed relentlessly on justifying and cataloguing the workings of the modern state and later its purported democratic institutions. It spoke of a newly arrived public sphere guaranteed by the equality and autonomy of its members, yet their membership was contingent upon ownership of private property.

As such, liberalism failed to recognize other forms of democratic decision-making. Jack Weatherford has provided some evidence and plausibility for the thesis that several of the democratic concepts utilized by the founders of that continent's new nation were concepts borrowed from Cherokee and other Indians.[61] Whether borrowing democratic notions or not, classic liberalism in the end justified withholding self-determination from the indigenous peoples. "In misreading the so-called East, it misread itself and became a victim of double distortion."[62]

The colonial experience profoundly affected and shaped Lockean and Millian liberalism. For example, historian Orlando Patterson has traced the concept of freedom, so fundamental to Classical liberalism, to the institution of slavery:

> and so it was that freedom came into the world. Before slavery people simply would not have conceived of the thing we call freedom. Men and women did not, could not value the removal of restraint as an ideal . . . an ideal cherished

in the West beyond all others emerged as a necessary consequence of the degradation of slavery and the effort to negate it.[63]

Prior to the slave trade, the concept of the individual, free from community, did not exist. Rather, freedom referred to the "freedom of a tribe, a nation, or as city from the domination of another such group."[64] In this form, it resembles only slightly our present concept of freedom as personal liberty. Through the experience of colonization freedom went from being conceived as referring to group-based sovereignty to the notion of freedom as personal liberty.

Law defines the formal relationships among individual, state, and intermediary groupings and the land. And law changed in response and as part of the experience of colonialism and the emerging European philosophy of the time. In the past, social control was informal and leadership involved consensus-building. Individuals lived within a collective social canopy that was so fundamentally constitutive of their experience and thought as to permeate it. Nils Christie states that in this collective reality, ownership of conflicts accrued to the participants rather than the sovereign/state.[65] In contrast an individualistic notion of society moved ownership of conflict upward.

The relationship between the human community and land was transformed by this same transformation of law. By the end of the sixteenth century, as local practices were set aside, Sir Edward Coke codified and reshaped common law at the same time Christopher Saxton developed a cartography of the kingdom.[66] In his zeal to impose a distant rationality on the legal system, Coke dismissed various place-specific customs. He selectively worked from heterogeneity to centralization and unity, disembedding law from locality. Saxton likewise served the centralization of state power. Land was formulated from the perspective of an independent, all-seeing cartographer—the view from above. These two projects irrevocably altered the particularized, localized, embedded legal space. They were substantial contributors to the process of "enframing, in which the world is set before the autonomous and detached self."[67] Until then, the law displayed notable local variations, as did methods of land measurement and mapping. Both were locally embedded, more subjective, and less universal in their establishment. Saxton and Coke were both engaged in representational projects that would recast space, place, and law into the modern, liberal format. Each was no longer viewed from the local perspective. Now each was objectively formulated from above. Space became something to be "measured, contained, divided, manipulated, and crucially, alienated."[68] Law became an ahistorical, placeless object while space became a neutral set of data to be fixed within a unitary perspectival grid. The geography of citizenship shifted from the local to the universal, and away from networks of kinship, manor, and church:

> The legal universe becomes at once totalizing and individualizing. Absent, of course, is the localized group. The local subject, situated within the spaces of feudalism, reemerges as an individualized citizen within a national system of law. This constitutes a radical departure from the premodern conception, in which the very idea of the individual as the locus of legal status is absent.[69]

The "mediating units" gave way to the "sovereignty of the individual" and the "sovereignty of the state." The overall process was one that universalized law and space, but paradoxically fragmented and decentralized the populace into less connected individuals. At the same time, the relatively informal social control slowly broke down in response to increasing trade relations and other economic changes. Industrial transformations were to follow the conquest of the land. As labor moved to the city and transferred skills from farm to factory, corporate bodies were organized to both counteract the growing power of the business corporation, and to build meaningful places to live and work.

Notes

1. Paul Theobald, *Teaching the Commons* (Boulder, Colo.: Westview, 1997), 66-70.

2. Benjamin R. Barber, *Strong Democracy* (Berkeley: University of California Press, 1984), 34-35.

3. Jack Weatherford, *Indian Givers: How the Indians of the Americas Transformed the World* (New York: Fawcett Columbine, 1988), 123.

4. Loren Wilkinson, *Earthkeeping in the 90s,* rev. ed. (Grand Rapids, Mich.: Eerdmans, 1991).

5. Kathy Laster and Padma Roman, "Law for One and One for All," in *Sexing the Subject of Law,* ed. Ngaire Naffine and Rosemary J. Owens (London: Sweet and Maxwell, 1997), 193-312.

6. Jürgen Habermas, *Theory and Practice* (Boston: Beacon, 1973), 61, emphasis in original.

7. Heidi R. Ballard, "The Ideology of Development," (Ph.D. diss., University of New Mexico, 1997).

8. Peter Hulme, "The Spontaneous Hand of Nature," in *The Enlightenment and its Shadows,* ed. Peter Hulme and Ludmilla Jordanova (London: Routledge, 1990), 16-34.

9. Fritjof Capra, *The Turning Point* (London: Fontana Flamingo, 1983).

10. Thomas Hobbes, *Leviathan*, ed. Michael Oakeshotte (New York: Collier, 1962).

11. Robert A. Nisbet, *The Quest for Community* (New York: Oxford University Press, 1953).

12. Ellen Meiksens Wood and Neal Wood, *A Trumpet of Sedition* (New York: New York University Press, 1997), 98.

13. Vernon Van Dyke, "The Individual, the State, and Ethnic Communities in Political Theory," *World Politics* 29 (1977): 343-69.

14. Nisbet, *The Quest for Community*, 133.

15. Wood and Wood, *A Trumpet of Sedition*, 99.

16. Habermas, *Theory and Practice*.

17. Patricia Hill Collins, *Fighting Words: Black Women and the Search for Justice, Contradictions of Modernity*, vol. 7 (Minneapolis: University of Minnesota Press, 1998), xiv.

18. Joan C. Tronto, *Moral Boundaries: A Political Argument for an Ethic of Care* (New York: Routledge, 1994), 8.

19. Tronto, *Moral Boundaries*, 6.

20. Tronto, *Moral Boundaries*, 8.

21. Tronto, *Moral Boundaries*, 93.

22. Virginia Held, *Feminist Morality: Transforming Culture, Society, and Politics* (Chicago: The University of Chicago Press, 1993), 220.

23. Held, *Feminist Morality*, 223.

24. Collins, *Fighting Words*, xiv.

25. Nisbet, *The Quest for Community*, 133.

26. Hobbes, cited in Peter Fitzpatrick, *The Mythology of Modern Law* (New York: Routledge, 1992), 75.

27. Wood and Wood, *A Trumpet of Sedition*.

28. P. S. Ayitah, *The Rise and Fall of Freedom of Contract* (Oxford: Clarendon Press, 1979), 36-37.

29. R. Jeffrey Lustig, *Corporate Liberalism* (Berkeley: University of California Press, 1982), 47-48.

30. Tronto, *Moral Boundaries*, 50.

31. Tronto, *Moral Boundaries*, 51.

32. Tronto, *Moral Boundaries*, 56.

33. Tronto, *Moral Boundaries*, 63-64.

34. Collins, *Fighting Words*, 199-200.

35. Tronto, *Moral Boundaries*, 9.

36. Martin Jay, Sidney Hellman Ehrman Professor of History, University of California at Berkeley. "Must Justitia Be Blind: Challenges of Images to the Law, (Presentation at Calvin College on April 21, 1998, NEH-funded Visual Rhetoric Series).

37. Rita C. Manning, *Speaking from the Heart: A Feminist Perspective on Ethics* (Lanham, Md.: Rowman & Littlefield, 1992), 66.

38. Tronto, *Moral Boundaries,* 9.

39. Carole Pateman, *The Sexual Contract* (New York: Cambridge University Press, 1988).

40. Lisa J. McIntyre, "Law and the Family in Historical Perspective," in *Families and Law,* ed. Lisa J. McIntyre and Marvin B. Sussman (New York: Haworth Press, 1995), 5-30.

41. Margaret Thornton, "The Cartography of Public and Private," in *Public and Private,* ed. Margaret Thornton (Oxford: Oxford University Press, 1995), 2-17.

42. Sheldon Wolin, "Contract and Birthright," in *Communitarianism: A New Public Ethics,* ed. Markate Daly (Belmont, Calif.: Wadsworth, 1994), 181-90.

43. Elizabeth Wolgast, *Equality and the Rights of Women* (Ithaca, N.Y.: Cornell University Press, 1980).

44. Nel Noddings, *Caring: A Feminine Approach to Ethics and Moral Education* (Berkeley: University of California Press, 1984), 6.

45. Held, *Feminist Morality,* 194.

46. Held, *Feminist Morality,* 195.

47. Held, *Feminist Morality,* 203.

48. John Locke, *An Essay Concerning Human Understanding* (Chicago: Encyclopedia Brittanica, 1952).

49. Susan Leeson, "Philosophic Implications of the Ecological Crisis," *Polity* 11 (1979): 303-18.

50. Paul Marshall, "John Locke: Between God and Mammon," *Canadian Journal of Political Science* 12, no. 1 (March 1979): 73-96.

51. Bhikhu Parekh, "Liberalism and Colonialism: A Critique of Locke and Mill," in *The Decolonization of Imagination,* ed. J. N. Pieterse and B. Parekh, (London: Zed Books, Ltd., 1995), 81-98, 85.

52. Theobald, *Teaching the Commons,* 67.

53. Parekh, "Liberalism and Colonialism," 85.

54. William Cronon, *Changes in the Land: Indians, Colonists, and the Ecology of New England* (New York: Hill and Wang, 1983), 63.

55. Fitzpatrick, *The Mythology of Modern Law,* 65-66.

56. Fitzpatrick, *The Mythology of Modern Law,* 67.

57. Fitzpatrick, *The Mythology of Modern Law,* 81.

58. Bhikhu Parekh, "Liberalism and Colonialism: A Critique of Locke and Mill," in *The Decolonization of Imagination*, ed. J. N. Pieterse and B. Parekh, (London: Zed Books, Ltd., 1995), 81-98, 85.

59. Bhikhu Parekh, "Decolonizing Liberalism," in *The End of "ISMS?": Reflection on the Fate of Ideological Politics after Communism's Collapse*, ed. Aleksandras Shtromas (Cambridge, Mass.: Blackwell, 1994), 85-103.

60. John Stuart Mill, *On Liberty*, ed. Elizabeth Rapaport (Indianapolis: Hackett, 1978).

61. Weatherford, *Indian Givers*.

62. Parekh, "Decolonizing Liberalism," 93.

63. Orlando Patterson, *Slavery and Social Death: A Comparative Study* (Cambridge, Mass: Harvard University Press, 1982), 340-42.

64. Weatherford, *Indian Givers*, 121.

65. Nils Christie, "Conflicts As Property," *The British Journal of Criminology* 17, no. 1 (1978): 1-15.

66. Nicholas Blomley, *Law, Space, and the Geographies of Power* (New York: Guilford, 1994), 67-105.

67. Blomley, *Law, Space, and the Geographies of Power*, 67-105.

68. Blomley, *Law, Space, and the Geographies of Power*, 91.

69. Blomley, *Law, Space, and the Geographies of Power*, 102.

CHAPTER 3

INDUSTRIAL TRANSFORMATIONS

As law in spirit is individualistic . . . and as unions are formed to escape the evils of individualism and individual competition and contract . . . [u]nionism is in its very essence a lawless thing, in its very purpose and spirit a challenge to law.[1]

Christopher Tomlins

THE TIME OF HOBBES, Descartes, and Bacon corresponded to the shift from the raiding of outposts of the "guns and sails" era to the consolidation of such outposts into settler colonies. Changes in one domain worked hand in hand with changes in another. Relationships with nature changed as the world was transformed into plantations and North American lands were "rationally" surveyed and sold. The groundwork of empiricism furthered society's conceptual move toward reductionism in knowledge and societal concepts of humans. The law and laissez-faire economics followed suit, leading to the further demise of mediating institutions. Corporate bodies such as labor unions attempted to counter the social reductionism and the diminishing public-trust responsibility of business corporations. But their lack of legal standing made their attempts to focus on community and place difficult.

The time of Newton and Locke saw the establishment of monocrop plantations and the increase in the slave trade. By 1700 some two-thirds of the land in England had been enclosed. Peasants who worked the land found they could not support themselves in the same way as past generations. To survive, many uprooted themselves and moved to the cities where new industries produced goods for wider and wider markets.

In North America, the commercial corporation continued its westward appropriation. It drove early migration from the settler colonies:

One of the first was the Loyal Land Company, chartered in Virginia in 1749 to sell land to the south and west of the settled areas. This was followed in other years by the Ohio Company, the Vandalia Company, the Mississippi

Company founded in Virginia, the Susquehanna Company, Lyman's
Mississippi Company, and the Ohio Company of Associates.[2]

The culture would imagine and mythologize the expansion in individualistic
terms. In doing so it would forget the foundational role of the chartered
corporation in effecting increasing scales of operations. Cultural mythmaking of
the day would ignore the corporate composition of the pioneering forces—many
of the early trappers were corporate employees or agents—but would embrace
and assimilate the more encompassing colonizer worldview.

In 1719 Daniel Defoe's *Robinson Crusoe* inaugurated the novel genre in
England.[3] The book was unthinkable without the mercantile European outreach
of the day and its structure was in accord with accounts of recent exploration
voyages. Defoe's book exhibited an ambivalence regarding the relationship
between the individual and the community. It echoed the values of the nascent
capitalism, supporting the extant notion of *homo economicus* and the protestant
ethic. Thrown into savage existence on a Caribbean island, Crusoe first
establishes his autonomy and embodies the sober, calculating work ethic, the
industrious spirit, and furnishes a literary parallel for the colonizer.

Western Europe was shifting culturally from rootedness within place,
within a particular encompassing locale, toward a dependence upon faroff
colonized lands. Self-sufficiency was giving way to dependency on the far-
reaching market. Colonial endeavors deeply underwrote how literate members
of the mother country understood themselves and their increasing good fortune.
Voltaire's *Candide* of 1761 paralleled *Crusoe* in its voyage to the New World
for the protagonist's transformation. America was a requisite backdrop for
several developments in the journey.

Edward Said makes a strong case that the literary form of the novel itself,
as a cultural artifact of the ascending bourgeois society, was deeply tied to
colonial expansion. The latter fortified the former, and the former helped
legitimate the latter. The nineteenth century was a time of intense imperial
activity, from the Chinese Opium Wars to the Crimean War, from the conquest
of lower Burma to the military campaigns in Canada, West Africa, and Egypt.
Novels and essays recurrently served to confirm empire and all its implications.

Said shows that the massive work of the plantation workers and others at
the opposite end of the colonial corporate yoke was conceptualized as a mere
convenience for the European race.[4] The colonized races, constructed as
secondary, again served to furnish a people with its own sense of being primary.
Said also argues that Jane Austen's *Mansfield Park* (1814) and Kipling's *Kim*,
along with Conrad's *Heart of Darkness* served as examples for the English.

Mansfield's work on social order and moral priority presumed overseas possessions that generated the wealth, social status, and particular values as embodied by Sir Thomas Bertram. Empire was an important backdrop for many of the novels, and its role increased with writers like Kipling and Conrad.[5]

Two decades after *Crusoe*, David Hume articulated some of the most important cornerstones of subsequent thinking about knowledge and science. Distinguishing sensory impressions from ideas, he laid the groundwork for empiricism. While Europe busily distinguished itself from encountered others, Hume demarcated the solidly empirical from that which is built upon it. His emphasis on uniting facts and logic set down the basic tenets of empiricism. Empiricism to this day distinguishes theory from data, seeking ways to solidify the less tenable former by association with the less arguable latter.

Hume demarcated how things are from how they should be. This welding of sense data to logic generates privileged knowledge about what is; to speak of what ought to be is to enter a different domain. Knowledge about how things are does not secure conclusions about that which ought to be. Empiricism continues to find discourse about the "ought" to be unsusceptible to rationality and discourse about the "is" to personify rationality. The former is thus conceived to be fundamentally arbitrary and the latter to be fundamentally exemplary.[6]

Many changes marked the European economy in the decades after Hume. Subsequent mainstream European history noted the shift by the early nineteenth century from the rural to the factory and industry. The region's economy also accelerated toward one of global economic predominance. Such history purveyed many different theories to account for the economic takeoff and the related societal changes. For all its scholarly variation, such history held to a common assumption. Whether emphasizing scientific expertise, military superiority, a religious ethic, or an entrepreneurial spirit, such history attributed the takeoff to factors internal to Europe. On such a view, the region pulled itself up of its own accord. It built upon its own strengths, capitalizing on them.

Some of the chartered corporations became quite successful and influential during this era. France and Scotland had followed the lead of the Dutch and English with corporate entities of their own, though with less support from state and military resources. The business corporation itself furnished the basis for a distinctive means of generating capital—the modern banking system and the stock market. The Dutch established a stock market to finance the East India Company in 1602, and by the end of the century the Bank of Amsterdam and the Bank of England had been formed.

New Land

Correlates of Enlightenment assumptions, over time, contributed to visible changes on the American landscape. William Cronon gives some indication of the magnitude of the changes wrought in a short time period.[7] Native Americans' practices could deplete the land but not quite in the way those of the newcomers did. The Native Americans that the Puritans encountered heavily relied on wood for fuel in homes and so needed to move every so often to a new supply. The Native Americans first thought that the Europeans arrived due to their own fuel shortage. The Europeans, however, were more interested in lumbering. Timber at first seemed endless and it was heavily used in building and sent across the Atlantic to meet the need there.

Farming required more destruction of forests. Colonists used fire to clear the land, burning forests to make room for agriculture. Clearing altered ground level ecology, warming and drying the soil, thus altering the microclimate of the soil surface. The land got hotter in the summer and colder in winter. In winter, snow melted more quickly and soil froze to deeper depths. Since frozen ground was unable to retain water as easily, flooding increased. Similar to the Europeans' impact in the Canary Islands, stream and spring flows became more irregular. Some streams dried up, even as the total amount of water flowing off the land and into streams and rivers increased. Edge-dwelling animal species were adversely affected. Tree species changed.

The newcomers exerted more year around control over animals' lives, compared to their Native American neighbors. European animals trampled, tore the ground, and compacted the soil, destroying native grasses and curtailing the root growth of higher plants. Plowing also was destructive of native species, which were replaced by European species that had adapted to the requirements of pastoralism. As elsewhere, weed plant species thrived at the expense of native ones; European animal species gained at the expense of indigenous ones. The changes were so dramatic that by 1768, John Bruchner wondered if the English expansion transforming the American wilderness was breaking down the "web of life" and plan of Providence.[8]

The newcomers introduced ecological hardships but sought to retain local communal connections that were dissipating in the face of the transition from feudal to industrial economy back home. The Puritan collectivity centered around the concept of a covenantal community where all members were part of the covenant of grace. Their villages were compact and homogeneous. Puritan leaders linked aspects of everyday existence with the religious, societal, and familial institutions of the community. The individual existed in the context of the covenantal community and its network of relationships. The early Puritan tradition emphasized the rights of institutions such as family and church. The location of school and religious reserves reflected the communal values of the system. Public order, exhibited for example in provisions for the establishment of new towns, superseded private property. The Massachusetts Bay Colony General Court prohibited speculation in land and town building.[9] The New England system of settlement required the process to take place at a township rather than an individual level. When more land was needed, a six-square-mile township was laid out and settled as a whole with the granting of land left to the corporate body of the town itself. Purchasers of land in new towns were required to erect houses and enclose some farmland for their use. Ownership of land in the town was tied to membership in the community. Once one town was settled and the land distributed, further settlement could only take place in the context of finding a minister and building another town and community. Settlements as the result of individuals' moving out on their own was not allowed.[10]

J. B. Jackson has described the society and landscape as one where space is hierarchical and centripetal. The center of the town was the most sacred and prestigious area. It contained the church, the center of community life, and the most respected people of the community. The sacredness of space, tied to community life, diminished with distance from the center.[11] The emphasis was on the question of "where"—where one belonged in the organic social order of things.[12]

Changes in American colonial society were taking place by the mid-1700s in response to the unfolding of Enlightenment's individualism and the economic and social class transformations it served. Land and people increasingly came to be extricated from community. Evidence on the landscape of these changes included the growth of isolated farmsteads, the sale of common lands, and the privately financed speculative settlements. Jackson has traced the origins of this change to Enlightenment reductionism and rationalism and has interpreted these changes as representing

> a break of traditional ties, social and environmental, and the forming of new relationships based on independence and mobility and rationality, on the release of forces, both destructive and creative, destined in time to alter society and the face of the earth. Relationships, and especially the relationship to the environment, tended to assume a new, more impersonal, more abstract and legalistic form. Land was possessed and exploited not by merely physical means but by contract.[13]

Thomas Jefferson became the originator of and advocate for the land policy that reflected individualistic Enlightenment ideals. He advocated the building of a nation of self-sufficient, independent farmers in tune with the earth that supported them. This was accomplished with an emphasis on economic rationalization as expressed through the United States National Land Survey, whose grid pattern was perfectly suited for quick disposal of public lands to individuals. This way of life, represented by the separate farmstead, was considered the norm and the Ordinance of 1785 took it as its model. It was confirmed by the Preemption Act of 1841, which required one to live on the land he or she claimed.[14] Land became another commodity that was valued for its economic possibilities. Historical constraints to individual materialistic gain were minimized, and American law began to assume the superiority of individual private property over every other social good.

In the meantime, Adam Smith was finding value in a free-flowing lack of regulation. He said that the discovery of America and a passage to the East Indies were the two most important events in the history of human society and noted that the discovery of America opened up a new, inexhaustible market that was leading to the expansion of wealth. He argued that Britain should free itself from the American colonies in part because the colonies failed to provide military support for the empire itself. India had come to furnish troops in service of the British East India Company, but the Americans were less productive in that respect.

Smith conceived exchange to be the core of economic life and held that the exchange between the old world and the new one would benefit both, not just the former. He formulated a portrait of the evolving economy as one of autonomous individuals. In this way, Smith-influenced economics came to mirror the individualism of philosophy that dwelled on Descartes, Hobbes, Locke, and others. Social life increasingly became one of freely contracting individuals, which resulted in a diminished understanding of the collective good. Value came to lie in exchange rather than use. Liberal thought increasingly bypassed classical notions of a transcendent moral order and the limits it would place on self-interest and desire for consumption. Relatively unlimited laissez-faire supplanted organic images of the natural and social order.

Smith's *Wealth of Nations* mentioned the new corporate entity twelve times but not once favorably. He held that wealth obtained through the free market was deserving and was in keeping with the natural order. He spoke of England as a nation of shopkeepers, locally rooted and subject to local community conscience. But corporations violated the natural order. They limited competition, countering the free flow of the market. Smith found the corporation to hold little promise, except by virtue of its monopoly privilege. He held that privilege to benefit the merchants but not the great body of the British people. The American colonies benefited a few English at the expense of the many. Smith decried the privilege, as did many others at the time. He derived imagery of the positive economic workings of an unrestrained invisible hand from his assessment of a largely precorporate world. Ironically, he supported freedom of trade in an increasingly globalized world that had already seen colonial corporations benefit one region of the globe.

Concurrently, the growing importance of science proceeded hand in glove first with military applications and then with industrial ones as well. Cities began to grow in an almost unprecedented manner and without respite. States burgeoned and empires expanded. From its beginning, the factory system had been met with popular resistance and grudging acquiescence on the part of much of the affected population. As the so-termed Industrial Revolution took hold, doubts continued to prevail in some quarters. Unions formed to redress the unequal power of individual workers with respect to their company employers. Riots were endemic in manufacturing districts. Early in the nineteenth century, Luddites vigorously and violently resisted the loss of control to factory owners, with extensive working class support in some areas. E. P. Thompson shows that they were, in effect, contesting the consequences of laissez-faire.[15] Before long utopians feared inequality and separation from nature; often leaving to form communal arrangements in Palestine and North America. Proudhon began developing modern anarchistic theory, emphasizing cooperation of workers in labor associations. Worker associations and others came to experience the state as a bulwark of inequality whose loyalty went to the larger business corporations rather than to their own collective associations.

Between Individual and State

A third of the way into the nineteenth century, at about the time of the dissipation of the Puritan communities, Alexis de Tocqueville came to North America from France for the purpose of examining how the societal changes of the day were playing out in the New World. His description of hiking for miles along a footpath to the last outpost in one direction, Saginaw, carries a certain poignancy. He said that in the forest, as in the ocean

> you are assailed by a sense of immensity . . . [I]n this ocean of leaves, who
> could point out the way? Whither turn one's looks? In vain to climb to the top
> of very high trees, for others still surround you. It is useless to climb the hills,
> for everywhere the forest seems to walk in front of you. . . . You can travel

> for thousands of leagues under its shade, and you go forward the whole time
> without appearing to change place.[16]

He was quite percipient about the forthcoming changes:

> One feels a quiet admiration, a gentle melancholy sense, and a vague distaste
> for civilized life, a sort of primitive instinct that makes one think with
> sadness that soon this delightful solitude will have changed its looks. In fact,
> already the white race is advancing across the forest that surrounds it, and in
> but few years the European will have cut the tree.[17]

But Tocqueville is more justly remembered for his numerous social observations in the new land. As had others, he often commented on its indigenous population's apparent lack of government, its equality, and its freedom. In the settlers he noted an interesting admixture of freedom and independence on the one side and conceptual conformity on the other. Those at the lowest social orders were able to have their say much more than in Europe, but at the same time individuals were reluctant to challenge the commonly accepted wisdom of their neighbors. In the shadow of liberty, fraternity, and equality, he also perceived a social leveling and concomitant changes in class dynamics. Tocqueville's analyses were among the first by thinkers whose work became foundational for the sciences of societal life.

Coming from a land renowned for its centralized bureaucratic administration, Tocqueville marveled at Americans' ability to solve problems on their own in concert and without recourse to a superior authority such as the state. He paired this capacity with Americans' propensity to join a multitude of political associations. He saw such associations as crucial in a democracy. Democracy is extremely vulnerable to a tyranny of the majority. The voluntary political associations form a countervailing influence against the potentially abusive majority power. On Tocqueville's experience, American voluntary associations were more peaceable than their European counterparts. The European ones were more oriented to immediate action, whereas the American ones entertained hopes of drawing their opponents over to their own side. The former were more centralized and oligarchic while the latter retained more individual independence.

For the visiting Frenchman, no lesson gained from the new land was more important. Political life in the motherlands was altering itself portentously as monarchy in the name of democracy. Citizens had become aroused, and the power of the mob alarmed political analysts as much as the power of the despot had in previous times. The structuring of political power was shifting.

De Toqueville unearthed multiple considerations, but pinpointed voluntary associations. They constituted a check on power, which had absolute importance. Such associations amounted to a mediating force between the individual and the sovereign, much as corporations had in earlier times. But they also furnished a preemptive force against the increasing danger of individual isolation, a central tenet of what would later be indicted as the danger of mass society: that individuals in an increasingly transformed world become isolated, sundered from the bonds of community.

Inevitably, the principle strategy of unitary democracy came to be fixed with the individual as the sole unit and the state as the sole association in society.[18]

The Economic Imperative

Writing in the decades following the publication of Tocqueville's treatise, Karl Marx added further insights into the societal transformations. Many recognized that the shift from local subsistence to the larger market economy initiated latent social consequences. By the time Tocqueville was being read, other authors were proposing various utopian alternatives. Many individuals were drawn to the agrarian, socialist, and religious communes of the 1840s. Marx proposed that the nonaristocratic portion of the population, found working in the factories, experienced alienation. Such persons were alienated from a meaningful relation to work. The developing economy further alienated the worker from his or her own body and separated the individual from the community.

Marx, and followers such as Lenin, pointed to the estrangement between colonizer and colonized as well as to the increasingly global influence of the market economy. They looked with less benevolent eyes upon the colonial expansion, finding more self-interest than many colonials at the time would acknowledge and pointing out that it was becoming evident that for the colonial endeavor, profits went to individuals, but costs went to society both abroad and at home. Lenin tied the imperialism of his day directly to the functioning of the European economy, so that the fortunes of far-off peoples and their colonial conquerors could be understood as connected.

The Marxian clarification at mid century deepened the implications of the connection between the European core and its various peripheries. The ascending economy, by its very nature, increased inequality. By the nature of the workings of the process of capital accumulation, wealth and power increased in concentration. At the other end of the spectrum, poverty increased and continued to do so. Those limiting their focus of analysis to Europe per se missed the increase of inequality inherent in the arrangement. Marx and his followers focused more on social class, but the implications were there to be drawn regarding the business corporation.

On the Marxian analysis, the free market eventually became anything but free, and the playing field for economic entities became anything but level. The fundamental workings of the economy itself generated an increased inequality. The more successful economic entities grew in size; the less successful ones went to work for the former. Business corporations were pressured by the very structure of the economy not only to make profits, but to grow. Those that expanded in size accrued many benefits. Those that failed to expand were more likely to be incorporated by their competitors or forced out of competition. Exceptions to the contrary, the corporations that expanded were the ones that were the most successful. The ones that grew the most tended to be the ones accruing the most wealth and the most power. The intentions and personalities of the business leaders themselves were not particularly relevant; the structuring of the economy pressured them to behave in particular ways. Small businesses could survive, but they would be overmatched, as was the individual.

Political thinkers heretofore had been uneasy with the relations between the sovereign and the individual. Many sought protections for the individual from despotism, while others sought protection of the elite from the common hoard. To be feared were the monarch and/or the state, or else the great mass. Enlightenment thinkers minimally anticipated the dangers of the business corporation. Hobbes did fear that the new-styled corporation would take power from the sovereign but was less concerned about the potential power imbalance between the corporation and the individual citizen.

The Individual Transformed

The changes sweeping Western Europe and North America at the end of the nineteenth century were so massive and wide reaching as to dominate the social thought of the day. While not all agreed with Marx as to the causal efficacy of economics, many did concur that social relations were changing profoundly and were moving away from community. Europeans (and soon non-Europeans alike) were relating to each other more in terms of market and social-contract principles rather than those of kinship. Urban interactions with large numbers of strangers were increasingly displacing village interchanges with familiars. At the same time, the state and various other enterprises grew in size and took on a bureaucratic format.

Some found positive elements in the transformation of social relations. Reason appeared to be supplanting tradition. Achievement on the basis of merit gained at the expense of ascription of inherited traits; the bureaucracy moved in the direction of universal and objective procedures. In the work world, standardization offered the promise of more just treatment. The universalizing criteria of science overpowered other theories of knowing, utilizing science's pragmatic efficacy, and the newly cosmopolitan individual was less provincial in his or her thinking. Sophistication and tolerance replaced dogmatic certainty and narrow-mindedness. Such advances constituted double-edged swords, but regardless of the actual value of the positives, a collective wisdom developed as to the negative impact of the transformation on the social fabric.

Individual identity was shifting. During the feudal period, identity was ascribed in terms of belonging to a certain rank. Relationships to the state were mediated by ties to groups in a hierarchy of dependence and authority.[19] The French and American Revolutions, at least in theory, served to apportion rights beyond those who owned property to all individuals. The collective groups became less important for an individual's rights and obligations and identity. The individual came to expect certain rights on his or her own, with no reference to the larger group, leading in the direction of the basic unit of civic society—the individual.[20] Intermediate collective ties between the individual and society were formulated as a constraint on individual freedom. Society's interests were characterized as the aggregate of individual wills of all citizens. Such an equality had become shorn of the earlier collective aspects of society.

The development of a national identity filled the gap. The individual came to think of him or herself more by reference to the geographically larger national group, and less by feudal group status. However contentiously, that national group regularly enlarged as neighboring territories were incorporated under a single state banner. Culturally distinct peoples gradually came to identify themselves as German, French, or British. Colonial encounters generated counterposing identities (for both sides), and for the Europeans helped to consolidate national identity. The state system of social organization proved to be feasible for the wealthier classes and their business corporations, but also sufficed for many other newly uprooted people in Europe as well.

Many analysts at the beginning of the nineteenth century recognized that individuals were becoming disengaged from the community; they increasingly lacked roots and were no longer connected by tradition to a particular locale. Less attached to a kinship network, the individual was also less connected to mediating groups between the individual and state.

The rise of the state in a sense complemented the weakening of the individual. Political units continued the long extant trend toward enlarging themselves and thus decreasing in number. The states did this by abridging rights previously held by manors, communities, and other local political units. Political leaders sought to expand their domains into ever-more encompassing territories. Nations were welded together under states and the state system cemented itself as the principals mutually recognized one another.

The time of these social commentaries was a time in which some of the most important changes in the legal accouterments of the new entity were taking hold. For the business corporation, apart from the colonizer monopolies initiated during the mercantile period, one of the most important developments pertained to altered concepts of its responsibility in the mid-nineteenth century.

Corporation Infused; Responsibility Defused

In the 1500s, the great trading companies had been organized in such a way that most legal liabilities gave rise to actions against the members as individuals.[21] The scale of colonial adventures altered the corporation in the early 1600s. "Economies of scale" in shipping pointed toward larger ships and the need to raise capital. In the past, members of a corporation had often worked individually as entrepreneurs. But in 1612, the East India Company resolved that only the corporation could trade. Questions of liability became more complicated and less obvious. Doubts about the personhood of the corporation began to arise. Originally, charters could not be granted to just anyone; such privileges could only be granted when the enterprise served the public good. The crown had long granted privileges with exemptions from ordinary liabilities for the contracting parties.

Liability became far more complicated as the scale of corporate business operations began to increase. When the royally chartered company's bridge collapses, who is at fault?[22] If blame could be traced to a particular worker, that person might not be a wealthy entrepreneur but rather his or her relatively impoverished agent. Later complications of organizational format, in effect separating workforce, investor, and management, exacerbated the difficulty.

With the Act of Repeal of the Bubble Act and the Trading Companies Act of 1834, the English crown was given the power to allow for the differential liability of company owners.[23] In 1837, the British Parliament enacted the Chartered Companies Act. This act contained the first mention of liability limited by share of ownership; it also allowed for the termination of liability immediately upon an owner's sale of shares. Prior to the Joint-Stock Companies

Winding-Up Act of 1848, each shareholder in a corporation was responsible for all of a firm's debts, but the liability of investors from the lower and middle class was limited by their net worth. The richer shareholders then comprised a more lucrative target for debt collection. This act served to restrict investment in corporations to those who were already well off. In this context, John Stuart Mill held that less stringent conditions should be attached to corporate status. Specifically, conditions should be relaxed for the purposes of generating operations of a larger scale.

The "scale" argument had noticeable plausibility to those who presumed it valuable and important to exceed current dimensions. Life insurance, railroads, colonial explorations—all could be seen to require a level of capital formation not ordinarily available to the individual or ordinary collectivities of individuals.

In 1855, Parliament provided for limited liability of companies, given proof of financial soundness and the addition of Limited to the company name. A year later the Joint-Stock Companies Act omitted any requirements for external audit or public financial disclosure. The whole point of incorporation for many entrepreneurs was to minimize responsibility.

Business corporations in England began to separate themselves from responsibility. At the same time, legal reasoning shifted in its view of the nature of this incorporated company. The 1856 Companies Act characterized the company in terms of its members, but the 1862 Companies Act omitted this designation and indicated that the company takes on an existence over and above those members.[24] Incorporated companies gradually went from being referred to as "they" to "it." Shares of stock no longer necessarily pointed to shareholders who had formed themselves into companies, but merely those who happened to own such assets. The companies became external to those who initially comprised them.

Before long the corporation could be characterized as a separate personality, with this characterization constituting one of the foundations of modern company law. The corollary collective body to the business corporation, the labor union, took up a place between the individual and state. However, its form could not meet with the same success. Individuals who formed unions were held to embody an unfair advantage against the solitary, individual business corporation.

Law at Labor

In the social theory of the day, obstructions to the rights of individuals were obstructions to the free working of commerce. Individuals were in that sense free to conduct their livelihood activities as they chose. This combined conception of freedom worked well up until the Industrial Revolution, when changing work structures presented new legal challenges. An explication of the common law of torts clarifies the cast of individualistic and paternalistic assumptions onto which industrial accidents in particular and labor law in general was grafted. Servants held a right to sue their masters for damages; individuals hired by others held the same right in the case of damage due to employer negligence. Some precedent existed for employees to sue for damage from negligence caused by another employee as well as through the doctrine of *respondeat superior*.[25] A principal was liable for the negligent acts of his agent. In spite of these protections, courts began to lean more heavily on the fellow-servant rule, by which a servant (and hence, employee) was unable to sue his master (employer) for injuries generated by the negligence of another employee. The premise was that the relation between employer and employee was contractual and so subject to individual adjustment for risks.[26]

A principle that had applied nicely enough for small numbers of individuals left gaping holes in the factory system. The immediately negligent party was far less likely to be the employer than a fellow employee. A difficulty within the initial design of corporate bodies came into play. Corporate employer-owners became remote enough as to experience limitations in this form of liability as well as that pertaining to their customers. Lawrence Friedman and Jack Ladinsky point out that the fellow-servant rule can be traced to an opinion issued in 1837 that was based on the master-servant analogy. Industrial injury was framed in terms of relationships within the household of nobleman and his servants.[27] Legal matters that addressed commerce between ordinary individuals were permeated by two doctrines:

> The two legal doctrines . . . were those of conspiracy and restraint of trade. . . .
> The basic public-policy proposition underlying the conspiracy doctrine is that a number of persons acting in concert or combination possess power for wrongful accomplishment not possessed by individuals.[28]

"Combinations" were perceived as a very serious matter. The relatively isolated individual was at a disadvantage when facing a collection of others. One could defend oneself against a single adversary, but was unfairly matched against a combination.

In common law, sovereigns could charter collectivities for purposes beneficial to society, and in the nineteenth century these slowly became more business oriented. However, actions taken by self-established collective enterprises that affect another's livelihood comprised a danger to be prohibited.

The transformations launched by the incipient Industrial Revolution meant that commerce changed in myriad ways. The scale of commerce continued to increase with European expansion. Harris Millis and Royal Montgomery describe how relations between individual and collectivity were also transformed in a way not anticipated by common law: ·

> From the same fundamental premise—that the group, by the very fact of union, is more powerful and dangerous than are a number of isolated individuals—there ensues the second of the basic dicta of the conspiracy doctrine: that purposes lawful in the case of an individual are not necessarily lawful in the case of a number acting in concert.[29]

Statutes were enacted to address treason, breach of the peace, and "merchants who combined to disturb the market or fix prices" as well. The doctrine came to include not merely combination per se, but combination for "any purpose that might be deemed malicious" in nature. Common law also made it unlawful for one to "restrain another in the exercise of his trade or calling." One could reasonably continue one's own activities, up to the point of doing damage to one's neighbors. A combination of individuals that acted in their own commercial interests in such a way as to restrain those of another was unlawful. "A labor combination is lawful under conspiracy-doctrine principles when its aim is the mutual benefit if its members but is a conspiracy if the purpose is injury to the reputation or property of an employer or interference with the employment opportunities of a non-union man."[30] To the extent that commerce activities entailed competition, they risked conspiracy and restraint of trade when performed by a combination rather than a single individual.

Legal analysis shows that the law eventually catches up with changes in society. Common law doctrines regarding conspiracy and restraint of trade were appropriate for a feudal world of individual merchants, but they were less appropriate for the world of the large-scaled corporation and its mass of employees:

> Responsibility of all conspirators for the acts of any one of them, while a logical implication of the conception of conspiracy, has been regarded by organized labor and by some jurists as unrealistic under modern conditions, since these members frequently are widely scattered, many neither knowing about nor having personal participation . . . in the acts of their officers and agents.[31]

For this reason the doctrines were modified. But the fundamental asymmetry of the individual and the corporation remained, and the latter benefited greatly from the conspiracy doctrines at the expense of the former. Restraint of trade became more complicated and more finely tuned as a doctrine, but the double standard of sovereign-chartered business corporations on the one hand and aggregates of individuals needing to form combinations on the other only intensified.

Britain had long enacted statutes against concerted action by laborers. The Ordinance of Labourers of 1349 and the Statute of Labourers of 1351 had decreed it unlawful for them to make concerted efforts to increase wages. The Combination Acts of 1799 and 1800 outlawed all concerted action by workers or employers. "Though equally applicable to combinations of employers and to combinations of employees, the Acts overlooked the fact that with the development of large-scale production a single employer might have many employees and be a sort of combination in himself."[32] A legal statute that prima facie treated each side of the equation equally (not counting inequities of class or feudal station) generated the opposite when applied to commerce relations conducted on the new corporate scale of the mid-nineteenth century. Not infrequently a so-called combination held less power, not more, than a single person when the person was to be a corporate entity.[33]

David Hume, Francis Place, and others noted the unfairness for unions, and soon the Combination Act of 1824 repealed the limits on labor combinations. The similarly named act of a year later quickly subtracted some of the new rights. It banned the closed shop and concerted actions other than those for wages and hours. In the United States, many workers were not accorded on-the-job rights because the constitution applied only to governments, not to private employers.[34] There the conspiracy doctrine was quite compatible with the individualism of laissez-faire economics and antagonism toward monopolies. The collective-rights issue of one employer being wrongfully hampered by a combination of his or her employees continued to remain an issue. Labor disputes meant that workers acting concertedly rather than individually in pursuit of their goals were ganging up on an individual employer and limiting that employer's right to free, unobstructed commerce. The default option for the judiciary was conspiracy. The employer rights were long established in the law of property and contracts, while those of the employees were new.

Unsympathetic judges treated combinations' very existence as a challenge to the law of the land. More sympathetic ones determined that whether combinations by their very existence were tantamount to conspiracy depended upon their purposes, which often appeared to be legal.[35] Even voluntarist associations were criticized for seeking the regulatory privileges of chartered corporations.

Judges held that contracts originated in courts, so regulatory control over corporations soon shifted from politics, responsive to popular pressure, to the courts, which were less vulnerable to such influence. The Kentucky Court of Appeals and subsequent courts ruled that workers were responsible for their own job injuries; personal damage must be expected when one goes to work for a corporation. The burden of damage that had been placed on the institution's liability was undone as well:

> [J]udges creatively interpreted the commerce and due process clauses of the U.S. constitution. Inventing a new concept which they called substantive due process, they declared one state law (controlling corporations and protecting workers) after another unconstitutional. Judges also established the managerial prerogative and business judgement [sic] doctrines, giving corporations legal justification to arrest civil rights at factory gates, and to blockade democracy at boardroom doors.[36]

They also construed the common good in terms of maximum production, irrespective of damage to land or community. States passed laws addressing the imbalance of power, protecting the individual, and curtailing the power of supra individual businesses, but courts invoked distinctive legal reasoning to strike down numerous laws that regulated the workplace and protected collective bargaining.

The law itself increasingly came to favor corporation business interests. Mill owners were given the legal right to destroy other's property by flood in order to conduct their business; eminent domain was used to condemn farm land for canal and railroad companies; the concept of a fair price for goods gave way to that of buyer beware. The courts ruled that a worker who contracted to work for a year and left before the year was up was not entitled to any wages for work done, but a building business that broke a contract was entitled to be paid for whatever had been done. The "pretense of the law was that a worker and a railroad made a contract with equal bargaining power."[37]

Boycotts were rendered legally inappropriate. Common law and then statute law ruled the boycott an attempt by the union to coerce third parties in its dispute with the corporation. Unions pressured others not to do business with the corporation, thus engaging in "secondary" boycotting. The courts ruled that such boycotts were malicious and unlawful—the threat and coercion deprived the third party of the right to patronize whomever or whatever it so pleased.[38] Furthermore, the courts claimed that the union had caused a breach of contract between the third party and the employer. Such cases again turned on unreasonable restraint of trade.

The great majority of labor injunctions in the United States have been designed, not to protect tangible property from loss or destruction, but to protect business from interference. Given the individualist background of common law, the right to business easily trumped the right to work in disputes between corporations and unions. The corporation's rights might have been initially tied to social benefit, but this conditionality had faded by the turn of twentieth century.[39]

Trade agreements raised a related problem for the courts. Since the unions were voluntary associations, they lacked legal personality (unlike business corporations). For this reason they lacked legal standing to assert property rights. Agreements with them carried no contractual weight.[40] Individual members could sue, but the associations were not empowered to contract for the collective body.

Without incorporating, unions were gradually pushed into the position of bureaucratic administration. Groups continued to increase in scale. Owners wanted more predictability over the workforce and appreciated the potential advantages of working with labor hierarchies to control the rank and file. The courts increasingly treated unions as a de facto legal personality furnishing them with contractual authority.[41] However, their members still faced structural disadvantages. An influential state court decision in 1842 held that since some work is more dangerous than other work, workers would choose less dangerous work and thus employers would need to provide higher pay to fill the more dangerous slots. In other words, the market compensated workers for the risk of injury.[42] Workers were entirely free to enter into the risky employment due to liberty of contract.[43] To hobble companies with injury claims was thought to slow economic growth.

Today the collective-bargaining contract functions to separate employees from their statutory rights. By signing, workers regularly waive such rights as the ability to participate in establishing working conditions, as well as the right to strike.[44] Management in turn agrees to review its actions in arbitration. This trade-off presumes an equality of contractants. "[C]ontractualist labor cases are at some pains to reassure that labor and capital ordinarily bargain from an initial position of parity."[45] The obvious asymmetry is minimized, cloaked by its participation in a legal procedure with guarantees of due process. Labor conflict has largely been routinized—contained within legal procedure. The assymetry of the contractants has been de-emphasized in favor of administrative procedure. The remarkable power differences of parties are subordinated to the purported values of neutral administrative procedure. The formal process obscures fundamental inequalities. Democratic decision-making is relegated to state administration, an apparatus that is subject to the influences of the asymmetries of power and wealth.

For labor, the lesson might be to rethink its relationship to law. Collective bargaining exemplifies

> alienated politics—the process by which people's communal, self-governing capacities are absorbed and returned to them in a form that while falsely pretending to serve universal needs, in fact atomizes their sociality and collective sense, induces their consent to illegitimate hierarchy, and substitutes heteronomous control by the powerful for autonomous self-direction by the people.[46]

The history of the legal basis of labor unions illustrates the legal decline of mediating institutions. This history, like all other histories of its kind, is deeply intertwined with conceptions of human nature, of democracy, and with conceptions of humans' relationships with place. Historian Robert Gottlieb has chronicled how community organizers such as Alice Hamilton, who was involved with the Hull House in Chicago, organized and worked out of a vision that linked community organizations, public health research and information, and the reconstruction of urban places. The key to this Progressive Era movement and many since, has been the conceptual linking of workplace hazards with community and consumer concerns. The purpose of Hamilton's research, and others that followed, like Rachel Carson, was to challenge the fundamental production choices of business corporations—the way society was organized. Corporate accountability to the local community was key to Hamilton and Carson's strategies. However, Gottlieb shows how the system has continued to usurp the critique. Labor unions have traded off critique for higher wages. The public-health movement, largely arising in response to the work of Alice Hamilton, quickly moved to a science-based, expertise-driven movement that treated symptoms of the system rather than fundamentally reform the structures of society.[47] Rather than ask why so much garbage was produced, rationalized and efficient garbage collection was introduced. Rather than look at the fundamental organization of social and corporate systems that polluted waterways, water treatment plants have been built. The system of management and control of by-products of the industrial transformation of society and nature has remained within the dominant paradigm of business corporation dominance, community dissempowerment, and the commodification of nature and place.

The transformations touched upon in this chapter are myriad. Europeans came to treat far off lands as their due, and their economy took off in no small measure as a consequence of their colonial extractions. The far off land itself suffered from their arrival. The scale of political and commercial arrangements greatly enlarged. Tocqueville and others noted the need for voluntary associations to mediate between the mass of individuals and their sovereign polities. Voluntary associations in commerce met with differential treatment depending upon whether they were incorporated companies or combinations of employees. Labor unions formed and inserted themselves between the lone individual and the rising states, but faltered within the established legal and social framework of society.

Notes

1. Christopher L. Tomlins, *The State and the Unions* (New York: Cambridge University Press, 1994), 58.

2. Frederick Jackson Turner, *The Frontier in American History* (New York University: Holt Rinehart & Winston, 1920), 123 in Jack Weatherford, *Indian Givers: How the Indians of the Americas Transformed the World* (New York: Fawcett Columbine, 1988), 36.

3. Daniel Defoe, *The Adventures of Robinson Crusoe* (New York: Crown Publishers, 1986).

4. Edward Said, *Culture and Imperialism* (New York: Knopf, 1994).

5. Said, *Culture and Imperialism*.

6. David Hume, *Theory of Knowledge*, ed. D. C. Yalden-Thompson (New York: Nelson, 1951).

7. William Cronon, *Changes in the Land: Indians, Colonists, and the Ecology of New England* (New York: Hill and Wang, 1983).

8. Roderick Frazier Nash, *The Rights of Nature* (Madison: University of Wisconsin Press, 1989).

9. Gwendolyn Wright, *Building the Dream* (New York: Pantheon, 1981), 9.

10. Wright, *Building the Dream*, 9.

11. J. B. Jackson, "The Order of a Landscape," *The Interpretation of Ordinary Landscapes*, ed. Donald W. Meinig (New York: Oxford University Press, 1979), 153-63, 156.

12. Jackson, "The Order of a Landscape, 161.

13. Jackson, "The Order of a Landscape, 155.

14. Hildegard Binder Johnson, *Order upon the Land* (New York: Oxford University Press, 1976), 39.

15. E. P. Thompson, *The Making of the English Working Class* (New York: Pantheon, 1963).

16. Alexis de Tocqueville, *Journey to America* (Garden City, N.J.: Doubleday, 1971), 384.

17. De Tocqueville, *Journey to America*, 372.

18. Robert A. Nisbet, *The Quest for Community* (New York: Oxford University Press, 1953), 252.

19. Peter Worsley, "The National State, Colonial Expansion and the Contemporary World Order," *Companion Encyclopedia of Anthropology*, ed. Tim Ingold (New York: Routledge, 1994), 1040-66.

20. Worsley, "The National State, 1057.

21. Christopher Stone, *Should Trees Have Standing?* (New York: Avon Books, 1975), 14.

22. Stone, *Should Trees Have Standing?*, 23.

23. Christin E. Amsler, Robin L. Bartlett, and Craig J. Bolton, "Thoughts of Some British Economists on Early Limited Liability and Corporate Legislation," *History of Political Economy* 13, no. 4 (1981): 774-93.

24. Paddy Ireland, Ian Grigg-Spall, and Dave Kelly, "The Conceptual Foundations of Modern Company Law," *Critical Legal Studies*, ed. Peter Fitzpatrick and Alan Hunt (New York: P. Basil Blackwell, 1987), 149-65.

25. Lawrence M. Friedman and Jack Ladinsky, "Social Change and the Laws of Industrial Accidents," in *Law and Society*, ed. Stuart Macaulay, Lawrence M. Friedman, and John Stookey (New York: Norton, 1995), 211-32.

26. Mark V. Tushnet, "A Marxist's Analysis of American Law," *Marxist Perspectives* 1 (1978): 96-116.

27. Friedman and Ladinsky, "Social Change," 211-32.

28. Harry A. Millis and Royal E. Montgomery, *Organized Labor* (New York: McGraw-Hill, 1945), 499-500.

29. Millis and Montgomery, *Organized Labor,* 500.

30. Millis and Montgomery, *Organized Labor,* 501.

31. Millis and Montgomery, *Organized Labor,* 501.

32. Millis and Montgomery, *Organized Labor,* 491.

33. Millis and Montgomery, *Organized Labor,* 504.

34. Staughton Lynd, "Towards a Not-For-Profit Economy: Public Development Authorities for Acquisition and Use of Industrial Property," *Harvard Civil Rights-Civil Liberties Law Review* 22 (1987): 13-39.

35. Tomlins, *The State and the Unions*, 43.

36. Richard L. Grossman and Frank T. Adams, *Taking Care of Business: Citizenship and the Charter of Incorporation* (Cambridge, U.K.: Charter, Inc., 1993), 19-20.

37. Howard Zinn, *A People's History of the United States* (New York: Harper & Row, 1972), 234.

38. Millis and Montgomery, *Organized Labor,* 584.

39. Karl Klare, "Labor Law and the Liberal Political Imagination," *Socialist Review* 43 (1982): 45-71, 43.

40. Tomlins, *The State and the Unions,* 83.

41. Tomlins, *The State and the Unions,* 92-93.

42. Friedman and Ladinsky, "Social Change," 211-32.

43. Lisa McIntyre, *Law in the Sociological Enterprise: A Reconstruction* (Boulder, Colo.: Westview, 1994), 182.

44. Klare, "Labor Law"; Lynd, 45-71. "Towards a Not-For-Profit Economy," 13-39.

45. Klare, "Labor Law," 53.

46. Klare, "Labor Law," 63.

47. Robert Gottlieb, *Forcing the Spring: The Transformation of the American Environmental Movement* (Washington, D.C.: Island Press, 1983).

CHAPTER 4

A NEW LEVIATHAN IN THE NEW WORLD

"Somewhat ironically . . . the philosophy of extreme economic individualism triumphed in America just as the corporations were in fact wresting the field from individuals."[1]

R. Jeffrey Lustig

THE CORPORATION DEVOLVED from a servant of the public good to a unit that functioned primarily for economic purposes. The entity's supraindividual legal body was matched in power only by the sovereign. The corporation conceptually accorded a level "between" individual and state that embodied a new institutional life in terms of its influence. Likewise, corporate loyalty was tied more to the state and the economy than to local place. Community embedded in nature suffered in as much as detachment from place grew.

The corporate entity had been conceptualized as an association of individuals (akin to a municipality or partnership) but soon transformed itself into a legal fiction and then by the end of the nineteenth century into a personal entity. It metamorphosed from the artifice of crown privilege as a chartered corporate entity into one that embodied the workings of the economy of the day, the appropriate form of commerce.

The corporation's structural advantage vis-à-vis the individual did not go unnoticed. Early on, many citizens decried the corporation as "communist" and "in violation of the social contract."[2] Local hostility to the corporation arose among New World settlers, who expressed their belief that this was an alien institution operating from London or somewhere else overseas.[3]

Although the corporate institution had great success in India, it was met with a different configuration in North America. Much resistance was present early in North American history, and this was directly due to fears that community life was being threatened. A large number of alternate supraindividual legal devices such as farmer cooperatives were created—a direct

63

result of settler unease with the business corporate form. Colonists formed cooperative associations that were neither individual operations nor chartered corporations; such arrangements were closest to trusteeships. In retrospect, they were far more democratic and self-managed than were the entities that soon surpassed them.

The new Constitution avoided the mention of corporations. Fearing the dangers of corporate *imperiums in imperio*, the Constitutional Convention denied the federal government the power to charter them.[4] Mediating institutions between citizen and sovereign had accrued power equal to that of the monarch, and the same held true when the citizenry became the sovereign.

Legislators at this time regularly restricted corporations. They denied charters to entrepreneurs who incurred community resistance. Charters typically specified that a corporate entity was created to serve the public interest. Legislative bodies dictated rules "for issuing stock, for shareholder voting, for obtaining corporate information, for paying dividends and keeping records. They limited capitalization, debts, landholdings, and sometimes profits."[5]

Given the Constitutional avoidance, states rather than the federal government chartered corporations and each act of incorporation required scrutiny. Clauses often were inserted to limit the concentration of power and wealth. Mechanisms included everything from a prohibition of interlocking directorates and corporate ownership of other corporations, to limits on capital accumulation, to regular shareholder meetings.[6] Large shareholders were limited by scaled voting so that large and small investors had equal voting rights. Shareholders could also remove directors at will.[7]

David Scuilli likens the legislatively mandated limits and chartering debates to elaborate naturalization ceremonies.[8] Some corporations received self-destruction clauses that limited their time span.[9] At times owners were prohibited from owning stock in other corporations and for almost a century, no corporate entities were granted the right to accumulate private property without restriction.

Until 1837, each state required that corporations be chartered for a particular kind of business, specified in detail.[10] Virginia's Supreme Court of 1809 decreed that merely private or selfish enterprises had no claim on the legislature for charter privileges.[11] Pennsylvania and other states went so far as to siphon off corporate funds in order to purchase private utilities and make them public.[12]

Some argued that given our Constitution, no business could be granted special privileges. The Constitutional Convention discussed and rejected a motion to place the power of incorporation in the hands of Congress. Five states passed resolutions to ban Congress from chartering corporations,[13] although Congress did so upon occasion beginning in 1791.[14] Madison and Jefferson opposed the chartering of a national bank.[15] The antidemocratic potential of corporations was evident to elite and commoner alike; colonists did not resent the corporate form so much as its exclusionary power.

It was not that people were ever against corporations, because corporations were chartered to do worthwhile things; rather, they were against confining corporate authority to a few individuals. They were not against privilege, but everybody required a right to that privilege.[16]

For their part, craft and industrial workers feared for their fates in the face of absentee corporate owners. After the Revolution, a corporation in the States could only be chartered through a legal act at the state level, the product of a long debate. Donald Roy argues that this direction in the development of the corporation could have been otherwise, as well as the many social relationships that have resulted.

Liberal thought held all people to be created (as if de novo) equally; none embody privilege. The corporation managed to retain aspects of privatization in that it came to be distinct from those individuals composing it. It managed to retain aspects of democratization by purporting to not interfere with the leveling of all people. However, other legal distinctions became troublesome:

> [I]t clouds the distinction between personal rights (in personem) and rights in property (in rem). . . . [T]he corporation embodies a legal entity between the property and the owners. . . . As it turned out historically, states defined the relationship between the groups and their members as a relationship of property, thereby undermining accountability to the public and framing political discourse over the corporation within the language of privacy rights versus state interference. But it need not have been so.[17]

Resistance to corporations centered around their monopoly privileges. The outcome of this contention could have been, logically, that no individuals could accrue special privilege to incorporate, or, all could. Corporations were opposed by those who argued for the elimination of all such privilege and those wanting to extend such rights to all. However, "the latter group won; the government extended the rights and entitlements of collective ownership to all who could afford it, and retreated from demanding the responsibilities it once had. The corporation survived, but as a private rather than as a public organization."[18] States could have placed control over them in legislatures or municipalities.

Members need not have been defined as owners. The capital could have been raised by the state so that returns went to the collective.[19]

The limited liability that gained favor in Europe met with repulsion in the new land. Massachusetts, in 1822, insisted that each person comprising a manufacturing company was liable for all debts contracted by the corporation while the person was a member.[20] Ohio, Missouri, and Arkansas held stockholders liable over and above the amount of their stock ownership and seven state constitutions held bank shareholders doubly liable.[21] Citizens continued to exert popular sovereignty.

Voters in Wisconsin and four other states rewrote constitutions so that popular votes had to be taken on every bank charter recommended by their legislatures. Over several decades, starting in 1844, nineteen states amended their constitutions to make corporate charters subject to alteration or revocation by legislatures.[22]

Some states even vested part ownership in the public.[23] For example, the state of Maryland chose one-third of the directors for the Baltimore and Ohio railroad, and a bank charter in New Jersey required it to help local fisheries. Citizen authority clauses at times required a company's accounting books to be turned over to a legislature upon request.[24]

A New Scope and a New Scale

Ralph Nader, Mark Green, and Joel Seligman explain the metamorphosis of the corporation from an institution constrained by the public to one freed from public oversight.[25] Commerce and trade were the overriding concerns in the first decades of the new nation-state. To that end, infrastructure came first, along with banking and insurance institutions. States did not have the funds to underwrite turnpikes and canals without partners in capital. Having been impoverished from the Revolution, states invested in banking as an alternate source of revenue to taxation.[26] Such institutions were semipublic and presumed to operate for the greater good. States appointed directors, invested, and generated revenues when successful. In return for the latter, they granted charters and enabled investors to profit from administering essentially public enterprises.[27] These early collaborations between polity and collective unit contributed to building the government apparatus itself.[28]

By 1800, more corporations, most of them still nonprofit, existed in the United States than in all of Europe. However, too many applications were coming in for legislatures to handle them individually. Gradually, general incorporation laws evolved to handle the surging volume of requests. Corporate apologists asserted that too much in the way of legislative time was given over to individual chartering. In the milieu of such contentions, incorporation went from special privilege to general right.[29] The new entity became a legal individual rather than an extension of the collective will.

States began to require only that the investors fill out the appropriate form, meet certain standard requirements, and furnish the fees. Administration supplanted partisan deliberation. Incorporation went from a privilege to a right, and from a carefully granted sponsorship to an opportunity open to all holding the requisite capital. Standard charter licensing further implied that the new entity comprised an appropriate organizational form that was here to stay.[30]

Corporations became less embedded in the social relations of place as these corporate entities lost their obligations to the public. An embargo early in the nineteenth century and the War of 1812 led to an increase in the formation of business corporations to build factories that could replace English and French goods. The first large-scale enterprises were mills in which owners could invest without actually being responsible for their operations.[31] The merchants could buy shares and take a profit, if possible, but leave the daily operating of the mills to the corporate entity.

Legislatures vacillated on the corporation issue, reflecting the contention of the day. For the new corporate entities, a more secure route took them to the courts and with few exceptions, they proved more responsive to corporate power than did legislators. A series of decisions pertaining to constitutional law invoked the Constitution's "obligation of contracts" clause to say that no state could pass any law impairing the obligation of contracts.[32]

Donald Roy shows that ownership and control of corporations could well have come to reside with states rather than in private hands. Private ownership was not at all natural or inevitable; the citizenry actually favored public ownership. In some quarters, full public ownership and control made more sense than private or mixed public/private ownership. Control of paths of commerce such as tollways and canals amounted to control over the means of commerce. Should one group benefit by controlling the market access of others, or should not such access be available to all to the benefit of all? A nationalized railway network was imaginable.

The giant railroad companies epitomized the crucial transition in business format, from individual farm and manufacturing plant to corporate behemoth. Manufacturing entities were small and ordinarily unincorporated at the beginning of the nineteenth century. The workforce was portrayed as a host of individual entrepreneurs, rather than a class of wage earners dependent upon supraindividual business entities.[33] The railroads became the bases for massive landholdings and resource development in the West and began an era of federally funded corporate subsidies. Since all community-level management of resources had disappeared from the legal and social imagination, the federal government's role was to encourage the economic exploitation of western resources for the purpose of national strength. This was done through the subsidization of private, largely corporate, development. Mineral lands were sold (and continue to be sold) at below-market value. Every other section of land within six miles of either side of railroad lines were granted to the railroad companies, thus forming massive holdings that became forest resource corporations. This empowering of corporate interests entrenched a system of interest called the Iron Triangle that continued up until the 1970s. This three-party coalition, consisting of corporate interests, related federal agencies, and appropriate congressional committees dominated by representatives from the West, made all decisions regarding resource management. Community interests were absent from the discussion.

Railroads furnished new means by which commerce could expand. They provided the transportation network requisite to the expansion of trading opportunities and trading operators, and they embodied an innovative organizational format, one that small manufacturers gradually came to emulate. Corporations no longer needed to be quasigovernment institutions. Earlier populist legislative controls on the entity were largely rescinded when states sought to establish and/or benefit from the steel rails.

Turning Point

The public's suspicion of monopolistic charters continued in the century after the Revolution. Farmer populists ran candidates who pledged popular, legislative control over the new giants. Such movements were aware of counterparts in Europe, in the Luddites, and in others. In Great Britain in 1844, the Rochdale Society of Equitable Pioneers established consumer cooperatives. In doing so, the group initiated a substantial cooperative movement that exemplified an alternative collective body. In both Europe and the United States, a substantial part of the appeal of such cooperatives was that they exemplified a more democratic, egalitarian alternative.

The purported social contract between freely entering parties of approximately equal wealth clashed with the increasing reality of the inequality among parties. The corporate entity gradually won freedoms from restrictions on its being able to concentrate wealth and power. It was able to form factory towns, threaten unemployment, and use its resources to influence newspapers and political figures. Taking powers heretofore limited to the sovereign, it issued its own scrip, built its own private roads, and could and did hire private detectives and armies for labor control.

At a time of rapid economic change, corporations pushed the gray areas of their limitations, and the courts granted increasing latitude regarding corporations' specified purposes. Beginning with the Jacksonian era, state courts increasingly took on a Lockean cast in that they began to concede that private commercial enterprises held a natural right to accumulate wealth.[34] Corporate law was moving away from a context of public-law norms and toward one of private-law contracts. Courts increasingly presumed that the institution's agenda would coincide with that of the larger social order. Spokesmen for the "artificial persons" characterized their institutions by reference to Locke and capitalized on a Supreme Court decision that asserted that corporations should have a natural freedom from political regulation.[35] In this way, individualism culminated in a triumph at the expense of the individual.

Corporations took on monopoly or oligopoly status beyond the arena of public transportation and resource development.[36] A grain elevator company argued that it was a "person" deprived of property by state laws that regulated prices charged to farmers. The Supreme Court disagreed, holding that grain elevators were not simply private property but were invested with a public interest and so could be regulated. The American Bar Association began campaigning against such reasoning, and succeeded within a decade. Responding to farmers, state legislatures passed laws to regulate rates that railroad corporations charged the farmers. In 1886, the Court disallowed states that regulatory power, and did away with 230 state laws passed to regulate corporations on the ground that they deprived corporations of their property without due process of law.[37]

The Fourteenth Amendment's protection that no state shall deprive any person of life, liberty, or property without due process was given its distinctive extension in the Supreme Court's case of *Santa Clara County v. Southern Pacific Railroad* in 1886. The amendment, adopted to protect recently emancipated slaves, now applied to corporations as natural "persons," so that California could not tax corporations differently from individuals. Qua legal "persons," corporations now gained First Amendment rights and legislatures lost many of their controls. With the Santa Clara decision, corporations held few or none of the limitations placed on individuals but most of the individual's legal protections. The due-process clause, as now interpreted, protected property such as corporate shares.[38] Until 1938, the Fourteenth Amendment was rarely used to protect African-Americans, but it was invoked to protect the personhood rights of corporations.[39]

Courts interpreted common law strictures to keep the corporation from owning stock in related businesses, unless permitted by legislative statute. Proponents successfully argued that corporations should be able to own property in that they legally were individuals. Such ownership proved useful for controlling competition in the latter half of the nineteenth century. Individuals suffered; a partnership could not own another partnership, but an artificial person now could.[40] Partners shared full liability, as did corporations in some states in the first half of the century. Until then, some states made stockholders liable or even doubly liable.

By the early twentieth century the courts were treating the corporation as a "natural entity" apart from the shareholders. Indeed, the entity was coming instead to be identified with its board of directors. Likewise, incorporation came to be regarded not as a special privilege conferred by the state but as a normal or natural business activity.[41] What had recently been encountered as artificial and in need of oversight, became what was natural and prior to the law, such that the presumption of corporate regulation was shifted against the state.[42]

Substantial populist resistance developed in the 1880s and 1890s. Nationwide movements were formed and populist books, magazines, newspapers, and songs caught the interest of millions. The first Farmers Alliance formed in 1877 in Texas and, within ten years, three thousand suballiances existed. Individuals increasingly banded together into a different form of supraindividual group, buying and selling cooperatives, in order to better leverage themselves against the ascending corporate entities. Alliancemen and Alliance-supported candidates won several governorships and came to control several state legislatures in the 1890 elections. Entire communities often supported striking workers against corporations and absentee landlords.[43] Public takeover of railroads and return of corporate lands "in excess of their actual needs" were advocated by the Populist Party and others.[44] But bankers refused to loan capital and racism undermined populists' collective feeling. Much of the movement's energy was routed into electoral politics and the Democratic Party, where the populist vision of cooperative collective entities responsive to the public interest foundered with the election of McKinley over Bryon in 1896.

States began to compete with each other by limiting liability and granting various other freedoms from popular control. President, and former New Jersey governor, Woodrow Wilson, proposed a series of controls for that state, thereby making it momentarily less attractive to capital. With its miniscule size, Delaware looked to be far more dependable/dependent, and took the opportunity. By the Depression, twelve thousand corporations claimed legal residence in a single office in downtown Wilmington.[45] Other states gradually revised their laws in the same direction, but Delaware would continue to provide a favorable legal climate at least into the 1950s.[46]

Corporation loyalty to local place receded with the loss of popular control. By the turn of the century, twenty-six corporate trusts controlled 80 percent or more of their markets.[47] Localities were played off against one another. In spite of this, around 1900, state legislatures were still enacting laws holding corporations accountable to public interest. But the general charters of New Jersey and Delaware placed the others at a disadvantage and signaled the direction of the future.

State courts and legislatures had been applying both the common law tradition and the U.S. constitutional system, both designed to mediate conflicts between individual citizens, between individual citizens and the state, or between state agencies.

> None had been designed explicitly to address the place and purpose of large intermediary associations within society, whether for-profit commercial enterprises or nonprofit associations . . . New Jersey and Delaware now took the lead in fashioning in practice what essentially would become U.S. constitutional law for intermediary associations, for corporate persons.[48]

The state courts of New Jersey, Delaware, California, and New York took the lead in establishing the "corporate judiciary" overseeing legal reasoning pertaining to the corporation. Courts and legislatures began deferring to corporate agents under what became known as the "business judgement rule."[49] That is, such business judgments were immune from judicial review if they avoided conflict of interest, acted in good faith, and acted in the best interest of the corporation. In a short time, states became nearly powerless to restrict the entity. The corporation became constitutionally protected, and it became the referent for legal discussions on collectives lodged conceptually between the individual and the state.

Changes in Theory

Due to the nature of the developing economy, the more successful charter operations grew into giants who were minimally influenced by the market restraints that had been postulated by classical economic theory. Their market position, absolute size, and internal organization created a set of problems essentially unknown to the world of the early nineteenth-century family-type corporations, and even less familiar to the earlier world of chartering monarchs.

While much of European social and political theorists continued to watch for possible abuses in the relation between sovereign and subjects, English Pluralists, such as G. D. H. Cole, R. H. Tawney, John Neville Figgis, and Harold Laski, registered their own unease with the newly rising business corporation. Most British businesses were in the hands of individual entrepreneurs in 1870, and most corporations remained small until the late 1800s.[50] Thirty-five hundred new companies registered in the first four years after the new Companies Act of 1862. In 1865 *The Times* lamented the "growing mass of impersonalities."[51] Virtually all major British businesses had switched to the corporate format by the end of the century. Mergers and amalgamations led to further increases in corporate size and influence. Smaller businesses lost to those gaining the advantages of scale.

The English Pluralists noticed the rapid accrual of power and the corporation's ever-increasing ability to tilt the social contract of approximate equals. They proposed that collective entities such as churches should be accorded legal rights. Their view was that the capacity to be a rights-bearing agent should not be limited to the individual and to the state. Entities such as the church and the community were important in their own right. The Pluralists took pains to insist that the human group marked out an existence of its own and that it could not be adequately characterized as simply a collection of individuals.[52] In this way, they joined early sociologists such as Emile Durkheim in attempts to counter the individualism of the day. Groups could not be reduced to aggregate collections of their individual members. Building on German legal scholarship, F. W. Maitland held that groups merited legal status as actual social phenomena, not just as fictitious entities. Harold Laski extended the notion of the group's tangible reality, arguing that groups must be held responsible for their actions.

The Pluralists pointed out that legal individualism led to a mismatch with social reality. Their claim that groups were more than fictitious entities akin to persons held particular import for business corporations. At the time, corporate persons were held to be incapable of committing acts that involved a guilty intention or crimes that involved *mens rea*.[53] Business corporations enjoyed the best of both worlds, social actuality and legal fiction.

Collective groups such as churches did not reap the long-standing legal benefits that the business corporation did. Corporations positioned themselves especially well to be able to grow beyond the previously established scale, and they continued to procure particular legal privilege, while their counterparts held relatively steady by comparison. Other groups increasingly modeled themselves upon the corporation. Colleges, churches, hospitals, municipalities, and cooperatives took on the corporate organizational structure and its imperatives, in turn contributing to an ever more business-focussed, individualistic culture. Toward the end of the century, business corporations took an interest in the "scientific management" innovations of Frederick Taylor. Applying the empirical methods and precision of science, Taylor studied worker performance and measured the time it took to perform tasks. In keeping with Bacon and Descartes, he used this examination to break down worker tasks into smaller individual components that could be repeated over and over. Such research established appropriate production rates, while at the same time increasing the rate from that which had existed before the research. Individuals could more quickly perform a small number of repeated tasks than they could work at a large number of tasks. In a sense, work performance was universalized.

At the same time, more managerial oversight was required. Decision making and control shifted away from the egalitarian and democratic and toward the hierarchical. More vertical structures replaced horizontal ones. Top managers consulted scientific expertise. Taylor's scientific management caught on in the industrial workplace, soon contributing to a Fordist—mass production—organization. But the tenets gradually came to pervade increasingly larger domains than the industrial. The ethos of scientific management would show up in many other arenas where increasingly efficient productivity was wanted. In time, it also worked to enable difficult value decisions to be toned down by being relegated to the domain of technical expertise.

The diminishment of the middle institutions would have consequences for the structure of environmental management. Individual property rights and corporate power would necessitate the growing centralized control of the federal government. Scientific management would replace the meaningful involvement of local resource-dependent communities. And the larger sense of public responsibility—the commons—would diminish as well. The following chapter's history of forest management in the United States is a story that involves all these forces.

Notes

1. R. Jeffrey Lustig, *Corporate Liberalism* (Berkeley: University of California Press, 1982), 54.0

2. William G. Roy, *Socializing Capital* (Princeton, N.J.: Princeton University Press, 1997), 53.

3. Oscar Handlin, "The Development of the Corporation," in *The Corporation: A Theological Inquiry,* ed. Michael Novak and John W. Cooper (Washington, D.C.: American Enterprise Institute for Public Policy Research, 1981), 1-17, 3.

4. Lustig, *Corporate Liberalism,* 47.

5. Richard L. Grossman and Frank T. Adams, *Taking Care of Business: Citizenship and the Charter of Incorporation* (Cambridge, UK: Charter, Inc., 1993), 8.

6. Roy, *Socializing Capital,* 54.

7. Grossman and Adams, *Taking Care of Business,* 8.

8. David Scuilli, *Corporations vs. the Court* (Boulder, Colo.: Lynne Rienner Publishers, 1999), 86-87.

9. Charles Derber, *Corporation Nation* (New York: St. Martin's Press, 1998), 123.

10. Jonathan Rowe, "Reinventing the Corporation," *The Washington Monthly* No. 11 (1996): 16-23.

11. Derber, *Corporation Nation,* 123.

12. Grossman and Adams, *Taking Care of Business,* 12.

13. Roy, *Socializing Capital,* 50.

14. Edward S. Mason, "Corporation," in *The International Encyclopedia of Social Sciences,* ed. David L. Sills (New York: Macmillan, 1968), 396-403.

15. Derber, *Corporation Nation,* 124.

16. Handlin, "The Development of the Corporation," 6.

17. Roy, *Socializing Capital,* 46-47.

18. Roy, *Socializing Capital,* 46.

19. Roy, *Socializing Capital,* 47.

20. Grossman and Adams, *Taking Care of Business,* 9.

21. Grossman and Adams, *Taking Care of Business,* 10.

22. Grossman and Adams, *Taking Care of Business,* 11.

23. Rowe, "Reinventing the Corporation," 16-23.

24. Grossman and Adams, *Taking Care of Business,* 8.

25. Ralph Nader, Mark Green, and Joel Seligman, *Taming the Giant Corporation* (New York: Norton, 1976), 34.

26. Morton J. Horwitz, *The Transformation of American Law, 1780-1860* (Cambridge, Mass.: Harvard University Press, 1977), 100.

27. Nader et al., *Taming the Giant Corporation,* 34.

28. Roy, *Socializing Capital,* 50.

29. Roy, *Socializing Capital,* 53.

30. Scuilli, *Corporations vs. the Court,* 97.

31. Handlin, "The Development of the Corporation," 12.

32. Joel Bleifuss, "Know Thine Enemy: A Brief History of Corporations" *In These Times* 22 (Feb. 8, 1998): 16-17.

33. Lustig, *Corporate Liberalism,* 90.

34. Scuilli, *Corporations vs. the Court,* 89.

35. Lustig, *Corporate Liberalism,* 54.

36. Harvey Wasserman, *Harvey Wasserman's History of the United States* (Evanston, Ill.: Harper & Row, 1972), 26.

37. Howard Zinn, *A People's History of the United States* (New York: Harper & Row, 1980), 255.

38. Derber, *Corporation Nation,* 130.

39. Greg Coleridge and Jan Goodman, *Citizens over Corporations* (Akron: Ohio Committee on Corporations, Law, and Democracy, 1999), 35.

40. Roy, *Socializing Capital,* 157.

41. Horowitz, *The Transformation of American Law,* 73.

42. Derber, *Corporation Nation,* 128.

43. Lustig, *Corporate Liberalism,* 90.

44. Wasserman, *Harvey Wasserman's History of the United States,* 75.

45. Rowe, "Reinventing the Corporation," 16-23.

46. Nader et al., *Taming the Giant Corporation,* 59.

47. Grossman and Adams, *Taking Care of Business.*

48. Scuilli, *Corporations vs. the Court,* 96.

49. Scuilli, *Corporations vs. the Court,* 96.

50. P. S. Atiyah, *The Rise and Fall of Freedom of Contract* (Oxford: Clarendon Press, 1979).

51. Atiyah, *The Rise and Fall of Freedom,* 597.

52. David Nicholls, *The Pluralist State* (New York: St. Martin's Press, 1974), 7.

53. Nicholls, *The Pluralist State,* 8.

CHAPTER 5

THE INDIVIDUAL AND NATURAL RESOURCE MANAGEMENT

> Legislation can do little that is effectual to arrest the progress of the evil, except where the State continues proprietor of extensive forests. Every proprietor will, as a general rule, fell his woodlands unless a stronger motive of self-interest impels him to preserve them. The right to do what every man will with his own is regarded as the most sacred among civil rights.

> Congressman Haldeman of Pennsylvania, 1872

WE HAVE CHRONICLED the growth of individualism in this culture over the last four hundred years with particular emphasis on Hobbes, Locke, the law, and the business corporation. We have shown the increasing privilege granted to corporations to operate as persons—persons who are protected from the consequences of their actions and with fewer and fewer obligations to the public good. This privilege displaced the rights of mediating and communal institutions. We have noted the detrimental effect on local social institutions and unions. The rise of Enlightenment thought and the resulting individualism of the culture have also particularly shaped our relationship to the natural world and our attempts at managing common resources.[1] The historical shift from the communal to the individual is evident in our changing sense of the environment around us.

Traces of the commons have remained. For example, in the early Puritan settlements, public order superseded private property. Although the settlers were influenced by Hobbes and Locke, they chose to live by reference to a covenant rather than the utilitarian social contract. They resisted the atomization of *homo economicus*, and opted to retain a centered emphasis on the collective good.

Soon this was to change. The emphasis on the individual and individual rights had its roots in the writings of Enlightenment philosophers John Locke and Adam Smith. Locke tied the individual will to the acquisition of private property, maintaining that society is a collection of individual beings and that the foundation of society is the will of the individual.[2] Ultimately, the individual was autonomous from the larger whole, finding expression and fulfillment only in private ownership. Similarly reductionistic was Smith's model of economic development: The economy emerges from the free actions of autonomous, self-sufficient individuals. Value, i.e., the value of goods, lies not in their use but only in (their value in) exchange between these autonomous individuals.[3] The concept of contract became the perceived basis of social and political institutions. The culture came to reflect Hobbes' societal conception of socially contracting individuals rather than Durkheim's view that social order preceeded the social contract. A simple, if not reductionistic concept of the state accompanied such notions.[4]

Locke conceived the state also in an economic, individualistic cast. Under the terms of the social contract, political association had no other purpose than the organized protection of the natural rights of property and liberty. The political order was now reduced to individuals acting in their own interest to create institutions through contractual agreements, with a diminishing concept of the collective good as a result. Such a portrayal of the state contributed to the classical school of economics and its hypostatization of the free market at the expense of community.[5]

The commons represented not a form of ownership but a way of being in community, one eroded by the subsequent economic and cultural developments that emphasized the individual over the communal.[6] By the time New England was well established, the seeds of change that ultimately undermined communal society had already been sown in Europe. Changes in American colonial society were taking place by the mid 1700s in response to the unfolding Enlightenment individualism and the economic and social class transformations it served. Land and people increasingly came to be extricated from community. The United States established its National Land Survey, whose grid pattern was perfectly suited for quick disposal of public lands to individuals. This way of life, represented by the separate farmstead, was considered the norm and the Ordinance of 1785 took it as its model. It was confirmed by the Pre-emption Act of 1841 which required one to live on the land he or she claimed.[7] Land became another commodity that was valued for its largely economic possibilities. Historical constraints to individual materialistic gain were minimized and American law began to assume the superiority of individual private property over every other social good.

Each cultural institution has changed as the commons has evolved into an arena of private consumption. Individuals in such a setting seek to circumvent their interdependencies. The skills of informal cooperation become atrophied;

individuals cut themselves off from others outside of the enclave so that the contacts that do take place are more abrasive.[8] It follows that these social issues have left their marks on private personalities. For the followers of Hobbes and Locke,

> competition has never been merely an impersonal mechanism regulating the economy of capitalism. It has been a guarantee of political freedom, a system for producing free individuals, and a testing field for heroes. . . In every area of life, liberals have imagined independent individuals freely competing so that merit might win and character develop: in the free contractual marriage, the Protestant Church, the voluntary association, the democratic state, as well as on the economic market. Competition is the . . . central feature of liberalism's style of life.[9]

With an atrophied sense of the commons and a fractured experience of social institutions, the competitive culture has come to generate a narcissistic quality in the modal individual personality.[10] Liberal theorists would expect competition to form the crucible for a strengthening of character; current analyses of the modern character suggest that the competitive worldview spawns the opposite. Current environmental problems indicate that many people compartmentalize parts of their lives and fail to see interrelated connections between their actions and environmental consequences. This deficiency in outlook is traceable in part to the same Enlightenment and pre-Enlightenment tradition.

> A[n] assumption about society, characteristic of classic liberalism, has been the stress upon the autonomy of different institutional orders. In the beginning, as with Locke, it would split off religious institutions from the political, so that the political justifications . . . had to be secular. Later on, the economic order was split from the political order, in the classic case of laissez-faire.[11]

Today's environmental concerns also reflect an increasing separation of values and the concept of "the good" from a religious basis.[12] The moral order has gradually been relegated to the periphery of everyday life, with less recognition of personal responsibility as a result. The culture's compartmentalizing of moral order from everyday life reflects a more general lack of awareness of interrelationship, for example, between personal consumption and ozone depletion.

The Enlightenment's individualistic concept of natural right derived in part from an atomistic and mechanistic interpretation as well as emulation of the successes of the natural sciences. For this reason, they eventually framed ways the culture would think about natural resource management. The methodology of the natural sciences was based on "splitting phenomena into their simplest elements and deductively explaining their interrelations from a few simple principles."[13] This methodology was extended to the social sciences; society came to be viewed as one large machine analogous to the subject matter of Newtonian physics. The reductionist, atomistic interpretation of science and its subject matter went hand in hand with the individualistic treatment of natural right.[14] Portrayals of biological, social, and political phenomena took on a mechanistic cast while more overarching concepts of the social, political, and religious order lost favor. Such a worldview worked against the recognition of community or institutions as concrete realities.[15]

As developed by Descartes, Hume, and others, rationalism replaced religion as the basis for the social and political institutions of modern democracy. The belief that rational thought (later, science) will bring about common acknowledgement of certain truths underlies the resulting concepts of society and polity. Such thinkers emphasized adherence to logic and science more than to dialogue; rationality meant a correct application of individual reasoning more than a satisfactory communal decision making. The method of thinking (and then of doing science) took precedence over the method of conflict resolution, which read as irrationality to doubters or outsiders. With the Cartesian method of harnessing reason for the elimination of doubt came the inference that diversity of opinion exists only as evidence that our powers of reason have been insufficiently applied.[16] In reality, perceptions of ecological problems such as land use and forestry vary and show themselves today to be points of contention.[17] Habermas[18] has shown such an assumption to be an Achilles' heel for Hobbes and others; to acknowledge a genuine public as the audience would require a fundamental reworking of the entire framework.

Politics, a domain for the Greeks pertaining to the good and just life and necessarily entailing the cultivation of character, now became the arena of manipulation for Machiavelli. For Hobbes, More, and others, politics became the science of administrating the rationality of the new order. Ethics became sundered from politics in order to take on the cast of science. Often, the formulated ideal was associated with a personal rejection of the mundanely political.[19]

Historically, the laws governing the use of this "environment as commons" short-circuited the complex web of interdependencies to be found there and favored the more powerful. After enclosure, environment as commons was transformed into environment as resource. Resources were removed from their social context in order to serve the needs of consumers.[20] Environmental historian William Cronon sees the definition of property as ultimately representing societies' views on the boundaries between people and between people and nature.[21] He contrasts Native American and European property concepts in early New England, and destroys any notion of the noble savage as being motivated by some innate goodness not shared by Europeans. New England Native Americans had an intricate system of overlapping but well-defined usufruct rights, or rights of usage, that involved complex social relations within a village and between villages. These usufruct rights defined boundaries between various social groups and arose out of the characteristics of the resource itself. For example, on the one hand, individuals had a right to plant a field within a village territory and an exclusive right to the crops from that field, while other village members had the overlapping right to continue to hunt on the same land. On the other hand, rich fishing grounds on one village's territory were shared with other villages. Colonists, in contrast, owned land in its totality. The property boundaries reflected social boundaries that emphasized the individual as being separated from other individuals, with the state serving as mediator among individuals to uphold individual property rights. In addition, the nature of the ownership was not connected to the ecological characteristics of the resource. In essence, land and people were abstracted from their niche in a community. Land divisions increasingly ignored actual topography. The movement toward viewing environment as resource reflects and parallels a move toward a social reality preoccupied with only two levels—that of the individual acting in his/her own self-interest (reflected in interest groups, corporations, and so forth)—and that of the centralized state power. Increased economic productivity has been purchased at a cost.

As the discussion of Tocqueville noted, America's individualism has been accompanied by a distinctive mix in political practice. The small landowner, resolutely independent of the centralized state, displayed a curious societal conformity. Physical and psychological dependence on the state has steadily increased, while the same cannot be said of mediating communal political institutions. The impulse of conformity has endured, housed for example in the enclave, paradoxically heightening the isolation of the individual.[22] The outward-looking, autonomous individual sees beyond communal institutions and increasingly focuses on the state. Informal communal social controls have evolved into the formal social controls of the state, as have communal patterns of conflict resolution.

More recently, the rise of industrial capitalism has led to the increased size and functional importance of the state—a state less and less answerable to that individual. The state and the multinational corporation increasingly impact on the everyday life of the individual, with consequences insufficiently anticipated by the Enlightenment thought that helped give rise to these developments. As Mills indicates,[23] liberalism attributed too much to the individual. Today, in the hands of a state particularly responsive to the concentration of power and wealth in the uppermost social class, liberalism faces obsolescence. The processes increasingly bifurcated the culture into the level of the individual who acted in his or her own self-interest, on the one hand, and that of centralized state power, on the other. Buttel ties further structural changes in industrial capitalism, evident by the 1990s, with the rise of a neoconservative society characterized by differentiation, a pluralistic class structure, global industrial multipolarity, and emphasis on national competitiveness.[24] These changes make groupings below the level of the nation-state even more difficult. Physical and psychological dependence on the state has steadily increased, while the same cannot be said for mediating institutions that stand between the state and the individual.[25] Informal communal social controls have increasingly evolved into the formal social controls of the state. Likewise, communal patterns of conflict resolution have increasingly required third parties in the person of the state. Nowhere is there a better example of the impacts of this rising individualism on land and conceptions of community than in the development of forest policy in the United States.

The Individual and Forest Policy

The changes wrought on the land can be seen through the presentation of a case study of the evolution of forest policy in the United States. Early forest policy in New England reflected the communal nature of the societies that grew up there prior to major influences of the Enlightenment. Restrictions on timber cutting and usage came early as population increased and lumber became scarce. Colonies typically put restrictions on the use of common timberland. Several colonies forbade the sale of lumber outside the colony without government approval. A typical strategy was to restrict the use of common lands by making them less common.

Massachusetts Bay Colony officials in 1632 and New Haven, Connecticut, officials in 1639 forbade cutting from common lands except with permission of public officials. Further restrictions were imposed in Rhode Island where, by 1638, several men from the colony determined what amount of timber from the commons was best suited for each person. By 1660, Massachusetts Bay Colony went so far as to restrict the right of commonage in wood to those already having rights, and extended it to others only by vote of the inhabitants.[26] During this period, there was little debate about the rights of the colonies to restrict cutting on common lands.

Early United States forest policy was limited to concerns over timber supplies for the development of the United States' naval fleet until 1816 when the U.S. Attorney General pointed out that no law existed to protect naval timber or other timber on public lands.[27] In March of 1817, Congress authorized the reservation of lands consistent with earlier policy but also added penalties for anyone who removed timber from these or "any other lands of the United States."[28] This law was the first that extended the penalties for cutting timber on public land to all public lands and not just those reserved for naval purposes. The federal government had begun to exert its right to protect all its timberlands.

The general public did not share the government's views about timber reservation and protection during this time. Individuals continued to challenge the state's right to prevent them from taking public timber despite a ruling from the U.S. Attorney General that the rights of the United States were essentially the same as those of a citizen, i.e., the government had the right to protect its property.[29] Just as corporations took on the identity of a rarified form of the individual, so too did the federal government in order to gain the right to protect its own property. Alternative legal concepts that might have recognized a variety of institutional forms were missing.

The timber conflict illustrates the forces at play during this era. Settlement was carried out largely by individuals and corporations who were exerting their presumed right to use the commons as they pleased. This was based on the idea that the social contract that led to the creation of the state did not include the protection of public lands but only the protection of private interests. In fact, the judgment of the U.S. Attorney General did not give the state a right to protect its lands. He had to interpret the right to protect U.S. lands in the same way as a private individual could.[30] The norm for government action was not expressed as justice but rather as a private right.

Congress acted on its right to protect federal property in the act of March 2, 1831, by providing for further penalties.[31] The United States Supreme Court, in *United States vs. Briggs*, interpreted the law as applying to all public land of the United States, whether reserved for naval purposes or not.[32] What had started out as purely a naval concern was extended to all public lands through the law of 1817 and through judicial interpretation of the law of 1831.

The move toward executive power versus individual interests illustrates the problem of a society that lacks a belief in a common interest. Competing interests raise particularly heavy and conflictual expectations for the state.

> [T]he sovereignty of the state power results from the necessity to enforce the validity of the system of contracts; . . . the contract system itself follows from the necessity of making survival in peace and order possible; and finally, . . . the common interest in peace and order follows from the necessity of removing the contradictions existing in the state of nature.[33]

The adoption of liberal concepts of natural law and individual rights were sufficient enough to generate major strains on the agent to whom the residual communal elements were accorded—the state. It becomes inevitable that the executive function is required to balance the forces of rival human wills, especially when these wills were increasingly those of corporations.[34]

The United States forest policy continued to reflect the strain between the power of the state versus the rights of the individual or corporation. The individualism of the American mind expressed itself in the desire for the state to leave the forests as unregulated commons, resources open to individual or corporate exploitation. There was no expressed desire to make forests into commons tied to communities. Groups of individuals desired state intervention only where a corporate monopoly developed that interfered with their perceived rights, or where the results of the exploitation of the forests led to negative effects on the third party. The state, as reflected in congressional policy, responded to the problems of forest destruction and management within the bounds of the Lockean worldview. Privatistic policies were continually initiated, and state management of the resource continued to be tempered by interest-group politics.

The first major concerns over forest destruction gained a hearing as demand for timber increased due to prairie settlement expansion. Given the constraints resulting from a failure on the part of Congress to obtain information about forest lands, the solution to forest destruction lay in private, individualistic policies: Sell the lands so that they would be put to their best use and be protected by the owners. The lands would have to be sold cheaply; otherwise huge appropriations for appraisal would have to be made. The General Land Office administered the laws passed by Congress that moved these lands into the hands of private individuals or corporations. The decision that Congress made to dispose of lands in this way was in itself a reflection of the pervasiveness of the ascending cultural individualism.

In the 1860s, largely influenced by George Perkins Marsh's book *Man and Nature*, discussion about forest destruction turned to a concern over the destruction's effects on climate and stream flow. Again the solution was relegated to the private domain. Many proposals were made to encourage individuals to plant trees and years of debate finally ended in the passage of the Timber Culture Act on March 3, 1873.[35] The law gave individuals 160 acres of free land if they planted forty acres in trees for ten years and reflected the ideology of the time in several ways. First, it targeted individuals as the sole actors, and railroad companies were also encouraged to plant trees. It also was based on the assumption that these individuals or corporations acted only in their own interest and thus needed to be rewarded for what might in this case be socially responsible behavior—perhaps a fair analysis given the assumption that no other level of social response existed outside the individual or state and given the direction of law that negated corporate responsibility to the public good.

The reduction of social realities to the level of the individual created an apparent contradiction in forest policy. Congress encouraged tree planting in one region at the same time that settlers and corporations were allowed to strip timber from other areas. Both were premised on the belief that the exclusive role of the state was to protect personal rights, particularly in property. The state treated businesses the same way it treated individuals, although the businesses were accruing increased power and influence with the state.

Mounting public pressure continually brought the matter of timber use before Congress[36] and several bills were passed that opened up the land for sale during this era.[37] Public pressure had started to rise, even from western states, in support of protection and management. Nevertheless, Congress passed acts that ensured either the sale of public timber lands below their market value or their free use.[38]

Congressional speeches during this era illustrate the perceived choices in dealing with the issue of forest management. Senator Howe of Wisconsin expressed the sentiments of many, maintaining that if a man could pay for timber and thought he needed the resource he should be able to buy it. After all, Howe concluded, nobody consumed more than he actually needed. In response to a reference to the needs of future generations he pointed out that future generations had as of yet done nothing for him.[39] Congressmen holding such a point of view maintained that there existed a "right" to engage in lumbering.[40] The only solution to public forest destruction lay in private ownership, a belief expressed by Senator Sargent of Oregon: "The wanton destruction by men who have no ownership in it will be very much diminished when private individuals can get possession of these lands by paying the Government."[41]

Some other congressmen were a bit more reserved about the ability of private ownership to ultimately solve the problem of timber destruction. But Representative Haldeman of Pennsylvania expressed well the context for the next policy era:

Legislation can do little that is effectual to arrest the progress of the evil, except where the State continues proprietor of extensive forests. Every proprietor will, as a general rule, fell his woodlands unless a stronger motive of self-interest impels him to preserve them. The right to do what every man will with his own is regarded as the most sacred among civil rights.[42]

Business interests advocated, and congressmen and the general population acknowledged, the right of every man to do what he willed with his own property. Under such conditions, the state gradually became the proprietor of the commons.

The concern of public welfare and forests was first clearly articulated in 1888, in the report of the Senate Committee on Public Lands. This report linked government involvement in the protection of forests with the idea of promoting the public welfare. However, reservation of forest lands by the federal government only gained acceptance when the effects of cutting were felt by third parties.

On March 3, 1891, the president of the United States signed a new public lands bill into law. The act repealed past laws relating to the sale of timber and/or timberlands as well as to the Timber Culture Act of 1873. To replace these laws, citizens could now obtain timber through the licensing provision and perhaps most importantly, forests could be reserved with permanent government ownership in mind.[43] The 1891 act continued two already well-established trends—centralized control at the federal level and the free use of public timber. The secretary of the interior issued broad rules for cutting timber under the 1891 act because of its broad specified purposes. He placed only one limitation on commercial operations: Rather than provide proof that the preservation of the trees was not essential for the public good, operators were required to show that the use of the timber was a public necessity.[44] By the late 1890s, a two-tier system of government ownership of forestlands existed. In contrast to reserved lands, which Congress had now appropriated money to manage, unreserved timberlands remained as a generally unregulated commons with timber either free or underpriced. In 1905, Congress transferred the administration of national forest reservations from the Department of the Interior to the Department of Agriculture.[45] The year 1924 marked a changing interpretation of the judicial interpretation of the public good when Congress amended the Weeks Act to allow the National Forest Reservation Commission to purchase lands suitable for producing timber rather than merely for watershed protection.[46]

The Depression led to default on property taxes by private owners of cutover lands, causing acute distress in forest regions, especially in the Great

Lakes. Public support for the acquisition of cutover land was strong in these areas because the federal government gave one-quarter of its forest production receipts to the counties. Problems generated by the emphasis on individual rights again became the province of the state. The federal acquisition program, begun to protect stream flow and watersheds and to ensure timber production, became intertwined with the need to relieve local economic problems. The Commission usually anticipated its purchases each year by the amount of private timberland that would be logged that year, a practice that could be viewed as a subsidy for corporate lumber interests. The Commission went so far as to purchase lands that had mature trees in order to provide receipts for the local community as soon as possible.[47] In the meantime, the state increasingly subsidized the business interests of the timber industry.

The increased involvement of the federal government in forest management was a result of the rise of new philosophies of resource management and changing perceptions of the land, both evolving around the year 1900. The conservation movement reflected the former and was concerned with both the need for the long-term sustainability of production of goods from the nation's public lands and the need for these goods to be protected from corporate monopolies. The establishment of national forests and the United States Forest Service was the direct result of the conservation movement. The work of John Muir, preservationist and founder of the Sierra Club, paralleled the conservation movement, but represented a different perspective. Muir emphasized the preservation of nature for its spiritual qualities. Grounded in Transcendental thought, Muir's preservationist movement called for the isolation of large tracts of land from any economic use. The establishment of national parks and the U.S. States Park Service was one of the outcomes of the work of John Muir.

The idea of preservation was at odds with those who sought to conserve in order to better serve human material utilization of the land. Theodore Roosevelt, who appreciated both qualities of land and resource, expressed support for the conservation movement and their goal of the scientific management of resources. He appointed Gifford Pinchot to head the new U.S. Forest Service. Pinchot was committed to managing forests for the material needs of the general public. Although strongly committed to scientific management, he was also in favor of limiting the power of large corporations who threatened to monopolize the country's resources. His view was that public lands should be managed for the greatest good, for the greatest number, over the longest time. Pinchot's commitment to scientific management led the Forest Service's appropriation of a centralized model of management akin to the one Frederick Taylor had been finding effective in the factory sphere.

Preservationists, though focused on setting aside nature for its own sake, shared certain limitations with conservationists. While conservationists included humans in their management systems largely as consumers of products, preservationists excluded humans entirely. Nature was viewed as a resource for individuals to use to experience the divine. Both ideologies failed to incorporate both communal understanding of society and meaningful human-land relations into their thinking. Historian Robert Gottlieb shows how both became captive to corporate interests and technical expertise. Their individualistic worldviews in the end led them inevitably to Washington to shape policy rather than to local communities.[48]

Throughout the history of forest management in the United States, solutions to problems have collected around two poles. Either private individuals or corporations have been seen as the solution to the problem, or the federal government has been called on to intervene. In an important way, one is but the mirror image of the other; one necessitates the other. When the effects of the actions of such strong individual and corporate interests have led to third-party problems (tax forfeiture, erosion, depletion of supplies, higher prices) the call has gone out for federal intervention to solve the problem. Where the state is perceived as only the protector of individual interests, it becomes inevitable that centralized state functions are required to balance the forces of individual and increasingly strong corporate interests. Nowhere in this history did legislators or others articulate a policy to encourage the moderation of individualistic tendencies or a strong sense of the commons.[49] And in the end, forest policy became the arena of the Iron Triangle of the U.S. Forest Service, the corporate forest interests, and congressional committees dominated by congressmen from districts dependent on the forest industry.

Notes

1. David W. Orr and Stuart Hill, "Leviathan, the Open Society, and the Crisis of Ecology," *Western Political Quarterly* 31 (1978): 457-69, 462.

2. Bernard Zylstra, "The Bible, Justice, and the State," in *Where Are We Now?* ed. William A. Harper and Theodore R. Malloch (Washington, D.C.: University Press of America, 1981), 185-211.

3. David J. Woods, "'Nature' in Adam Smith's *Wealth of Nations*," Paper series, (Toronto: Institute for Christian Studies, 1985), 7.

4. Orr and Hill, "Leviathan, the Open Society, and the Crisis of Ecology," 462.

5. Herman Dooyeweerd, *A New Critique of Theoretical Thought*, trans. by David H. Freeman and H. De Jongste (Philadelphia: Presbyterian and Reformed Publishing, 1955), 360.

6. Ivan Illich, "Silence Is a Commons," *CoEvolution Quarterly* 40 (1983): 5-9.

7. Hildegard Binder Johnson, *Order upon the Land* (New York: Oxford University Press, 1976), 39.

8. Philip E. Slater, *The Pursuit of Loneliness: American Culture at the Breaking Point* (Boston: Beacon, 1979); Robert N. Bellah, Richard Madsen, William M. Sullivan, Ann Swidler, and Steven M. Tipton, *Habits of the Heart* (Berkeley: University of California, 1985).

9. C. Wright Mills, *Power, Politics, and People,* ed. Irving Louis Horowitz (New York: Oxford University Press, 1963), 263.

10. Brad Stone, "Modernity and the Narcissistic Self: Taking 'Character' Disorders Seriously" (paper presented to the Society for the Study of Symbolic Interactionism, Urbana, 1987); Christopher Lasch, *The Culture of Narcissism* (New York: Norton, 1989); Bellah et al., *Habits.*

11. Mills, *Power, Politics*, 292.

12. Bellah et al., *Habits.*

13. Woods, "Nature," 2.

14. Herman Dooyeweerd, *Intellectually Defenseless?* trans. John Vriend (Amsterdam: Uitgevers-Mij, Holland, 1937); Jurgen Habermas, *Theory and Practice* (Boston: Beacon, 1973), 41-81.

15. Herman Dooyeweerd, *Roots of Western Culture* (Toronto: Wedge Publishing Foundation, 1979), 176.

16. Evan H. Runner, "Scriptural Religion and Political Task," and "Anti-thesis: The Forms of Its Political Expression and Their Development in Modern Times," in *Christian Perspectives* (Hamilton, Ontario: Guardian Publishing Company, Ltd, 1963), 179-236, 204.

17. For example, in Louise Fortmann and John W. Bruce, *Whose Trees? Proprietary Dimensions of Forestry* (Boulder, Colo.: Westview, 1988).

18. Habermas, *Theory and Practice*, 70-81.

19. Robert D. Holsworth, "Recycling Hobbes: The Limits to Political Ecology," *Massachusetts Review* 20 (1979): 9-40, 23.

20. Illich, "Silence," 7.

21. William Cronon, *Changes in the Land: Indians, Colonists, and the Ecology of New England* (New York: Hill and Wang, 1983), 58.

22. Bellah et al., *Habits.*

23. Mills, *Power, Politics*, 293.

24. Frederick H. Buttel, "Environmentalization: Origins, Processes, and Implications for Rural Social Change," *Rural Sociology* 57, no. 1 (1992): 1-27, 9.

25. Peter L. Berger and Richard John Neuhaus, *To Empower People: The Role of Mediating Structures in Public Policy* (Washington, D.C.: American Enterprise Institute for Public Policy Research, 1977).

26. J. P. Kinney, "Forest Legislation in America Prior to March 4, 1789," *Cornell University Agricultural Experiment Station Bulletin* 370 (1916), 372.

27. U.S. Attorney General, *Official Opinions of the Attorney General*, ed. Benjamin F. Hall (Washington, D.C.: Robert Farnham, 1852), vol. 1, 137.

28. U.S. Statutes at Large, (Washington, D.C.: Government Printing Office), vol. 6, 474.

29. Attorney General, *Official Opinions*, vol. 1, 471-73.

30. Attorney General, *Official Opinions*, vol. 1, 471-73.

31. U.S. Statutes at Large, vol. 8, 461.

32. U.S. Statutes at Large, vol. 9, 351.

33. Habermas, *Theory and Practice*, 63.

34. Runner, "Scriptural Religion," 206.

35. *Congressional Globe*, (Washington, D.C.: Government Printing Office, 3 March 1873), 42-3, 2111, 2209.

36. *Congressional Record*, (Washington, D.C.: Government Printing Office, 2 February 1876), 44-1, 815-18; *Congressional Record*, (Washington, D.C.: Government Printing Office, 7 February 1876), 44-1, 906.

37. U.S. Statutes at Large, vol. 19, 73.

38. Janel M. Curry-Roper, "A Historical Geography of Land Ownership in Minnesota: The Influence of the Timber and Stone Act" (Ph.D. Thesis, University of Minnesota, 1985), 47.

39. *Congressional Record*, (Washington, D.C.: Government Printing Office, 15 February 1876): 44-1, 1085.

40. *Congressional Globe*, (Washington, D.C.: Government Printing Office, 11 February 1876), 44-1, 817.

41. *Congressional Globe*, (Washington, D.C.: Government Printing Office, 11 February 1871), 41-3, 1158.

42. *Congressional Globe*, (Washington, D.C.: Government Printing Office, 17 April 1872), 42-2, 2506.

43. *Congressional Globe*, (Washington, D.C.: Government Printing Office, 3 March 1981), 51-2, 3894, 3916.

44. United States General Land Office, *Annual Reports* (Washington D.C.: Government Printing Office, 1891), 52-1, Serial 2933, 329-30.

45. U.S. Statutes at Large, vol. 33, 628.

46. U.S. Statutes at Large, vol. 43, 653.

47. United States National Forest Reservation Commission, *Annual Reports* (Washington, D.C.: Government Printing Office, 1932), 72-2; Serial 9665, 20.

48. Robert Gottlieb, *Forcing the Spring: The Transformation of the American Environmental Movement* (Washington, D.C.: Island Press, 1983).

49. Janel M. Curry-Roper and Steve McGuire, "The Individualistic Imagination and Natural Resource Policy," *Society and Natural Resources* 6, no. 3 (1993): 259-72.

PART II

CURRENT CONSEQUENCES

CHAPTER 6

AGGREGATED IN THEORY

[T]he Japanese have little interest in abstract theory because theories are most useful to people who like to argue. People who do not like to argue have no use for theory.[1]

Richard Parker

[T]he proper metaphor for political reasoning is not concatenation but weaving—the interlacing of strands in a cable . . . rather than the forging of links in a chain.[2]

Benjamin R. Barber

With his self-isolated and self-scrutinizing individual mind, Western man was master of concepts and abstractions. He was the king of quantity and the driver of those forces over which quantitative knowledge gave him supremacy without understanding . . . [a] one-eyed giant.[3]

Thomas Merton

THE HISTORY CHRONICLED thus far has shown how the forces of economy and philosophy banded together to shape the modern Western worldview, especially as expressed in the United States. This worldview conceptualized society as being built on autonomous individuals at the expense of the community. Legal structures evolved that gave increasing power to a particular "individual," i.e., the business corporation, leaving the individual person increasingly powerless in light of the lack of mediating structures. The changes in scale, both the expanding scale of the corporation, and the diminishing scale to the level of the individual, diminished any relationship with nature. All sense of environment as commons was lost with the loss of communal societal concepts. Human nature went from being viewed as relationally constituted to individually conceived. The resulting effect was the similar flattening of the policy framework that regulated the environment. Within this societal conception, state centralized control was increasingly required to balance the utilitarian demands on nature by individuals and corporations.

Extensions to Social Science

A major portion of political and economic theory over the last century has extended the individualism of early Enlightenment thought. By the mid 1900s most political science and sociology theories worked under the rubric of "pluralism," but a pluralism at variance with the earlier English pluralists who recognized the existence of communal life. This extension of Enlightenment individualism held that state power reflected a plurality of competing interest groups, not social wholes. Like the exalted free market, the political arena of freely competing interest groups have presumed to result in favorable outcomes. Democracy as interest group politics was so constituted. The person who inhabits this assumed unidimensional world embodies the apotheosis of the rationalization process referred to by Weber and others as *homo economicus*— calculating a life of costs and benefits. A person's free choices lent themselves to a distinct form of social-science packaging, one that sought universality in the laws of behavior and scientific neutrality in the production of its scientific knowledge.

Garrett Hardin's paper, "The Tragedy of the Commons," exemplifies the predominate view of humans and their relationships with nature.[4] In this account (as in prisoner's dilemma games and in political-philosophy accounts) abstracted, universalized individuals were largely shorn of communal and familial context. *Homo economicus*, so shorn, then acted according to perceived self-interest. Individual competition overused the commons, leading to tragedy. Protecting the environment appeared to require privatization or a state that exerted control over otherwise errant individuals. Hardin's assumptions are the same assumptions as those that have informed forest policy as described in the previous chapter.

Academic sociology has retained comparatively more of the community focus of that discipline's founding fathers than have other social science disciplines. Throughout that time, disagreements as to the degree, universality, and desirability of something like the decline of community and the concomitant rise of individualism have regularly manifested themselves. More than once, reports of the death of community have been greatly exaggerated. But the concern remains—and for good reason. We find the recent analyses by Robert Bellah et al. (1985) and Wendell Berry (1977) to be apt.[5] Community in North America and elsewhere continues to disappear. As Daniel Kemmis shows, the awareness of personal responsibility has atrophied.[6] In municipal conflicts in Montana, disagreeing parties *could* work out their own, satisfactory settlements, but instead have given over that responsibility to the formal process. Common ground exists but goes unrecognized by the unencumbered self of the modern citizen. In turn, facing away from personal responsibility offers minimal recognition of humans' inherent mutuality.[7]

Many of the important discussions of civil society, democracy, and the state of community make reference to the "self."[8] Some find the self to be a prepolitical constellation of nonrationalizable interests, akin to a Hobbesian vision. Others have a more optimistic view of the self and hold that democracy itself transforms the self in positive ways. Setting aside for the time being the ultimate nature of the self, we concur with extensive social-scientific literature that the modern self of *homo economicus* perceives itself to be unencumbered and cut off from much collective obligation. Moderns increasingly enact the life of a contained insular self artfully limned by T. R. Young and Robert Bellah.[9] Legal discourse reflects this concept as well. "The public subject of Western law was born out of this way of thinking about the self: as one who is sovereign to himself, a self-possessing being, essentially a creature of reason—of the mind—autonomous and self-determining."[10] Put another way, the modern self is increasingly uprooted, severed from place.[11] Place is universalized as a featureless space on which individual humans make self-interested moves. Commitment to a particular place has diminished. The individual's place is arbitrary and his or her home can be anywhere. To feel rooted increasingly strikes moderns as an odd, antiquarian notion.

In previous chapters we have sought to highlight particular aspects of the colonizer Enlightenment self, with implications for its current progeny. The Enlightenment self constituted its own identity by contrasting itself with the indigenous populations on the receiving end of the colonial adventure. The native was read as brutish, unconceptual, and stagnant in contrast to the colonizer who was civil, learned, and open-minded. The colonizer exemplified the endpoint of a trajectory upon which the native was embarked but had minimally traversed. They universalized a vast range of experience into a perceived stagnant uniformity. A raison d'être was to enable those encountered to make progress toward the civilizing goal. All conquistadorean savagery of self went unfaced, projected onto the other. The demarcations were crucial. Jennifer Nedelsky has shown the political fallout of conceiving the self by reference to its boundaries.[12]

Today's self looks notably insular. "The quest for self then, pursued under the predominant ideology of individualism, involves separating out from family, religion, and calling. . . . It means autonomously pursuing happiness and satisfying one's own wants."[13] "Radically private validation" is its mode of constitution. The individual thinks his or herself strong to the degree that it is autonomous and not dependent upon family and community. A democratic and culturally pluralistic self would require more connection than that which is characteristic of our times. The modern self regularly limits its involvement in the public sphere.[14] Such individuals lie ripe for demagogic picking, the would-be substitutes for family and community. Our purpose here is not to operationalize these claims but rather to note certain facets of the interrelated crises in community and the land and point toward the possibilities of more welcome outcomes.

How Not to Think about Knowledge

To talk about how to think is to raise the matter of science. Science has had enormous technical successes and contributed to higher standards of living among many on the planet, so much so that its criteria for knowledge production are sometimes thought identical with the criteria of knowledge production in general. As a way of knowing and as a knowledge production community, it has often been accorded exemplary status.[15] Religion, common sense, intuition, dialogue, and other nonscientifically measurable aspects of reality have at times been placed in competition with science and found wanting. A host of issues have been raised over the years, but for our purposes it will suffice to allude briefly to science's role in the chronology of the matters at hand, as well as to their proposed resolutions.

A millennium ago, Europeans utilized organic metaphors to frame their experience. Organic imageries gradually gave way to more mechanistic ones. Machinery proved successful for adapting nature to human purposes. Francis Bacon and others sought to improve their knowledge of divine creation, and soon, to improve upon creation itself. Everyday knowledge-production practices were deemed deficient and powerful new procedures were developed. Nature came to be accorded female characteristics and was interrogated for its secrets. Bacon's experimentation opened nature to a surveilling and controlling gaze. Experimentation led to taxonomy. Taxonomic scrutiny into the order of nature led beyond understanding that order to improving upon it.

Knowledge had been a communal product and in some senses continued to be one. By its nature, human knowing engenders disagreement. The European Age of Reason sought to reduce such disagreement, and in doing so brought an individualistic cast to knowing. René Descartes focused on that which eliminated doubt. To remove doubt, he found it necessary to proceed qua an individual, "I think therefore I am." The successes of Isaac Newton and others supported the idea that a distinct new and successful way of producing knowledge was in the offing. Later, David Hume and others took that possibility of a particularly efficacious procedure and tied it to empiricism.

Empiricist thought, at pains to yoke more dubitable theory to less arguable sensory impressions, came to emphasize the perceptions of the individual scientist. Empiricism extolled scientific successes as resultant from the ascension of actual experience at the expense of unsecured theory. In making that point, its later philosophers would regularly invoke individualistic imageries. The perceiving scientist was framed in the singular. The body of knowledge so generated by science was formulated by logical positivism with the imagery of a "wall" of science secured by empirical building blocks at the base, or a "layer cake" again secured by a foundational empirical base upon which the more tentative thinking could be anchored. Each of the latter would stand as a visual edifice readily inspected or ascertained by a lone knower.

Bacon, Descartes, and Hume emphasized differing particulars but, in common, helped Europeans to think that a new, nonreligious-based certitude existed. Science gradually proved successful enough and useful enough to fill the bill of providing "The One Right Description," to use Richard Rorty's terms.[16] In the twentieth century, science was recurrently articulated in empiricist, and for a time, logical positivist terms. Those terms could have emphasized science's continuities with other methods of knowledge production. For the most part they instead worked to demarcate differences. Empiricist understandings of science did not so much negate its communal aspect as downplay that aspect in favor of emphasis on the empirical foundation, the application of logic, and the articulation of the appropriate procedure.

The notion of foundation deserves consideration. In scientific and political discourse alike, foundationalism perceives, fears, and so seeks to avoid the possibility that decisions will be made irrationally.[17] Thus it seeks to establish universal bedrock principles. Dissatisfied with the certitude obtained by ordinary discourse, Descartes, and most since, sought to establish a foundation of one sort or another. Procuring such a foundation has been presumed crucial to most attempts to move beyond ordinary discourse to enhance certitude. The specification of the foundation itself might vary from qualitative social science to Husserlian phenomenological philosophy within academe, to Talmudic scholarship and investigative reporting outside it. But the notion of a foundation itself has been central to many otherwise disparate knowledge-production projects within modernity. Foundational enterprises are invoked for their mythological power. They show common family resemblances and difficulties.

Foundational enterprises such as the empiricist one do not isolate themselves from that which they proclaim to transcend. The realm or sphere of sensory impressions or empirical data embodies theoretical aspects. Empirical observations are not ordinarily theory free or even theory neutral. Scientific practitioners, as do other knowers, perceive from some package of worldview or paradigmatic presuppositions. Their culture and their scientific community frame their purported "blank slate" or perceptual template. Empiricism's doctrine of immaculate perception has insufficiently appreciated the impact of such differential socialization of thought.[18] For practitioners, the current belief system does not determine that which they will perceive in the future, but it deeply influences and limits that which will be perceived.

The individualist cast of science has contributed to its latter-day apologists by treating it in pictorial terms. The metaphor of mapping is used to characterize scientific knowledge and correspondent models of truth, models that focus on the degree to which a formulation corresponds with reality. The assumption is that social scientific works can be compressed into snippets of language, and that those snippets can be judged in terms of how well they correspond with reality as codified into a body of (scientific) language.

Science/Democracy

Science often has been invoked as a means to democracy. The invocation is based on science's capacity to provide a solid knowledge base, rather than its exemplification of a democratic procedure. That is, many visions of democracy look to science as a source of secure knowledge on which an informed public may base its opinions.

Recent decades have made the opposite possibility increasingly evident. The content of science has become increasingly technical and specialized and the sheer amount of information has escalated to extreme proportions. But it is not just the matter of amount and difficulty of content that creates problems. Technical expertise has come to take on a different role than that of mere knowledge provision. For example, modern society has become "medicalized," such that problems are increasingly attributed pathological qualities and medical solutions. Their management is increasingly turned over to medical expertise. Emotional problems become mental-health matters in which decisions about their resolution are turned over to experts. Technical expertise does not merely generate knowledge; it becomes so positioned as to make decisions. It does not merely inform the citizenry in order to provide the information for democratic decision making; it accrues many of the decisions themselves. "All anti-democratic arguments, if they are serious, are arguments from specialized knowledge," according to Michael Walzer.[19]

In vitro fertilization, egg fusion, cloning, surrogate mothering, and other childbirth technologies provide examples by which the search for knowledge for its own sake stretches and threatens to break down science's accountability to democratic decision making. These also exemplify the extremes to which a contract model of social life exalts individual need at the expense of the traditional framework of familial and collective institutions. Scientific advances are fostered, and then in retrospect, the citizenry attempts to exert popular control over the directions they are taking.

The lack of accountability of science shows parallels to the lack of accountability of corporations. Both are supposed to be neutral and their existence is intertwined with issues surrounding the environment. Turn-of-the-century community organizer Alice Hamilton, 1960s author Rachel Carson, who began the modern environmental movement with her book *Silent Spring,* and contemporary grassroots movements such as the Citizen's Clearinghouse for Hazardous Waste question this objectivity of science and corporate action. More so, they question whether science and corporations should be above community accountability. All these movements call for the democratization of information and the placement of that information within a community context.[20]

We agree with Paul Feyerabend that science and social science should be less exempt from popular control.[21] Science's technical expertise does not warrant a carte blanche search for knowledge and control. Science has too often acted as though there should be no limits to where the search for knowledge should go, irrespective of the side effects. Just as its precursor Descartes emphasized certainty via the mind at the expense of ordinary dialogue, science sometimes emphasizes the knower at the expense of the community. In areas such as the Manhattan Project's testing of the atomic bomb, the Tuskegee Institute's study of African-Americans who were syphilis-infected but left untreated, and the launch of the Cabrini space shuttle with its load of lethal radioactive plutonium, science seeks knowledge regardless of extraordinary risks and/or side effects. Many examples abound in which knowledge has been privileged over wisdom. Successful technical expertise has enabled science to continue its agenda almost irrespective of democratic popular control.

Thus, the democracy that science exemplifies is a limited one. The institution largely provides open access to knowledge and its generation. But that same institution is usually responsive to the influence of elites, pointing away from popular control toward technical expertise. Science purports to comprise a tool for the common good, and at times is put to such use. But since its early days, science has exhibited an individualist facet, a facet that seeks control rather than coexistence, and a facet that serves the few rather than the many.

Valuing Commitment

Who should science serve and how? The goal of a body of knowledge might appear straightforward enough for the natural sciences, but science applied to social behavior shows complications. Is not advocacy work at cross-purposes with understanding? Does not value commitment interfere with attempts to depict accurately? The founders of European social science a century ago, from Max Weber to Karl Marx to Emile Durkheim, acknowledged the issue to be a serious one and engaged it in different ways. Social science sought to institutionalize itself as a scientific discipline. To do so, it was deemed imperative to distinguish social science from social work, for the latter more readily embraced advocacy. The goal was to address social problems from a stance of neutrality rather than advocacy. Just as classic liberalism split off morality from politics, value decision had to be bracketed off from science.

Subsequent academic social science largely opted for and refined a three-stage Weberian position, with minor variations. The selection of topics for social scientific analysis was to be guided by value commitment. At the end of the work, social science could be put to uses governed by value commitment in the form of advocacy. However, the middle stage of the work itself had to be governed by the values of science only. Partisanship was set aside for the search of accurate portrayals. Following Hume, social science would speak only to the "is," not the "ought"; the former would not dictate responses to the latter. Useful, accurate work would neutrally provide the empirical basis. Advocacy and value commitment could then make use of the objectively furnished material. Social science would speak to issues of ought, but only by providing the information with which to make such decisions. The predominant value-neutral position seeks to speak neutrally only the facts, momentarily setting aside human values, thereby giving the individual social scientist a bad case of role conflict. He or she gains the laurels of technical expertise at the expense of citizenship.[22]

Colonizers' worldview stance was a similar one of purported objectivity involving disinterested observation as to the ways in which colonially encountered peoples were deficient. The predominant stance on value commitment echoes the colonizers' Enlightenment one in several respects. The colonizers universalized themselves. Each veiled his or her constitutive role regarding the conclusions reached and attributed an irrationality to the people of color encountered. The colonizers accorded themselves a neutral standpoint, concluded that they themselves were to be crowned creators of civilization, and assessed others as to how far they yet were from their standard.

The Enlightenment individual seeks a knowledge that is universalized in the sense that it largely features generalizations that hold true irrespective of the preconceptions of different members of the scientific audience. The individual succeeds, sometimes generating interesting, useful knowledge with a value of its own. We argue that a tension exists between that which has been demonstrated to be true beyond doubt and that which is interesting. The more interesting the scholarship, the more its presentation embodies value implications. In other words, it is possible to report routine or passable social science in a way that does not generate the role conflict or that does not speak substantially to the value commitments of the speaker. The great works are regularly expressed in a manner that begins to speak to matters of value commitment and not just in a technocratic, neutral way, as Robert Bellah and many another have shown.[23] Some of them stop short of advocacy, but others more openly address the "ought" that Hume and pure empiricist sociology would not address.

Social scientists conduct their discourse in language. Logical positivism of the Vienna Circle and many of its social scientific heirs attempted to construct a methodological "language" of lawlike propositions, snippets supported or produced by the empirical gaze. But the work of social science itself, the human production aspect, against the body of knowledge in and of itself, is conducted in something closer to ordinary human communication. Monographs are put forth and reviewed, papers are given and responded to, summary compilations are generated and themselves judged. The nature of human communication conveys commitment. It embodies the commitment stances of its speakers. To speak or write is to create a relation between speaker and hearer(s) or reader(s). To speak is to request from the audience such actions as listening. Ordinary human speech does not bracket or set aside its value commitments but rather exemplifies them.

The most basic commitment identifies the heart of any conceptual perspective. The underlying theoretical basis of what is important and what is good and how knowledge is done animates and orders the rest.[24] The guiding source embodies the ground from which the remaining specifications of the perspective stem. Social studies of science have articulated numerous instances of a principle: To the degree that outside criticisms touch inwardly to the fundamental, its practitioners will dismiss or fail to even perceive the criticisms. Newcomers to a school of thought, tradition, or paradigm often shift their stance or allegiance while those steeped in it ordinarily do not.

The universalizing gaze embodies a distinctive self and self (mis)-understanding as it searches to catalogue in order to control. Clarity regarding self and other suffers. Some knowledge gains are made, but one particular kind of knowledge is systematically minimized and sometimes distorted.

Local Knowledge

Work that has opted for universalistic explanations and translocality has involved loss of context and applicability. For instance, forest management that seeks to achieve a maximum sustainable yield of timber grapples with a "wicked problem" that entails groups of variables that may be unique in time and space.[25] Analysis and solutions continue to resist standardization into general laws or theories.[26] Studies by Kloppenburg and Curry-Roper have exemplified commonalities in the thinking of theorists of sustainable agriculture and feminism.[27] Feminist concerns about context-dependence substantially mirror the perspective of agroecologists such as Wendell Berry and Wes Jackson as well as echoing a long line of work in ethnomethodology and epistemological reflections on history and anthropology.[28] The reductionism of science based on the search for universality sharply contrasts with both sustainable agriculture proponents of local knowledge and feminist epistemology that emphasizes situated knowledge, limited location, and the inability to split subject and object.[29] Evelyn Fox Keller goes so far as to claim that the traditional approach of science hampers questions related to humans' relationship to natural systems.[30] Her proposed alternative goal of understanding over prediction entails empowerment rather than power to manipulate, and reflects and affirms humans' deep connection to the land.

To use grounded theory of this sort is to acknowledge the situated and continually evolving nature of group life. We do not suggest the abandonment of theory, but rather a way to formulate a more complex and yet tentative theory that more closely addresses questions about experienced social life rather than what is externally deduced.[31] Michael Burowoy's extended case method similarly allows for specificity through focusing on those aspects of a situation that do not fit present theory. This focus allows for the reconstruction of already existing theory.[32] Agricultural research of the sort performed by experiment stations can have only limited applicability to the wide diversity of actual farming operations. Much of it retains methodological individualism. Studies of the diffusion and adoption of agricultural innovation work with an individual as the unit of study.[33] This technique misses the culturally situated meaning of discourse. The alternative perspective, that of "local or indigenous knowledge," dwells on understandings arising only out of particular places—turning the agricultural establishment on its head. This perspective argues that knowledge, just like social and economic life, is embedded in specific localities.

Agricultural research in the past fifty years has been characterized by a commitment to an ends-means reductionistic scientific rationality commonly associated with the physical sciences.[34] That is, scientists assign one outcome, such as increasing yields, as a deterministic end. They then manipulate various experimental treatments to determine the most effective method to reach that end in order to produce general universal knowledge. It represents a way of relating to nature through its goal of control. By contrast, local knowledge generated by the farmer allows for practical experience as a valid measure of success and incorporates detailed knowledge of local ecological and environmental factors.[35] Knowledge that is usefully applicable to a particular place demonstrates a value of its own, albeit a departure from knowledge that is universalistic. Agricultural research minimizes local specificity in order to control as many locales as possible. Local agricultural study more readily incorporates the agenda of those who live directly on and by the land. The former seeks uniformity and efficiency; the latter more readily speaks to matters of ecological health. Local agricultural study mirrors "applied" social (and probably natural) science everywhere in that it emphasizes useful application over more abstract, universal generalization.

The matter pertains to more than agricultural research. In North America, social science as a whole has sought to institutionalize itself as science for close to a century. To do so it delayed holistic understanding at the expense of certainty. At Columbia, the survey research of Paul Lazarsfeld and others opted for a method that sacrificed history and the broad scope of societal dynamics for a narrower certitude as to the attitudes and traits of aggregates of individuals. Such work settled for secure but partial understanding of widely dispersed phenomena at the expense of a more complete, holistic understanding of a specifically situated phenomenon. These empiricist-spatial perspectives often see the geographical world as space and particular places as simply the locations of spatial attributes. In doing so, this perspective echoed the reductionism of Descartes. The work breaks down complicated phenomena into discreet components, often analyzing them as if in isolation from each other, hoping in the future to reconstruct the system with the analyses of the parts. Descriptions and analyses of human responses to environmental and societal change quite often center upon individual responses. Scholars with this perspective tend to use quantification in order to find generalizations that apply across space and to simplify human experiences in order to isolate those aspects deemed most essential.[36] The human model often assumed is one of utility-maximizing beings whose relations with others are largely instrumental.[37]

The individualist influence is methodological as well as theoretical. Survey research in particular, and "variable analysis" in general, focus by their methodological nature on the responses of individuals.[38] The realm of the social is only remotely tapped by reference to the traits of individuals. Just as historical process is stunted by a method that frequently settles for data from one point in time, social interaction is flattened by methods that, in the name of science, settle for the attitudes and traits of individuals.

Dennis Wrong and Alfred McClung Lee hold that much social scientific work portrays experience in terms of acquired customs, habits, or norms that followed without much thought or sense of choice, again utilizing the focus of the individual, atomized "actor."[39] Humans make choices, act collectively, bend, and go beyond their constraining influences, while those studying them often focus on cataloguing the influences on individuals. Much social scientific work today has avoided such oversocialized and unhumanist treatments, but a substantial amount remains exemplary of that which Wrong, Lee, and Blumer critiqued. The sense of embeddedness in relationships as the result of choice is minimally developed. Behavior is seen rather as the result of a set of roles where decisions involving more than one individual are the result of role-prescribed behavior.[40]

A related problem is the empirical challenge of separating the effects of individual attributes from the effects of social context in the determination of individual outcomes. The potentially rich notion of social structure regularly dilutes into group-level properties that are measured as mere aggregations of individual attributes. Places reflect a hard-to-grasp quality and a sense of something more in culture than can be described with useful nuance by purported lawlike generalities or overly abstract theoretical concepts.[41] In line with this perception, in a study across Iowa, Curry-Roper found evidence for the existence of distinct community-wide world-and-life-views that were grounded in common belief systems and physical places.[42] They were community wide, concerned fundamental commitments, included elements of commitment to place and relationship to the natural world, and affected agricultural worldviews and patterns of farming. These worldviews were not merely attributable to class, gender, or educational level. Where it has grown strong, the communal sense of place constitutes a formative, influential phenomenon of its own, rather than a mere appendage to such variables.

Atomization in orthodox economics results in narrow pursuit of self-interest while the usual alternative sees behavior as so internalized that relationships have only marginal effects on actions.[43] Once someone can be characterized by social class or some other measurable variable, all other behavior is predictable and automatic.

Values, spirituality, and related phenomena are often utilized as reflections of other measurable forces such as socioeconomic status, or educational attainment, and are ordinarily divorced from truth content and from decision making or interpretive work. Morality has often been individualized and addressed apart from societal context.[44] It is also ordinarily addressed apart from the truth value of its content. Colonizers dismissed the truth value of most indigenous theorizing that it encountered. Their social science heirs often look to the factors that would explain particular beliefs, implicitly dismissing their truth content.

Indeed, the social contract model of community as articulated in earlier chapters with its assumption of the self-interested nature of humans, has become so thoroughly accepted that the establishment of just such a true and satisfying community is dismissed as regressive thinking.[45] The colonizers' Enlightenment model of community is a narrow, anemic one, in sharp contrast with that of the peoples that European adventurers encountered.[46] Central to a meaningful recognition of commitment, community, and the relational aspects of reality is the concept of covenant. Robert Bellah has clarified the conflict between the Lockean, reductionistic notion of society and covenantal concepts of society. The covenant is a relationship between parties that, unlike the parties in the Lockean contract, belong to one another by virtue of a prior relation. The covenant is not a limited relation based on self-interest but an unlimited commitment based on loyalty and trust—personal relationship. It involves obligations to each other that transcend self-interest, while it promises a deeper sense of self-fulfillment through participation.[47] Covenantal community embodies more than organizational belonging for members. A community is a group with whom one regularly interacts and shares space. Individualism leads to equating community with organization.[48] A good organization is one that serves well the persons involved. Community, on the other hand, is something we are; it is a property of our personhood. To clarify this further, we may say that an organization is a rule-governed framework of human invention for ordering human affairs. A community is a human organism constituted of the shared life of a number of persons.[49] Social scientists other than Bellah and his coworkers have minimally utilized the concept of covenant and the related concept of birthright.

A world that has become globalized will likewise have atrophied its sense of place. A world in which transnational business corporations increasingly predominate will be a world increasingly unrooted from place. The "great good places," will become increasingly transformed into the narrow lifestyle enclave described by Bellah et al.[50] The concept of place is intertwined with assumptions on the nature of humans, of communal bonds, and humans' relationships with nature and place. In this chapter we have identified how social science understands community and the individual. From here we will address assumptions about how science and social science are generated in ways that continue individualist thinking.

Notes

1. Richard B. Parker, "Law, Language, and the Individual in Japan and the United States," *Wisconsin International Law Journal* 7, no.1 (1989): 179-204, 200.

2. Benjamin R. Barber, *Strong Democracy: Participatory Politics for a New Age* (Berkeley: University of California Press, 1984), 32.

3. Thomas Merton, *Gandhi on Nonviolence* (New York: New Directions, 1964), 1.

4. Garrett Hardin, "The Tragedy of the Commons," *Science* 162 (1968): 1243-48.

5. Robert N. Bellah, Richard Madsen, William M. Sullivan, Ann Swidler, and Steven M. Tipton, *Habits of the Heart* (Berkeley: University of California Press, 1985); Wendell Berry, *The Unsettling of America* (New York: Avon Books, 1977).

6. Daniel Kemmis, *Community and the Politics of Place* (Norman: University of Oklahoma Press, 1990).

7. Kemmis, *Community and the Politics of Place*, 110.

8. Mark Warren, "Democratic Theory and Self-Transformation," *American Political Science Review* 86 (1992): 8-23.

9. T. R. Young, *The Drama of Social Life* (Somerset, N.J.: Transaction Books, 1990); Robert N. Bellah, "The Quest for Self," in *Rights and the Common Good: A Communitarian Perspective*, ed. Amitai Etzioni (New York: St. Martin's Press, 1995), 45-57.

10. Ngaire Naffine, "Sexing the Subject (of Law)" in *Public and Private*, ed. Margaret Thornton (Oxford: Oxford University Press, 1995), 18-39, 23.

11. Berry, *The Unsettling of America*, 53.

12. Jennifer Nedelsky, "Law, Boundaries, and the Bounded Self," *Representations* 30 (1990):162-88.

13. Bellah et al., *Habits of the Heart*, 48.

14. Bellah et al., *Habits of the Heart*, 48.

15. Wendell Berry, *Life Is a Miracle* (Washington, D.C.: Counterpoint Press, 2000).

16. Richard Rorty, *Contingency, Irony, and Solidarity* (Cambridge, UK: Cambridge University Press, 1989).

17. Mark Warren, "Nonfoundationalism and Democratic Judgment," *Current Perspectives in Social Theory* 14 (1994): 151-82.

18. Norwood Russell Hanson, "Logical Positivism and the Interpretation of Theories" in *The Legacy of Logical Positivism,* eds. P. Achinstein and S. Barker (Baltimore, Md.: Johns Hopkins, 1969), 57-84.

19. Warren, "Nonfoundationalism and Democratic Judgment," 152.

20. Robert Gottlieb, *Forcing the Spring: The Transformation of the American Environmental Movement* (Washington, D.C.: Island Press, 1983).

21. Paul K. Feyerabend, *Against Method: Outline of an Anarchistic Theory of Knowledge* (New York: Verso, 1975), 96.

22. Bellah et al., *Habits of the Heart,* 299.

23. Bellah et al., *Habits of the Heart.*

24. Alan Blum, "Criticalness Prejudice: Science As a Perfect Art for Our Times," *Canadian Journal of Sociology* 2, no. 1 (1977): 97-124.

25. Michael E. Patterson and Daniel R. Williams, "Paradigms and Problems: The Practice of Social Science in Natural Resource Management," *Society and Natural Resources* 11 (1998): 279-95.

26. Cornelia Butler Flora, "Reconstructing Agriculture: The Case for Local Knowledge," *Rural Sociology* 57, no. 1 (1992): 92-97; Ann Reisner, "Tracing the Linkages of World Views, Information Handling, and Communications Vehicles," *Agriculture and Human Values* 9, no. 2 (1992): 4-16.

27. Janel M. Curry-Roper, "Alternative Agriculture and Conventional Paradigms in United States Agriculture," in *Contemporary Rural Systems in Transition: Agriculture and Environment,* vol. 1, ed. Ian Bowler, Chris Bryant, and Duane Nellis (Wallingford, UK: CAB International, 1992), 254-64; Jack Kloppenburg Jr., "Social Theory and the De/Reconstruction of Agricultural Science: Local Knowledge for an Alternative Agriculture," *Rural Sociology* 56, no. 4 (1991): 519-48.

28. For example, Shelley Feldman and Rick Welsh, "Feminist Knowledge Claims, Local Knowledge, and Gender Divisions of Agricultural Labor: Constructing a Successor Science," *Rural Sociology* 60, no. 1 (1995): 23-43.

29. Donna Haraway, "Situated Knowledges: The Science Question in Feminism and the Privilege of Partial Perspective," *Feminist Studies* 14, no. 3 (1988): 575-99, 581.

30. Evelyn Fox Keller, *Reflections on Gender and Science* (New Haven, Conn.: Yale University Press, 1985), 147.

31. B. G. Glaser and A. L. Strauss, *The Discovery of Grounded Theory* (Chicago: Aldine Publishing Company, 1967); D. Harper, "On 'Methodological Monism' in Rural Sociology," *Rural Sociology* 56, no. 1(1991): 70-88, 83.

32. Michael Burowoy, "Reconstructing Social Theories," in *Ethnography Unbound: Power and Resistance in the Modern Metropolis,* ed. Michael Burawoy (Berkeley: University of California Press, 1991), 8-27.

33. Harper, "On 'Methodological Monism' in Rural Sociology," 74.

34. Reisner, "Tracing the Linkages of World Views," 7.

35. Reisner, "Tracing the Linkages of World Views," 8.

36. Robert D. Sack, "*The Nature*, in Light of the Present," in *Reflections on Richard Hartshorne's "The Nature of Geography,"* eds. J. Nicholas Entrikin and Stanley D. Brunn (Washington, D.C.: Association of American Geographers, 1989), 141-62, 144.

37. J. Friedman and B. Hudson, "Knowledge and Action: A Guide to Planning Theory," *Journal of the American Institute of Planners* 10, no. 3 (1974): 3-16, 3.

38. Herber Blumer, *Symbolic Interactionism* (Englewood Cliffs, N.J.: Prentice Hall, 1969).

39. Dennis Wrong and Alfred McClung Lee, *Toward Humanist Sociology* (Englewood Cliffs, N.J.: Prentice Hall, 1978).

40. Mark Granovetter, "Economic Action and Social Structure: The Problem of Embeddedness" *American Journal of Sociology* 91, no. 3 (1985): 481-510, 486-87.

41. Kathleen Stewart, *A Space on the Side of the Road* (Princeton N.J.: Princeton University Press, 1996), 5.

42. Janel M. Curry-Roper, "Worldview and Agriculture: A Study of Two Reformed Communities in Iowa," in *Reformed Vitality: Continuity and Change in the Face of Modernity*, eds. Donald Luidens, Corwin Smidt, and Hijme Stoffels (Lanham, Md.: University Press of America, 1998), 17-32; Janel M. Curry-Roper, "Community-Level Worldviews and the Sustainability of Agriculture," in *Agricultural Restructuring and Sustainability: A Geographical Perspective*, ed. Tim Rickard, Brian Ilbery, and Quentin Chiotti (Wallingford, UK: CAB International, 1997), 101-15.

43. Granovetter, "Economic Action and Social Structure," 485.

44. Tom Kitwood, "What Does 'Having Values' Mean?" *Journal of Moral Education* 6, no. 2 (1977): 81-89, 82.

45. J. P. Cordella, "Reconciliation and the Mutualist Model of Community," in *Criminology As Peacemaking*, eds. H. E. Pepinsky and R. Quinney (Bloomington: Indiana University Press, 1991), 30-45, 30.

46. Ifeanyi A. Menkiti, "Person and Community in African Traditional Thought," in *African Philosophy*, ed. Richard A. Wright (Lanham, Md.: University Press of America, 1984), 171-81; Stuart Fowler, "Communities, Organizations, and People" *Pro Rege* (June 1993): 20-32.

47. Robert N. Bellah, "The Church in Tension with a Lockean Culture," *New Oxford Review* 57, no. 10 (1990): 10-16, 11.

48. Fowler, "Communities, Organizations, and People," 25.

49. Fowler, "Communities, Organizations, and People," 26.

50. Ray Oldenberg, *The Great Good Place* (New York: Paragon Press, 1989); Bellah et al., *Habits of the Heart*.

CHAPTER 7

MONAD LAW

The catalog is lengthy of instances where the Supreme Court has had difficulty bringing into focus the social dimension of human personhood, and also the kinds of communities that nourish this aspect of an individual's personality. Except for corporations . . . groups or associations that stand between the individual and the state all too often meet with judicial incomprehension.[1]

Mary Ann Glendon

Environmental and consumer rights . . . appear to fall outside the traditional division of rights. This has been into either rights enforced by the state (public rights) or by individuals (private rights) because environmental interests do not slot neatly into the category of either public or private rights.[2]

Marie Fox

IN PREVIOUS CHAPTERS we looked at law primarily as it applied to two institutions between the individual and the state—the labor union and the corporation. We showed that the corporation prevailed at the expense of labor unions due to the individualist assumptions underwriting legal discourse. Contractual relations, with their assumed autonomous individual contractors, also contain a gender bias. The social contract's sociality is one of adult males competing within the market, rather than a sociality of humans born to women and dependent upon family. Liberalism has subordinated the private (family) realm to the public (male) domain of civil society. Collective bodies such as the family have been rendered largely invisible. And just as contract law saw the laborer and the corporate person to be equal in theory in their negotiated contract, the marriage contract was legally construed to treat the wife as if she freely and equally entered into that contract, though the reality was quite different. Each party was purportedly uncoerced by economic realities or injustices. Each was free to submit to the conditions of contract.[3] As women have entered the public sphere, and as men have become more involved in child rearing, the Enlightenment view of the person has encountered complications.

111

The individual employer, who is increasingly a corporate employer, has held on in the face of challenges from the employee to include the consideration of family matters.

Ruth Colker shows that today, U.S. courts devalue birthright whenever it collides with the laissez-faire economic doctrine of "hyper-capitalism with its assumptions of the human person."[4] Women and children have been lumped together as a unitary entity in considerations of family leave, and the interests of young children largely have been ignored in favor of a focus on the economic impact on employers for granting maternity leave to working mothers.

In contrast to Canada and numerous European countries, the U.S. courts reject the claim that pregnancy-based discrimination falls under sex discrimination. The U.S. courts have been on the lookout for special treatment of the mother as against other employees, and in doing so have neglected the care of newborns. For example, in the *Maganuco* case, the Seventh Circuit Court ruled against a schoolteacher who wanted to use her accumulated paid sick leave before taking an unpaid maternity leave. The court found that it was her free choice to stay home with her newborn. The Pregnancy Discrimination Act pertaining to her case allowed for only ten days of recuperation from childbirth, yet daycare centers usually do not take such children until they are at least six weeks old. Hearing a similar case, an Ontario court concluded in a different direction, deciding this constituted sex discrimination. Pregnancy, in the reasoning of the Canadian court, benefited the greater society enough that employers and others should shoulder some of its costs—children embedded in communities and families are considered part of the commons.

Cases that involve reproductive hazards in the workplace are similarly decided without offering satisfactory protection to fetuses. For example, in *American Cyanamid*, a court of appeals ruled that a company could prohibit female employees of childbearing age from holding jobs exposing them to high levels of lead unless they had been sterilized. The women could have chosen employment elsewhere rather than opting for the sterilization procedure. However, the problem was seen as entirely the women's and not the company's. After *Johnson Controls*, pregnant women who worked at a toxic workplace had to choose between unemployment and signing a waiver disclaiming the right to sue if a disabled child was born as a consequence. In the United States, pregnant women are granted the choice between job and health of fetus, rather than accorded any preferential treatment that would discriminate against nonpregnant workers. In contrast, the European Union requires the removal of pregnant or breast-feeding women from such conditions, without loss of employment.

Until recently, United States federal law furnished no protection for employees needing to miss work due to family responsibilities or illness. The

Family and Medical Leave Act (FMLA) of 1993 entitles parents to unpaid leave up to twelve workweeks, although many employers are exempt. Also, many family situations have been found inapplicable. Most European states provide at least six months leave and small businesses are not exempt as they are in the United States. Canada offers antidiscrimination protections, parenting-leave legislation, and often collective-bargaining protection. Expert congressional testimony that newborns require a minimum of six months of quality parental care failed to withstand political compromise in the procuring of the FMLA. Children remain the individual burdens of particular parents.

Society needs to invest in its children. The general citizenry holds an interest in how children are raised, and myriad social science researches make it patently clear that social problems correlate with suboptimal child development. Yet laissez-faire-influenced law fundamentally neglects children. The social problems consequent to neglected infancy and childhood are enumerated many times over, but legal discourse in the United States finds the human rights of newborns hard to visualize when they clash with business interests. They are relegated to the individual problems of individual parents.

Most countries in the West subsidize all families by way of child allowances or basic income guarantees to all families with children. The United States limits these to the poor. European laws and policies readily draw a distinction between households that are engaged in child rearing, and other types of living arrangements, whereas such a contrast has been difficult to establish in the United States.[5] But in the land where marketplace outshines all others, legal protections for infants and legal understandings of the collectivities to which they are born are proving difficult to attain. The rights of one individual to freely contract with another or with a corporate individual are guaranteed to do business, but not the health rights of newborns and their mothers.

The self-sufficient economic man flourishes more readily in the texts of the philosophers and the modelings of the economists than in the concrete realities of most human experience. Such unfettered self-sufficiency was not available to him in his youth, nor to his caretaker(s). The free-floating experience may hold for certain philosophers, social policy analysts, hermit mountain men, and their aspirants, but the human condition of many elderly or disabled people is far less autonomous, and the condition of their caretakers is far less unfettered. Choice is minimally available for some; others willingly choose a condition of inter-dependency.

Those who authored the legal and learned philosophical documents, in turn, comprehend the realm of interdependency as informal and within the private sphere, as well as implicitly beneath the contractual realm. Dependency itself is seen as pejorative—a failing. Just as European civilizers disparaged the prestate peoples encountered by colonizers as deficient versions of themselves, so, too, does the life of domestic dependency today look disdainful to those who codify the universal proscriptions of family policy.

> By making a radical version of individual autonomy normative, we inevitably imply that dependency is something to be avoided in oneself and disdained in others. . . . [T]he new freedom to terminate marriage is accompanied to a lesser degree in the Unites States than in most other Western countries by legal protections and social programs that respond to the needs of a spouse who has become dependent for the sake of child raising. . . . Similarly . . . with respect to parental leave, childcare, and other forms of family assistance, the United States lags behind many other liberal democracies in protecting motherhood and childhood.[6]

Although the trend is toward a concept of the individual as monadic, unfettered by family interdependence, it is not necessary to look far to find a more socially anchored concept of the individual. The European Social Charter and most post-1945 Western European constitutions articulate a relational, interdependent concept of the individual, not an isolated, sovereign one.[7] Several constitutions ensure or protect the family. The 1947 United Nations Declaration of Human Rights formulates the family as the natural and fundamental unit of society, thereby entitled to its protection.

"Family" has long typified the premarket ground of a communal web from which relations of commerce have evolved. For that reason, legal discourse was satisfied to treat the institution as precontractual, largely pertaining to the private, domestic sphere as opposed to the public, civil society domain. Law pertaining to family developed and reflected patriarchal assumptions, but treated the family as a marriage-based collectivity rather than a mere aggregate of individuals. Family law in the United States of late appears to be moving toward a more atomized, aggregated concept of disembodied individuals, or *monads*, to use the philosophy term.

Legally, marriage has been considered to be only secondarily a contract between spouses. More fundamentally it has been understood as a contract between the couple and the state, and as such regulated by the state. States are now diminishing the differences between informal and formal marriage. Family members are able to an increasing extent specify contractually their marriages in ways that begin to diverge from the traditional norm.

In constitutional law, the image of marriage has shifted suddenly "from a community of life to an alliance of independent individuals."[8] Within seven years, the Supreme Court went from conceiving marriage as a sacred, living harmony to an association of two individuals each with a separate intellectual and emotional makeup.[9] What appears to comprise family rights in Supreme Court cases now looks to be individual rights only. One can expect that with technological advances such as egg transfer and in vitro fertilization, the pulverizing of family as legal collectivity will continue. Such cases display a formidable capacity to unravel collective unity into individual rights.

Inscrutable Community

The legal discourse of community parallels the discourse of family. Mary Ann Glendon's metaphors succinctly and vividly distill the common outgrowths of several extensive historical dynamics. United States' legal discourse conceives the individual as "lone rights bearer" marked by a "missing dimension of sociality" with correspondingly anemic responsibilities to his or her fellows. The case of "Poletown" in Detroit illustrates this cultural stance. A score of years ago it became a parcel of land desired by General Motors for expansion, setting up an archetypal matchup of clashing rights among individual, state, and corporate bodies. Poletown residents vociferously resisted the General Motors incursion, but the corporation secured the support of city hall to displace thousands. Residents were uninterested in the quid pro quo of economic compensation for a ravaged community way of life.

> But our legal system did not afford them a ready way of talking about such harms. Pathetically, they [the residents] tried to construct an argument by analogy to environmental protection. But the environmental argument did not register in the minds of judges trained in a legal system that has difficulty both in dealing with long-term effects and with envisioning entities other than individuals, corporations, and the state.[10]

The Poletown judgement illuminated the limitations of the law's social body. Individuals stood as the repository of various rights and obligations. States regulated the conflict among individuals.

The more successful business corporations eclipsed the state in power and revenue accumulation, and shaped the latter's agenda and decisions. Communities found that legal discourse fundamentally limited their standing and rights. Western law has long proceeded with individuals as the norm. Community has been even less visible than family in Western law. In function and form, the corporation eclipsed all other collective bodies. The same legal discourse that found corporations to be individuals with free speech protections now finds community rights to be largely unavailable.

Regarding the Poletown case, the apparent rights of a corporation's larger societal "public use" trumped the rights of a sizeable, concrete community. The law had long found that in cases of public nuisance, the balance between one party's right to enjoy their domain and another's to use their domain was a balance tipped by the interests of commerce and economic growth. The clashing rights between one neighbor fouling the air while engaging in their livelihood and the other preferring clean air were initially fairly evenly balanced, much as the social contract presumes approximately equal participants. When the neighbor became a large-scale industry that promised economic growth and progress, the balance tilted in its favor.

Michigan Supreme Court judges held it was enough that Detroit's purpose was to alleviate unemployment and fiscal distress. The advantage to a private entity, General Motors, was incidental to this formulation of the public benefit and dubious assessments of that benefit.[11] The corporation's promises were not kept, but over four thousand people were relocated and their land paved over.

Corporations place communities at a disadvantage by invoking corporate transnational mobility over and against place-bound community. When it came to canal and railroad sites, they were able to play one locale off against another. In the 1890s, when populists protested over unequal distributions of economic power, corporations moved their legal residency to New Jersey and Delaware. No longer rooted at any particular locale, their political economy enables them to play one city needing jobs against others in similar straits.

Not all situations involve keeping corporations out of communities. In another case, Youngstown labor and community groups went to court to restrain steel corporations from leaving, thereby destroying their community. Their legal claims were as ineffectual as the Poletowners'. One thesis the citizens put forth was that they held a kind of "communal property right" that had arisen from the lengthy relationship between the steel corporations and Youngstown, so that the former were obliged not to leave the city in devastation.[12] The federal appellate judge, denying such groups relief, was sympathetic, but pointed out that "American law recognizes no property rights in the 'community'" and directed them to the legislative process.[13]

Fans of professional sports teams have long thought such teams to be "theirs" in some sense. In 1957, Walter O'Malley initiated a wave of sports team migrations, often leaving profitable locales. Many sensed a kind of violation of community right, but were unable to stem the migrations. Locales enabled teams to exist and enrich the owners but found they held no legal interest against owners. The national pastime that invoked communal values remained fundamentally a business. One owner recently held a strong enough sense of the inseparability of team and community to attempt to give her team over to its community, San Diego. But Joan Kroc encountered provisions within major league baseball, essentially a cartel, by which such a transaction required assent of a sufficient body of the other owners. Other owners dissented, and the deal was lost. The Green Bay Packers and certain minor league teams are minor anomalies, but the larger pattern remains. The law recognizes a minimal interdependence between community and its emblematic team.

Whether the contention is rust-belt corporate flight, baseball interdependence, Native American land ownership, or environmental standing, the law's communal body is nearly invisible.[14] The epigraph at the beginning of this chapter capsulizes a wide array of legal mismatches.

> The catalog is lengthy of instances where the Supreme Court has had difficulty bringing into focus the social dimension of human personhood, and also the kinds of communities that nourish this aspect of an individual's personality. Except for corporations . . . groups or associations that stand between the individual and the state all too often meet with judicial incomprehension.[15]

This judicial incomprehension becomes especially problematic when it encounters geographic notions such as the nature of the local community. In trying to make sense of local community, such discourse has become hostile to the claims of the small rural town in crisis.[16] Nicholas Blomley illustrated this in a comparison of two situations in Canada. In the first, the town of Kimberley, British Columbia, whose life has been tied to a silver, lead, and zinc mine, is faced with the mine's closure. The residents are left with no choice but to move away in order to survive, but are reluctant to do so. They experience a strong attachment to place, linked with a sense of shared history. In another situation, a court case involves a doctor's rights to practice in British Columbia in contravention of government regulation of physicians' licenses based on provincial need. In both cases the court formulates work as bound up in self-worth and esteem and some sense of community recognition. Loss of work, in both cases, was regarded not just as a loss of earnings but also as the loss of a way of life. However, one case is concerned with the right to move to a place, while the other case is concerned with the right to remain. Both court decisions presuppose what Blomley calls "the right to geography."[17]

In line with the Enlightenment's liberal notions of freedom, the courts perceived the community and/or state to be the oppressive force; its analysis based on the assumption that conceives of the individual as autonomous and self-sufficient. The courts remain more sympathetic to the doctors who are being restricted by government than to the residents of Kimberley. The doctors were given the "right" to move to British Columbia but Kimberly residents did not get a sympathetic ear in their desire to maintain their community. From this perspective the community is viewed with suspicion as a potentially oppressive force. Rather, it is only within the private sphere—the domain of liberty—where the individual is left unrestrained by the community and state, that the individual can "find" himself or herself.

The geography described by the courts treated geography in the language of space. The community perspective, conversely, is one of place:

> The court's geography is one of frictionless surfaces, reminiscent both of Lewis Carroll's global chessboard (upon which movement occurs in a frenetic hyper space); of the mythic isotropic plain of regional science, upon which self-willed individuals make rational and frictionless moves; and of the abstract and turbulent spatial geometries of Thomas Hobbes, in which the atomized individual is incessantly propelled by appetites and aversions . . . the account is simultaneously a heroic one—of the lone individual confronting all odds in pursuit of economic advancement or the abstract hierarchies of central place theory—and a profoundly lonely one.[18]

From the legal perspective, geography appears as a surface of opportunity for individuals—a frictionless surface on which self-interested individuals make rational moves. A geography that recognizes ties to real places is in turn tied to images of stagnation, lack of freedom, and feudalism. The same forces that treat geography as space treat nature as resource, abstracted from its context in ecosystem and human community. Nature is left with only its commodity value. Individual autonomous persons and corporate individuals lead in the same direction: to the demise of the rights of community and the value of nature.

The idea of living in places as leading to a lack of freedom permeates the culture. While it is clearly the case that places can be oppressive, it is also the case that families can be oppressive and dysfunctional as well. This does not lead us to conclude that we need to do away with families. Healthy families, like healthy places, at their best produce healthy and mature individuals. The point is to clarify that which is healthy; such a clarification requires an appreciation of the rootedness of humanity in place.

Is it possible to speak of individuals without giving attention to community and place? Personhood cannot be conceived of in abstract legalistic, individualistic terms because if it could, where would personhood originate? Just as the Hobbesian social contract becomes inappropriate for portraying the relation between mother and child, legal discourse fails to appreciate the essence of personhood. All persons stand grounded in community and place. The abstract concepts of legal personhood and geography as space insufficiently calibrate the actual practices of people who do not want to move in space but want to be able to choose particular places. America's image as being the land of the free is grounded in a freedom that is independent and autonomous.

We have already seen that the common-law tradition favored the rights of employer-individuals over those of employee-individuals. The Constitution did not expressly establish a right to unionize. Collective practices along the order of strikes and boycotts were often made tantamount to illegal conspiracy and unfair restraint of trade. At times, labor had utilized collective reasoning in order to resist corporate power. These movements have been associated with the anarchist, cooperative, and Christian communalist movements. For example, in the late 1880s Samuel Gompers appealed to the "natural law of collective action."[19] At the same time, courts that heard conspiracy cases presumed a backdrop of a free, unobstructed marketplace and individual rights, including the rights of those who did not wish to join the union.[20] The courts channeled the Sherman Antitrust Act away from limiting corporate monopolies toward restricting labor unions.

Labor itself utilized a more individualist stance. The Knights of Labor emphasized individual liberties as put forth in the Declaration of Independence and by the American Federation of Labor.[21] Corporatist or guildlike justifications were forsaken for the individual-based foundational rights of the Republic. The National Labor Relations Act (NLRA) of 1935 granted legitimacy to collective bargaining but not power for the collective per se. The Constitution's primary recognition of rights as the possession of individuals meant in practice that any rights are turned toward individual claims.[22] The NLRA, in fact, pushed the structure of organized labor into one of increased administrative control over the rank and file.[23] The dissent of unequals was channeled away from institutional power toward the right merely to present a case to a governmental agency. Environmental historian Robert Gottlieb has shown the connection between this legal situation and labor unions' diminishing interest in both the fundamental restructuring of industrial processes and the goals of enhancing community and health.

In contrast, states in Western Europe place numerous strictures on corporations and provide supports for the workforce. These supports, such as a prohibition on benefits discrimination between part-time and full-time workers, are not deemed prolabor so much as in the "the long-term general interest in maintaining the conditions that promote family life, community life, and a productive work force."[24]

The United States has become the only Western industrialized nation that operates under an "employment at will" doctrine that stipulates employers need not demonstrate "cause" to fire an employee. "The rationale behind the rule reflects the false presumptions underlying laissez-faire economics—that it is supposed to benefit worker and employer equally because they both are supposed to benefit equally from the flexibility to quit or be fired."[25] An assumption that might have been appropriate five hundred years ago between individuals of approximate equality falters in a world of individuals employed by giant corporations, minimally buttressed by labor unions. Thirteen of fifteen states of the European Union require good cause for termination and all require minimum pretermination notice periods. In the United States, employers are largely free from the need to justify terminations.[26]

The *homo economicus* reasoning supports the free-floating, individual entrepreneur/corporation, at the expense of family, community, and nature. The Supreme Court has favored protecting the employer's need to operate freely.[27] A federal statute in the United States now requires a sixty-day notice before closing or mass layoff, but exceptions and loopholes exist. In contrast, German employers are required to take "social aspects" into account in dismissing employees so that those who would suffer the most would be the last to go, and companies that plan to close plants must open their books to workers.

Many liberties are forsaken in the United States when one enters into employment.[28] Technically, employees have the right to free speech, but critics of employers can be fired. An employee directed to perform an illegal or unethical act is free to refuse but only in the sense that the employee is free to quit. It might appear that political rights such as freedom of speech, freedom of assembly, and privacy are disengaged at the workplace, but it is more accurate to say that corporations are free to fire employees for exercising their political rights. A worker employed by a private corporation does not have on-the-job constitutional rights because the Constitution applies only to governments, not to private employees.[29] In most states, employers are free to monitor employees' conversations on company phones without telling employees. Courts have blocked employers from unauthorized searches of desks, but they have also allowed "the smallest pretext" to suffice as justification.[30] The law has been reluctant to interfere with the voluntary agreement between employer and employee, with the civil rights of the latter suffering as a result. Polygraphs are usually not permitted as evidence in court, but some states permit employers to require them. A "Bill of Employee Rights" could become federal law, but only if the culture changes its model of individual/group rights.

Corporations have managed to gain many Bill of Rights protections, protections that were intended to apply to individuals. Beginning with the 1886 *Santa Clara* decision, the courts have held that a corporation is a person, with many personal rights thereby pertaining to it. Since then they have gradually won a series of court decisions freeing them from government regulation. They have done so by invoking Bill of Rights safeguards intended to apply to individual humans.[31] In *Lochner v. New York* (1905), Lochner, a bakery owner, challenged a state statue limiting the number of hours employees could work. He argued that the statute interfered with his freedom to contract, in contradistinction to the Fourteenth Amendment. This ruling did not involve a corporation but cleared the way for subsequent challenges to various laws that limited them.

As late as 1960, the corporation did not clearly benefit from many of the other Bill of Rights safeguards, other than due process. Since then, the Fourth Amendment was reinterpreted such that routine regulatory health and safety inspections required a warrant. Corporations have utilized the First, Fourth, Fifth, Sixth, and Seventh amendments in order to retain their business agendas at the expense of employees and the communities in which they base their operations.[32] Indeed, utilizations of the Second, Third, and Eighth Amendments may be in the offing in the near future. In turn, shopping malls have been ruled legally able to prohibit peaceful expression of free speech, in that they are privately owned businesses rather than the commons areas they appear to be.

While the newer leviathan of the business corporation deserves increased critical deliberation, the more classically conceived one, the state, should not be ignored when collective rights are discussed. The building of the European state and popular loyalty to the state system meant a correlative diminution of collective bodies between the state and the individual. The French Revolution sought to minimize guilds and other competing sources of traditional loyalty. Alexis de Tocqueville supported the American incarnation of mediating institutions to check the state. However, the scale and power of the states themselves increased as readily as the scale and power of business corporations. "The state would tend not to like group rights standing in the way of the nation-building enterprise, preferring direct lines of command to the social atoms, the individuals."[33]

Insularized Environs

Legal assumptions regarding the environment are parallel to the reasoning invoked in cases pertaining to family and community. One of the characteristics of environmental problems is that they transcend political demarcations. The direction to take in environmental litigation when faced with this difficulty is not immediately obvious.[34]

D. P. Emond found connections in the law between the persistent preoccupation with individual rights and the right to exploit the environment. One assumption underlying this theme is that land amounts to little more than one commodity or factor of production among others, with no special status. Another is that individual rights take precedence over public or community rights. "In fact, the law today seems to regard community rights at most as the sum of the rights of the individual members of the community, and not as something that may be greater than or in some way transcend individual rights."[35] The common law purports to maximize community welfare but does so by invoking a calculus of benefits and costs. Such cost-benefit analyses lack investigations into community-wide and environmental impacts per se. They merely measure impacts on the plaintiff. The individualist calculus latently functions to favor economic development over and against community and environmental preservation. The third assumption underlying this theme is that only legally recognized persons hold rights. The environment serves only utilitarian human interests. Protection for its own sake is not a legitimate goal of the law.

Human rights are usually constructed to protect individual integrity. This individuality can only be protected through being free from government: Individuals are to be left free of state coercion, secure in person and property, and at liberty to follow their own consciences. Environmental issues are not at all parallel. Just as welfare entitlements in the United States do not have constitutional status as human rights, so the basic right of a healthy environment does not exist.[36] The bias is in the direction that individuals should be free, with as little prior restraint as possible. The government begins with the obligation to protect individual freedoms and the right to legally acquire property before it enforces the rules for free exchange.[37] This framework of assumptions tilts us away from the conviction that human life should be governed in strict accord with prior environmental and ecological limits and that good stewardship of nature is a fundamental presupposition of public law.[38] What is needed is the clarification of what is more fundamental and prior, in contrast to what is less fundamental on the priority list. Environmental justice should not be a cause that remains in the hands of one interest group perpetually slugging it out with other interest groups. Recognition in basic law of the necessity of ecological health as the precondition of all public and market relations should become as fundamental as the recognition that certain human rights exist as the precondition of all public rules and market regulations.[39]

The issue of ecological health as a precondition to the market is fundamental to attempts by communities to control land-use. The legal concept of land-use controls a millennium ago meant community control of the medieval commons. After enclosures, the concept underwent a period in which cases dealt primarily with individuals and private nuisance. The rise of urban centers and industry in the United States led to enabling legislation at the level of the states that gave local governments the right to develop land-use plans and zoning regulations. These land-use controls had to be clearly tied to the legitimate use of police power—the constitutional mandate for government to protect the health, safety, and general welfare of the public. Zoning limitations are usually upheld if enabling statutes authorize them, if they are clearly tied to police power, and if they are reasonable and exercised in a manner that follows due process. Government taking of land is justified if it is for a public purpose, and it always requires compensation. The contentious cases fall into the gray area between legitimate use of police power and eminent domain. At what point does government land-use regulation lead to so many restrictions that it is, in essence, "taking" property from the owner? For example, do restrictions on wetland drainage, justified by the important ecological role of wetlands in water retention and purification, wildlife habitat, and so forth take away all economic value from the owner of the property? And is it a public purpose when the government condemns private land only to turn it over to a developer, all in the name of urban redevelopment? These are the areas where conflicts arise among private and corporate rights that are built on an economic valuing of nature, state rights that regulate and condemn with the goal of achieving some public good, and community rights.

The legal apparatus has found individuals more visible than groups. It has weighed the public benefit of industrial operations more heavily than its public nuisance aspects. Yet it has placed statute limitations against some larger-scaled uses, and it has utilized several concepts that acknowledge something like a communal right to appropriate the use of the land. In this sense, environmental law appears more open to notions of public benefit than, for example, labor law. It shows remnants of the "Lone Rights Bearer" model of law, but less so than does the legal discourse pertaining to family and community. The potential for a less individualist environmental law exists, but it also calls up fundamental individual/group issues.

Organizations such as colleges and unions can litigate with advantages that are less available to individuals, and that ability is important in and of itself.[40] Class-action lawsuits may be the arena that expresses collectivity. Class-action suits proceed on behalf of a large group of similarly situated individuals.[41] Such suits rework individualistic due process into a "complex mix of individual and social dimensions."[42] Individuals can initiate it for others without their consent and although the others can opt out, actions can still be taken for all. A grouping of individuals otherwise atomized with respect to each other can act collectively as a legal entity, say, as persons affected by a particular environmental degradation, to the benefit of the group.

Rights created for victims of environmental pollution appear to require new group-oriented rules for their enforcement.

> The problem is essentially that such rights do not fall into the traditional classification of either public rights enforceable by the state or private rights enforceable by individuals. . . . Environmental and consumer rights . . . appear to fall outside the traditional division of rights. This has been into either rights enforced by the state (public rights) or by individuals (private rights) because environmental interests do not slot neatly into the category of either public or private rights.[43]

The law's body in the new land works with a civil procedure mainly concerned with private individuals and private interests. However, it is an era of organizations and corporate organizations that have distended the human scale. The premonitions of the English Pluralists have come to pass. That which anemically functions for victims of environmental pollution myopically looks at collectivities merely as aggregates. Groups are reduced to collections of monads—multiples of insular man. Such thinking displays a "complete neglect not only of rights that are intermediate between purely public and purely private, but also of groups and organizations occupying the intermediate grounds."[44] The roots of the demise of the rights of institutions show themselves in two widely held formulations of nonpolitical institutions and their relations to the state—the fiction and concession models.[45] John Marshall held the fiction model: The individual was a real person in law, while an institution along the order of a business was a fictitious entity. The concession approach complemented the fiction model: Legal rights of artificial bodies were concessions from the state.[46] Though these models had their origins in Roman law, they were easily combined with the Enlightenment concept of human autonomy.[47] Although Tocqueville established long ago the importance of intermediate groups, legal recognition has lagged. Modern discourse lacks a language from which to be aware of the connection to those beyond the lifestyle enclave.[48] That connection and its otherwise attendant moral sensibility have faded and continue to fade, even as the aggregates long for something like that which has receded.

Traditional legal thinking disembodies the bipolar entities of individual and state in parallel ways. For each, the one is detached from the larger collective. The right to property defines a region of relative freedom from the constraints of others, while international law conceives the state to be largely sovereign over its territory, largely free of international control. Insular humans act as sovereigns for their home/castle while the recognized state largely controls its territorial property with limited meddling from the international community. As when colonial Europe encountered its neighbors, the boundary marking is crucial. The powerful state is self-contained in much the same way that (male) personhood stands apart from the private domain of the family.

This chapter has sought to show that the law operates primarily by reference to the individual and the state. The nonbusiness corporate body carries little legal purchase, as noted in the cases of family, community, and union. Birthright and covenant are increasingly eclipsed by contract. Collective health is scaled down to individual size. Collectivities find that the law that supports the corporate individual is more sympathetic and of more substance than the law that supports them. Environmental law displays some possible sites for collective action, but remains too individualistic to do justice to environmental problems. The difficulties transcend individuals and governmental borders, but the law addresses them in terms of individual and state rights. In this chapter we have focused on the community side of the current community-land nexus. Next, we examine more fully the effects on land.

Notes

1. Mary Ann Glendon, *Rights Talk: The Impoverishment of Political Discourse* (New York: Free Press, 1991), 114-15.

2. Marie Fox, "Earth Matters? Legal Regulation and Environmental Control," in *Law, Society, and Change,* ed. Steven Livingstone and John Morrison (Aldershot: Dartmouth, 1990), 71-95, 76.

3. Mary F. Brinig, *From Contract to Covenant* (Cambridge, Mass.: Harvard University, 2000).

4. Ruth Colker, *American Law in the Age of Hypercapitalism* (New York: New York University Press, 1998), 100-154.

5. Glendon, *Rights Talk,* 125-27

6. Glendon, *Rights Talk,* 73.

7. Glendon, *Rights Talk,* 70-75.

8. Glendon, *Rights Talk,* 123.

9. Glendon, *Rights Talk,* 123.

10. Glendon, *Rights Talk,* 30.

11. Glendon, *Rights Talk,* 30.

12. Glendon, *Rights Talk,* 111.

13. Glendon, *Rights Talk,* 111.

14. Glendon, *Rights Talk,* 113-14.

15. Glendon, *Rights Talk,* 114-15.

16. Nicholas Blomley, "The Business of Mobility: Geography, Liberalism, and the Charter of Rights," *The Canadian Geographer* 36, no. 3 (1992): 236-53.

17. Blomley, "The Business of Mobility," 244.

18. Blomley, "The Business of Mobility," 246.

19. Leon Fink, "Labor, Liberty, and the Law: Trade Unionism and the Problem of the American Constitutional Order," in *The Constitution and American Life,* ed. David Thelen (Ithaca, N.Y.: Cornell University Press, 1988), 244-65.

20. Fink, "Labor, Liberty, and the Law," 244-65.

21. Fink, "Labor, Liberty, and the Law," 244-65.

22. David Thelen, *The Constitution and American Life* (Ithaca, N.Y.: Cornell University Press, 1988).

23. Michael T. Klare, *Resurgent Militarism* (Washington, D.C.: Institute for Policy Studies, 1978); Carl Swidorski, "Constituting the Modern State," in *The Constitution and American Life,* eds. David S Caudill and Steven Jay Gold (Atlantic Highlands, N.J.: Humanities Press, 1995), 162-78.

24. Glendon, *Rights Talk,* 112.

25. Colker, *American Law,* 197.

26. Colker, *American Law,* 198.

27. Colker, *American Law,* 201.

28. Thomas Donaldson, *Corporations and Morality* (Englewood Cliffs, N.J.: Prentice-Hall, 1982), 130-32.

29. Staughton Lynd, "The Constitution and Union Rights," *In These Times* 12 (1987): 12-13, 12.

30. Donaldson, *Corporations,* 150.

31. Carl J. Mayer, "Personalizing the Impersonal: Corporations and the Bill of Rights," *The Hastings Law Journal* 41 (1990): 577-667.

32. Mayer, "Personalizing the Impersonal," 577-667.

33. Johan Galtung, *Human Rights in Another Key* (Cambridge, Mass.: Polity Press, 1994),17.

34. Malcolm F. Baldwin and James K. Page, Jr. eds., *Law and Environment* (New York: Walker and Company, 1970), 248-76.

35. D. P. Emond, "Environmental Law and Policy," in *Consumer Protection, Environmental Law and Corporate Power,* eds. Ivan Bernier and Andree Lajoie (Toronto: University of Toronto, 1985), 89-166, 108.

36. Joseph L. Sax, "The Search for Environmental Rights," *Journal of Land Use and Environmental Law* 6, no. 1 (1990): 93-105, 94-96.

37. James W. Skillen, "Environmental and Resource Ownership: How Can We Do Justice to Both Public and Private Trusts," (Pew Global Stewardship Initiative Conference, Gloucester, Mass., October 1996), 2.

38. Skillen, "Environmental and Resource Ownership," 3.

39. Skillen, "Environmental and Resource Ownership," 5.

40. Mauro Cappelletti and Bryant Garth, "Finding an Appropriate Compromise: A Comparative Study of Individualistic Models and Groups Rights in Civil Procedure," *Civil Justice Quarterly* 2 (1983): 111-47.

41. Emond, "Environmental Law and Policy," 118.

42. Cappelletti and Garth, "Finding an Appropriate Compromise,"134.

43. Fox, "Earth Matters," 76.

44. Cappelletti and Garth, "Finding an Appropriate Compromise," 118.

45. Rockne McCarthy, "Liberal Democracy and the Rights of Institutions," *Pro Rege* 8, no. 4 (1980): 4-11.

46. McCarthy, "Liberal Democracy," 8.

47. McCarthy, "Liberal Democracy," 9.

48. Robert Bellah, Richard Madsen, William M. Sullivan, Ann Swidler, and Steven M. Tipton, *Habits of the Heart* (Berkeley: University of California Press, 1985).

CHAPTER 8

LAND IN PRACTICE

The greatest wisdom has always been required to judge if nature acting alone
can meet our needs, or if our cleverness and effort are required.[1]

Wes Jackson

THE PREVIOUS CHAPTER showed the difficulty of conceptualizing community
and place within legal discourse, particularly in the United States. This same
discourse has shaped everything from privately held farmland, to commons such
as fisheries, to public grazing lands in this country. The significance of this
difficulty for nature is that it, like people, becomes abstracted and disembedded
from relationships under the present schema. Through this process, nature loses
any value beyond the economic, and policies affecting natural resources are also
abstracted out of the community context. Universalizing and reductionistic
science takes community's place. The next two chapters describe at length a
variety of human-land systems and how the dominating paradigm limits our
understanding of the relationships between human communities and nature.
These human-nature management systems cover a range of resources, from
those whose ownership has traditionally been federal (rangeland and forests), to
those that by their nature are common property (fisheries), to privately owned
agricultural lands.

Rangelands

The public rangeland management system in the western United States
illustrates how the Enlightenment framework shapes perceived policy options.
The Taylor Grazing Act of 1934 closed the open grazing land of the United
States, establishing a permit system that divided public lands into grazing
allotments managed by the Bureau of Land Management (BLM). Previous to
this, grazing land had moved from the public domain into private hands based
on the assumption that individual, private ownership would bring about the best

129

use of the resource. The tax forfeiture and wholesale abandonment of land during the Depression put an end to this assumption.

From the time of the passage of the Taylor Grazing Act through the mid-1960s, policy goals on these western lands emphasized both the stabilization of the rangeland industry and the stabilization of communities. Individual grazing allotments have been used to meet these objectives, thus creating a system where equity considerations in public rangeland management and development worked to the advantage of narrow, not community-wide, local interests.[2] The system remains to this day, with decision making continuing to reflect the interests of livestock operators who hold individual allotments.[3]

A 1974 court case, *Natural Resources Defense Committee v. Morton* (Secretary of the Interior), forced the Bureau of Land Management to prepare environmental impact statements on the effects of present and proposed grazing for specific sites of public lands.[4] The court held that the issuance of grazing permits by the BLM, collectively if not individually, constitute major federal actions affecting the human environment within the meaning of National Environmental Protection Act (NEPA) and thus required an Environmental Impact Statement (EIS).[5] Amidst growing public pressure, the Federal Land Policy and Management Act (FLPMA) of 1976 did not repeal the Taylor Act but superimposed a new system with more diverse goals and emphases, thus bifurcating power between the individual allotment holder and the federal government.

The Public Lands Improvement Act of 1978, and the amended FLPMA, made the improvement of range conditions to be the goal of rangeland management and the highest management priority.[6] Litigation continues over these legislative mandates, shaping land-use policies as they go. Public participation, mandated by FLPMA and NEPA, is allowed within the framework of individual comments or interest-group comments on large-scale plans, abstracted from the context of a local community.[7] The BLM has continued to exclude public participation even in comparison to most other U.S. federal land management agencies.

Allotments are authorized by a permit issued by the BLM for a maximum of ten years, but an existing permit holder has priority over other applicants. These permits have taken on the characteristics of private property rights. Permits can include additional management terms as specified in the permit itself or the allotment management plan (AMP). The BLM annually determines how many livestock will actually graze on the allotment.[8] In theory, the annual decisions allow flexibility and adaptation, but in reality, they supplant the permit and the AMP and become a blank check that allows the permittee and the BLM to agree privately each year on numbers of livestock.[9] Superimposed on this allotment system are larger scale land-use plans called Resource Management Plans. These plans are meant to meet FLPMA's mandate for multiple use.[10] Each resource management plan provides management direction for an area of BLM land called a "resource area." These areas typically comprise over one million acres of BLM land and include on the order of one hundred grazing allotments.[11] Meaningful discussion, community dialogue and consensus building is absent from the process in most cases. The BLM says that renewal of a permit is not an "action" within the meaning of its regulations so no notice is required.[12] The BLM allows public comment on area-wide resource management plans with an EIS, but these are so general in nature that public comment is ineffectual. Annual decision making is the crucial stage.[13]

In principle, resource management plans should be a major determinant of grazing management. In reality, resource management plans have had little effect on grazing management because they are vague and contain no specific prescriptions for grazing management.[14] The BLM has integrated EIS preparation with resource management plan development—all of which are highly generic with little or no detailed, site-specific environmental information or analysis.[15] Place, land, and community are abstracted from context.

Fisheries

Historically, the Atlantic coast of North America has been dependent on its fisheries. The state has largely captured management rights over fisheries in the past few decades, relying on strategies that continue to fall within the individual-state, bifurcated paradigm.[16] In cases where stocks of fish declined in the 1970s and 1980s, governments often imposed limited-entry schemes. These schemes allocated licenses to a limited number of individuals. The theory was that incomes would rise as the number of participants gradually declined. Moreover, investment would be instituted on an economically rational basis and overcapitalization would be avoided.[17] Peter Sinclair claimed that this policy, when implemented in Northwest Newfoundland, paid little attention to its social consequences. Like grazing allotments, the limited licenses conferred individual property rights to a specific group.[18]

While the income of license holders has increased, there has also been the tendency for capital cost and the catching capacity of the fleet to increase as well. Fishermen take advantage of higher profits and of government subsidies and invest in larger, more powerful boats equipped with expensive gear and fish-finding devices.[19] The social costs appear to be both an increasing social division and a reduced possibility for social mobility while protecting the local fishing elite.[20] In many cases, this has opened the way to increase the scale of fishing and possibly to corporate fleets. Local society has been thus divided into interest groups rather than being enabled to perceive of a larger community interest. Individual allotment by the state has conferred individual property rights because of an assumed individualistic institutional context. This approach has had ramification on social structure and has in fact aided in undermining community controls, creating an individualistic social structure that policy in essence had assumed into existence.

Another management strategy is the individual boat quota system. This system was established for the Atlantic snow crab in early 1990s by the Department of Fisheries and Oceans of Canada. Licenses had been limited earlier. Each licensed enterprise could then plan and distribute fishing capacity and effort, leading to economic efficiency.[21] This should have led to the sharing of risks and benefits, an organizational principle within coastal fishing communities. Instead, the establishment of owning shares resulted in a benefit that could be used as a lever for capital accumulation and enhanced earnings. Membership in families with high-value license-holding fathers now became the single social situation essential to accessing a position of captaincy/ownership within the fisheries.[22] This shows the complexity of attempting to construct a locally meaningful, but socially just, system of resource management.

In actuality, studies of fishing communities, particularly in Atlantic Canada, have shown how fishermen, through informal arrangements, are locally regulating their fishing. They control access and monitor each other. Increased capitalization has tended to undermine these informal norms much the same way as privileging corporation's rights in over community rights. The state has chosen to regulate fisheries directly rather than institutionalizing the informal fishermen-initiated regulations, again failing to recognize an already existing collective system. The government has become synonymous with collective action, not recognizing the existence of a system of mutually committed and cooperatively organized fishermen who could handle their own regulations if empowered to do so.[23] Government fishery advisory services play the role of assisting individual fishermen and fish processors, not collective groups.[24]

An alternative that will be discussed in later chapters is for the government to legally recognize the existence of the local social structure. A lack of such recognition means that no leadership role is institutionalized in the local fishery when collective entrepreneurship is needed. No one has the authority or responsibility to act on behalf of all members of the local industry when innovations and development projects require it. The community attempts to organize only in times of crisis.[25]

Agriculture

Societal norms and values of the eighteenth and nineteen centuries structured the development of farm enterprises and the landscapes that continue to dominate the midwestern United States. The ideology of farm culture includes: (1) a farmer should own his or her own land, (2) each farm should be economically self-sufficient, (3) the less government the better. These values and norms were grounded in the Enlightenment philosophy of Locke and Smith with their emphasis on rationalism, reductionism, and the individual.

We use several examples of a problem facing farming in the United States and show how the previous discussion relates to this. The first is the problem of the growing criticism of farming as the source of nonpoint surface and groundwater pollution from pesticides, nitrates, and sediment.[26] What assumptions about and responses to this concern within the farm community have remained tied to the conventional ideology of farming?

Locke's teaching promised individual freedom, the opportunity to compete for unlimited individual material wealth, and the limitation of government interference with individual initiative. It should come as no surprise then, that individual voluntary compliance and incentives have been emphasized, along with technical research, in economically viable alternative methods of farming. This approach has been part of United States farm legislation since its inception in the 1930s.[27] These alternatives, called sustainable or low-input agriculture, emphasize better management and reduced costs. Problems of agriculture, assuming the individual as the main building block of society, remain conceptualized at the individual level and thus as policy targeted at individuals. The individual is seen to respond only to immediate economic interests with no constraints of a larger community. The final result to date has been the institutionalization of the positive environmental image of sustainable agriculture within the Land Grant Universities, the USDA, and more recently, agro-chemical firms, without any fundamental change in the basic conventional ideology underlying the farm enterprise.[28] Sustainable agriculture has largely been defined as a set of techno-scientific practices, such as those that require more precision to lower chemical inputs, rather than a change in paradigm.[29] Thus, the term *sustainability* has been integrated into conventional agricultural discourse[30] and has become a symbol for advancing low-chemical agriculture within the conventional agriculture scientific and policy mode. This has led to strange bedfellows.[31] For example, DeLind's analysis of a state report on sustainable agriculture in Michigan shows that this practice is seen as a promising biological method for maintaining production and environmental quality techniques and technologies.[32]

The emphasis has remained on the farm and farm-level profitability, thus neglecting larger social questions.[33] The State of Iowa has been at the forefront of the move toward sustainable agriculture with the creation of the Leopold Center for Sustainable Agriculture. The center was created by a groundwater protection bill and emphasizes research and education rather than compliance. Dennis Keeney, former Director of the Leopold Center for Sustainable Agriculture described the key components of this method as being based on sound agronomic principles with cultural practices thus limited to management systems and cropping systems—farm-level patterns.[34] He did say that many farmers were concerned with control of policy and feared it might encourage a movement from individual to corporation farming.[35] The reductionism is evident in the way the concern is expressed—individual or corporation (not community). As with the Michigan report, agriculture is not seen as part of a social system of relationships, nor is sustainable agriculture seen as sustaining people, places, and communities.[36] For example, Welsh[37] has found that ownership arrangements are important determinants of economic outcomes in farming. He found that counties with higher percentages of nonfamily corporations have, on average, higher cash gains but lower percentages of farms realizing cash gains.[38] Yet the issues of community social structure are typically outside the "scientific" study of sustainable agriculture.

Although a great deal of attention has been placed on the means, sustainable agriculture has left the ends out of its analysis.[39] Sustainable agricultural technologies are seen as relatively neutral, with what is good for the environment being good for society at large.[40] The assumption is that the technologies or approaches to the solution of problems are neutral.

These attitudes show the conventional view of the environment—reductionistic, individual problems, and solutions in isolation. It fits well with the scientific view of knowledge inherited from Bacon, Descartes, and Hume.[41] Scientists assign one end, such as increasing yields, as a deterministic end. They then manipulate various experimental treatments to determine the most effective method to reach that end with the aim to produce general universal knowledge.[42] Ann Reisner's predictions have thus far proven true:

> It is likely that agricultural scientists trained in the means-ends reductionistic research tradition will try to redefine sustainable agriculture as a technical problem that requires a technical solution, an approach that would resolve several challenges to the reductionistic mode of science and retain scientists' control over information generation. Such a solution would define away many of the social implications of the sustainable agriculture belief system.[43]

The search for universal knowledge leads to farmers' becoming interchangeable, as knowledge of the local conditions is less relevant than following the best management practices and package directions for chemical fertilizer applications.[44] Furthermore, the emphasis on individuals and economic factors pervades both the economic and sociological literature on farmer decision making. Little attention is given to social organization and local culture as it affects agriculture.[45] Social scientists have tended to focus on individual-level characteristics of farmers such as attitudes, values, and management styles relating to technology adoption and agricultural production.

This individualistic conceptualization of sustainable agriculture is based on the assumption of the existence of rational decision-making processes among individuals that lead to profit maximization.[46] Within the standard scientific paradigm, the problem of sustainable agriculture then is a technical one that requires scientific methodologies. These methodologies lead to known solutions with the only problem being getting farmers to adopt the solutions.[47] This viewpoint denies agency to all except scientists.[48] In reality, little can distinguish science from nonscience in real practice.[49] The real problem is that though some would think otherwise, scientific and technical truths are partial.[50] What is needed is much more complex, entailing a multiplicity of approaches.

While agriculturists come from the perspective of voluntary compliance and incentives, environmentalists, who are now seeing agriculture as just another business, emphasize regulation.[51] In actuality, both of these attitudes are a reflection of the same conventional ideology. The ideology of individualism, as we have seen, has emphasized private ownership, speculation, and resource as commodity outside of community. These attitudes have limited the solutions to farm problems in the United States to two options. Either private individuals acting in a free market responding only to economic incentives have been seen as the solution to the problem, or the federal government has been called on to intervene, targeting individuals in its intervention. One is but the mirror image of the other; one necessitates the other. When the effects of the actions of such individual interests have caused third-party problems (water pollution, erosion, higher prices) we have tended to call for federal intervention to solve the problem through regulation, as many environmentalists desire. Where the state is perceived as only the protector of individual interests, it becomes inevitable that centralized state functions are required to balance the forces of individual interests. We would suggest we have presupposed a model of the state—one that is derived from such thinkers as Locke and the neoclassical economists such as Von Mises. Under this model, the function of government is to maintain the social system that allows individuals the freedom to pursue their own best interest usually expressed in private property. "Good" actions by the state are those that allow individuals to attain the ends they wish to attain. The forces of globalization may lead to the further hollowing out of the state and its displacement with other institutions that are more transnational in character.[52] The individual and the transnational institution may be the two levels of society left to negotiate the future.

This cultural ideal, with its emphasis on the individual and land outside the community, now permeates society. It is within the framework of this ideology that policy has been formed and constrained in the past. Federal farm policy assumes that the farm economy emerges from the free actions of autonomous, self-sufficient individuals and thus targets the individual. The primacy of private property rights has also been assumed, so policy has been based on voluntary participation in farm programs encouraged by monetary incentives.

An agriculture program that illustrates the conceptual problems of farm policy in the United States was the Conservation Reserve Program (CRP). The program offered farmers an annual rental payment and one-half the cost of establishing a permanent cover if they agreed to retire their highly erodible cropland for ten years.[53] Farmers submitted offers during a designated sign-up period. The offers contained the amount of eligible cropland the producer wished to enroll and the annual rental rate desired. Grazing or harvesting of forage or any other commercial activity was not permitted for the duration of the contract unless specifically granted by the secretary of agriculture. The cropland base and allotment history, used to figure price-support levels on specific crops for the farm, was to be reduced by the ratio of the land retired to total cropland acreage. Eligibility was determined by soil-loss tolerance levels and by an erodibility index that indicated the inherent erodibility characteristics of a soil relative to its natural rate of regeneration. Conservation Reserve Program participation within a county was limited to 25 percent of cropland unless a specific exception was made by the secretary of agriculture. The limit was designed to prevent adverse effects on the local community. Bid caps also established the maximum acceptable bids.[54]

The concept of these highly erodible acres is problematic because the idea of acres is abstracted from its geographic and social context. Geographers and soil scientists Gersmehl, Baker, and Brown show the difficulty in establishing erodibility criteria that are meaningful at the local level. Erodibility is a complex mix of management practices, specific soils, and policy and economic context as locally impacted.[55] This abstraction of the concept of erodibility and its focus on individual farmers led to unintended results from the CRP program. Seventeen and a third million acres were put into the CRP from 1985 to 1991, but harvested cropland went down by only 2.6 million acres during those same years. In areas of the country with the largest participation in CRP, the largest numbers of acres were plowed up to offset the CRP.[56] The program's problems are related to targeting individuals outside a community context and the abstraction of acreage. Rather than allocating money to communities that have some knowledge of the movement of land in and out of cultivation, individuals are targeted, which may even undermine community attempts at controlling erosion. For example, the Nebraska Sandhills have experienced reductions in farm size due to mechanization and intensified cropping that came with center pivot irrigation systems. These systems in turn increased erodibility. The CRP gave benefits to those who had developed pivots on Sandhill land rather than ranchers who did not; thus causing local tensions.[57]

In a related problem, the Conservation Reserve Program does not now permit entire farms to be enrolled in the program, only its highly erodible land. Thus, the CRP does not control production on an entire farm. A program must also control the level of production on cropland that is not idled. When some of their land is idled under government programs, farmers are constrained to plant and manage their remaining acreage more intensively. Such management techniques may result in greater soil damage to cropland and increased total production.[58]

In addition, highly erodible land is perceived as one clearly defined category of land from which cropland can be retired. The reality is that all types of land, from class I, the highest quality, to highly erodible, the lowest quality, are on a continuum and move back and forth between cultivated and noncultivated land uses. Taking land out of cultivation at the highly erodible end of the continuum, aggregated at the national level, merely means that other highly erodible lands or other lands that have not been in cropland, will be converted to cropland. The program is ineffective in changing both overall and local land-use patterns, ineffective for controlling the supply of grain, and ineffective in changing overall rates of erosion. Abstracting policy, land, and participants from community remains ineffectual in understanding actual problems and thus ineffectual in forming meaningful strategies for living with the land.

The structure of grazing allotments, state fishery management strategies, and the land-use change incentives of agricultural policy are all built on a similar structure. The approaches assume an individualistic notion of society that necessitates federal intervention. The abstraction of policy from local community also leads them down the road toward the abstraction of nature. Any mediating institutional structures, grounded in the community and nature of a place, are undermined by this view of the bifurcation of society. The "scientific" management paradigm upon which these policies are built cannot easily integrate social goals and effects because it involves nonquantifiable ends and values that fall outside the realm of science. These policy regimes remain views from nowhere that simplify relationships among nature, human communities, and the larger society. For a more extended look at these problems we now turn again to United States forestry.

Notes

1. Wes Jackson, *Altars of Unhewn Stone: Science and the Earth* (New York: North Point Press, 1987), 151.

2. Michael M. Borman and Douglas E. Johnson, "Evolution of Grazing and Land Tenure Policies on Public Lands," *Rangelands* 12, no. 4 (1990): 203-6, 203.

3. Joseph M. Feller. "Grazing Management on the Public Lands: Opening the Process to Public Participation," *Land and Water Review* 26, no. 2 (1991): 571-96, 572-73.

4. Borman and Johnson, "Evolution of Grazing," 203.

5. Feller, "Grazing Management," 579.

6. Borman and Johnson, "Evolution of Grazing," 204.

7. Feller, "Grazing Management," 579.

8. Feller, "Grazing Management," 575.

9. Feller, "Grazing Management," 576.

10. Feller, "Grazing Management," 576-77.

11. Feller, "Grazing Management," 577.

12. Feller, "Grazing Management," 583.

13. Feller, "Grazing Management," 585.

14. Feller, "Grazing Management," 577.

15. Feller, "Grazing Management," 579.

16. Anthony Davis and Conner Bailey, "Common in Custom, Uncommon in Advantage: Common Property, Local Elites, and Alternatives to Fisheries Management," *Society and Natural Resources* 9, no. 3 (1996): 251-65, 257.

17. Peter R. Sinclair, "Fisherman Divided: The Impact of Limited Entry Licensing in Northwest Newfoundland," *Human Organization* 42, no. 4 (1983): 307-13, 308.

18. Sinclair. "Fisherman Divided," 307.

19. Sinclair. "Fisherman Divided," 310.

20. Sinclair. "Fisherman Divided," 311.

21. Davis and Bailey, "Common in Custom," 252.

22. Davis and Bailey, "Common in Custom," 260.

23. Svein Jentoft, "Models of Fishery Development: The Cooperative Approach," *Marine Policy* 9, (1985): 322-31, 327-28.

24. Jentoft, "Models of Fishery Development," 330.

25. Jentoft, "Models of Fishery Development," 330.

26. National Research Council, *Alternative Agriculture*, (Washington, D.C.: National Academy Press, 1989), 3.

27. United States Department of Agriculture, Economic Research Service, "History of Agricultural Price-Support and Adjustment Programs 1933-1984: Background for 1985 Farm Legislation," *Agriculture Information Bulletin* 485 (1984).

28. C. E. Beus and R. E. Dunlap, "Conventional versus Alternative Agriculture: The Paradigmatic Roots of the Debate," *Rural Sociology* 55, no. 4 (1990): 590-616, 612.

29. Frederick H. Buttel, "Environmentalization: Origins, Processes, and Implications for Rural Social Change," *Rural Sociology* 57, no. 1 (1992): 1-27, 1.

30. Patricial Allen, Debra Van Dusen, Jackelyn Lundy, and Stephen Gliessman, "Integrating Social, Environmental, and Economic Issues in Sustainable Agriculture," *American Journal of Alternative Agriculture* 6, no. 1 (1991): 34-39.

31. Garth Youngberg, Neill Schaller, and Kathleen Merrigan, "The Sustainable Agriculture Policy Agenda in the United States: Politics and Prospects," in *Food for the Future*, ed. Patricia Allen (New York: John Wiley and Sons, 1993), 295-318, 299-300.

32. Laura B. DeLind, "Sustainable Agriculture in Michigan: Some Missing Dimensions," *Agriculture and Human Values* 8, no. 4 (1991): 38-45, 39.

33. Allen et al., "Integrating Social," 35.

34. Dennis R. Keeney, "Toward a Sustainable Agriculture: The Need for Clarification of Concepts and Terminology," *American Journal of Alternative Agriculture* 4, nos. 3 and 4 (1989): 101-5, 102.

35. Keeney, "Toward a Sustainable Agriculture," 104.

36. DeLind, "Sustainable Agriculture," 40.

37. Rick Welsh, "The Importance of Ownership Arrangements in U.S. Agriculture," *Rural Sociology* 63, no. 2 (1998): 199-213.

38. Welsh, "The Importance of Ownership Arrangements," 211.

39. Lawrence Busch, "Irony, Tragedy, and Temporality in Agricultural Systems, or How Values and Systems Are Related," *Agriculture and Human Values* 6, no. 4 (1989): 4-11, 6.

40. M. A. Altieri, "Beyond Agroecology: Making Sustainable Agriculture Part of a Political," *American Journal of Alternative Agriculture* 3, (1988): 142-143, 142.

41. Ann Reisner, "Tracing the Linkages of World Views, Information Handling, and Communications Vehicles," *Agriculture and Human Values* 9, no. 2 (1992): 4-16, 6.

42. Reisner, "Tracing the Linkages," 7.

43. Reisner, "Tracing the Linkages," 9.

44. Cornelia Butler Flora, "Reconstructing Agriculture: The Case for Local Knowledge," *Rural Sociology* 57, no. 1 (1992): 92-97, 93.

45. Miriam J. Wells, "Ethnic Groups and Knowledge System in Agriculture," *Economic Development and Cultural Change* 39, no. 4 (1991): 739-71, 739.

46. James Cruise and Thomas A. Lyson, "Beyond the Farmgate: Factors Related to Agricultural Performance in Two Dairy Communities," *Rural Sociology* 56, no. 1 (1991): 41-55, 41.

47. Joseph J. Molnar, Patricia A. Duffy, Keith A. Cummins, and Edzard Van Santen, "Agricultural Science and Agricultural Counterculture: Paradigms in Search of a Future," *Rural Sociology* 57, no. 1 (1992): 83-91, 87.

48. Jack Kloppenburg Jr., "Science in Agriculture: A Reply to Molnar, Duffy, Cummins, and Van Santen and to Flora," *Rural Sociology* 57, no. 1 (1992): 98-107, 101.

49. Kloppenburg, "Science in Agriculture," 99.

50. Kloppenburg, "Science in Agriculture," 99.

51. J. A. Zinn and J. E. Blodgett, "Agriculture versus the Environment: Communicating Perspectives," *Journal of Soil and Water Conservation* 44 (1989): 184-87, 185.

52. Luc Julliet, Jeffrey Roy, and Francesca Scala, "Sustainable Agriculture and Global Institutions: Emerging Institutions and Mixed Incentives," *Society and Natural Resources* 10, no. 3 (1997): 309-18, 311.

53. Robbin Shoemaker, "Agricultural Land Values and Rents Under the Conservation Reserve Program," *Land Economics* 6, no. 2 (1989): 131-37, 131.

54. Shoemaker, "Agricultural Land Values," 131-32.

55. Philip J. Gersmehl, Bryan Baker, and Dwight A. Brown, "Land Management Effects on Innate Soil Erodibility: A Potential Complication for Compliance Planning," *Journal of Soil and Water Conservation* 44, no. 5 (1989): 417-20, 419.

56. Philip Gersmehl, "Macro-geographic Patterns of the Conservation Reserve Program," Presentation at the Annual Meeting of the Association of American Geographers, (Boston, 1998).

57. Gersmehl, Baker, and Brown, "Land Management," 419.

58. Thomas L. Daniels, "America's Conservation Reserve Program: Rural Planning or Just Another Subsidy," *Journal of Rural Studies* 4, no. 4 (1988): 405-11, 409.

CHAPTER 9

FORESTRY MANAGEMENT PHILOSOPHIES

[T]he brute application of economic models to political activity systematically understates the value associated with participation in decision making . . . [but] participation of the local community is critical for the legitimacy of the choices made when the community will bear the consequences of those decisions.[1]

Gerald Torres

Bureaucracy is administration which almost completely avoids public discussion of its techniques, although there may occur public discussion of its policies.[2]

Robert K. Merton

THE TENSION BETWEEN INDIVIDUALS who are claiming their rights and a state that has been accorded the job of mediating the various interests has persevered throughout the history of forest management in the United States. Globalization has left clear markers of its impact as well. The environmentalist movement's highlighting of resource depletion has served to make forest management even more of a problem area than in the previous century.

Sociologist Frederick Buttel has shown that academic analyses of environmental policy have for the most part presumed a pluralist rather than instrumentalist or structuralist model of the state, ignoring most of the recent neo-Marxist work.[3] The same holds for environmental policy analysis in general. In recent years, solutions to forest management problems in the United States have collected around two poles, as indicated earlier. Either private individuals have been seen as the solution to the problem, or the federal government has been called on to intervene. As with fisheries and rangelands, one is but the mirror image of the other; one necessitates the other. Fundamental difficulties arise from the individualist cast and/or the assumptions about the nature and functioning of the state. These difficulties predispose the proposed

141

solutions toward failure in the long term. Some corporate and individual actors may find them beneficial, but the overall ecological and sociological outcomes have been deleterious. The initiatives of recent generations have insufficiently provided for a sense of the commons, for a sense of an authentic public (which would function as a kind of human commons), or for (local) collective rights other than those of the (globalizing) business corporation. At several points, the type of scholarship on which proposed solutions draw plays an important contributing role that provides a cloak of technical expertise rather than democratic inquiry. Colonizer Enlightenment-based presuppositions regarding knowledge, human nature and the relation of the people to nature continue to shape responses to ecological concerns.

Historically, the absolute belief in individual private rights as the basic building block of society, especially expressed in property, has led to the subsidizing of particular economic interests—often corporate ones. Be it through underpricing the resource for individuals and companies, reserving land due to desires of irrigation farmers, giving away land contingent upon people's planting trees, repurchasing lands after the timber had been removed, subsidizing the harvest of forests by underpricing the timber, or because of road building, state subsidy has augmented the imbalance between the few and the many.[4] When the effects of the actions of such individual interests have led to third-party problems (tax-forfeiture, erosion, depletion of supplies, higher prices) the call has gone out for federal intervention to solve the problem. Where the state is perceived as only the protector of individual interests, it becomes inevitable that centralized state functions are required to balance the forces of individual interests. Nowhere in history have legislators articulated a policy to dampen individualistic tendencies or reinvigorate a strong sense of the commons.[5]

Economist Efficiency

The primary focus of this chapter will be forest management philosophies and policies; the discussion will at times make reference to more general environmental policies while attending specifically to forest management. Attention will be directed primarily to the thinking of forest managers and related legislative policy analysts, but a brief consideration of economic thought merits consideration first.

Economists and others have questioned whether the federal bureaucracy can manage resources in an economically efficient manner. A second but related concern is whether the bureaucracy is susceptible to control by the more powerful economic interests. Several responses to these concerns have surfaced in recent years. Those economists interested in the problems of behavior and efficiency have proposed a property-rights approach as another response to current problems. This group holds that most natural resource problems are due to the breakdown of the structure of rights. While this approach has proven efficient in some cases, its assumptions deserve examination. Proponents of property rights believe that what the individual seeks is an indicator of what is good. Individual choices determine value.[6]

The approach fails to recognize social institutions as franchised entities in their own right, instead reducing them to composites of individuals. The neoclassical microeconomic framework presumed here is one that uses the simple motivational assumption of profit or utility maximization, which is either abstracted from institutional analysis or analyzed within a certain institutional framework. The framework invites simplification, and seldom focuses on the institution.

A further critical difficulty ensues. Property rights economists work with a myopic model of the state and its role in the economy of natural resources.[7] They presuppose a model derived from thinkers such as Locke and the neoclassical economists such as Von Mises. "Good" actions by the state are those that allow individuals to attain the ends they wish to attain.

A second response to the issue at hand has been to divide goods into public and private spheres. On such a view, private goods should be left to the market, with public ones subject to collective action. Public goods are those from which nonpaying users cannot be excluded, so there are no incentives for private firms to produce them; once the goods are provided to one individual, they can be provided to others at no additional cost. Goods come to be split between private and public. This response assumes that landowners hold almost absolute rights to their property, while society as a whole bears no interest in private property. Community again becomes relegated to the state, without reference to mediating social institutions in between.

Sustained Yield

Three systems have been used to manage U.S. public forests. Alterations to forest biology from the colonial period on had not gone unnoticed; timber shortages had long concerned the new settlers. Custodial management, which focused on protection, arose during the Progressive Era around the turn of the century in response to exploitation.[8] The United States Forest Service (USFS) was formed during this era under the leadership of Gifford Pinchot. Foresters themselves were viewed as neutral professionals who applied science in the utilization of natural resources, much as applicators of Frederick Taylor's scientific management were seen as neutral managers unearthing findings about human behavior in order to serve the common good of efficiency. Professional and scientific neutrality was believed to benefit all interested parties by providing the most accurate rendition, one that would result in increased utility for all. Exploitation issues at the turn of the century led to the marriage of science and government control, with the manifest goal being the management of natural resources for the long-term public good.[9]

The post-World War II system focused on sustained yield (SY) management of forests to yield sustainable timber volumes.[10] Sustained yield goals were tied, among other things, to the belief that the supply of timber would somehow translate into community stability.

The origins of this professional concern for community stability can be traced to the middle of the eighteenth century in northern Germany. The virtually undeveloped state of transportation and communication resulted in a widespread system of small, independent political units with high customs barriers that prevented any significant degree of regional trade. Local consumption depended directly on local production. Self-sufficiency was the rule, and the effect on forestry was the development of small units where production and consumption were closely regulated. The idea of the normal forest under the closed economies of the period became firmly established as the basis for management. More to the point, this philosophy, embedded in small German political entities, migrated to a vastly different ecological (and political) niche. The policy was imported to North American forestry in spite of the different context.[11]

The doctrine of sustained yield, as developed in the early post-World War II period, was thought to provide perpetuating forests stands, a continuity of wood supply, and regional stability of employment. Supporters of SY assumed that an even flow of timber would guarantee constant annual levels of production, employment, and incomes to the owner of the forest.[12] The reality is a dynamic system where transport routes, new industries and so forth affect employment.[13] Regulation of the supply of one input is simply inadequate to ensure constant production levels when demand fluctuates.[14] To the extent that community stability has been a related social objective, sustained yield has been neither necessary nor sufficient to attain it.[15] In reality, competitive pressure among privately held corporations pushed these firms toward innovation to increase their relative profitability. They worked to reduce their labor costs and went down the road of a technology treadmill.[16] With increasing economies of scale, individual mills extended their geographic limits and their numbers fell. Locally situated communities continued to feel the pulls and pushes of the far-reaching timber market. Internationalization of forest products capital occurred along with decreased union density.[17]

The failures of sustained yield to some extent reside in the minimal recognition of its social meaning concomitant to the technical aspect. By far the most evident social meaning embodied in such a practice is the region's commitment to creating a future by perpetuating basic biological conditions in such a way as to support important sectors of that region. Technical terms and functional definitions abound, while the symbolic meaning of sustained yield is the most subtly far-reaching. Sustained yield serves as a symbol for social continuity, the continuation of the biological basis for social continuity. It functions as an article of faith[18] at the expense of hope and charity.

While committed to sustained yield, those who use the concept invoke a view of society as an aggregate of individuals. However, sustained yield exemplifies a distinct myopia when its society is formulated this way. The individuals do not share anything like the same stature. Increased concentrations of wealth render an equation of individuals disingenuous. More important for present purposes, the business corporation incarnations of such concentrations necessitate a fundamental rethinking of the society's nature, and then its policy for land use. Likewise the unprecedented increase in the scale of business operations ascended hand in hand with a parallel increase in the size, scope, and functioning of the state apparatus.[19]

Sustained yield originally evolved as an instrument for ordering social and economic conditions, as well as for managing the production of wood from forests.[20] The incipient thinking that eventuated in sustained yield paralleled the shift in societal metaphors from organic metaphors of the body social to rationalized ones responsive to the new corporate and industrial forms. Out of an especially turbulent period in U.S. history, sustained yield was advocated by federal government officials as a means of creating social stability during periods of social unrest among citizens or workers.[21] Robert Lee suggests that sustained yield served as an institutional means for bringing order to relationships between corporations that had been engaged in mutually destructive competition. A legal means was found for collectively withholding wood from the market. Just as the state's invocation of regulatory agencies helped dissipate progressivist challenges to corporate malpractice, the doctrine of sustained yield helped head off unrest by workers and communities experiencing the side effects of corporate-scaled competition. In each case, the purported solution was held suspect in many quarters, and over the long term showed itself to benefit the (business) corporation rather than the collectivity.

While current SY advocates have manifested faith in the efficacy of the concept, rooted on a simple image of balance between wood supply and the material needs of a local community, they have not adequately examined the possibility that sustained yield originated in response to popular instability, and that the solution leads to further social instability at a later date. Historical studies show that debates over community stability have not simply centered on the dynamics of local social well-being, community development, political processes, or social change. Their focus has been on achieving economic stability by providing a cultural symbol for legitimating prescriptions for economic stabilization.[22] Community stability became a symbol for inspiring a political cause, regardless of whether this cause was expanding government ownership of forest land, eliminating destructive practices by corporate producers, or promoting increased timber harvest on public lands. Qua iconic symbol, community stability invited commitment to the nation-state rather than true dialogue at the local level of decision making. As such, the symbol incorporated the beginnings of its own subsequent decay.

Multiple Use Sustained Yield (MUSY)

The U.S. policy regime of the 1970s added a philosophy of Multiple-Use (MU) management of forests to SY, setting explicit goals of outputs that maximized social value when both market and nonmarket outputs were considered.[23] Congress was the source of authority for these changes. Prior to the 1970s, timber management was dominated by the forest service professionals with little input from the public. These managers emphasized timber as a resource. Multiple use was meant to break the Iron Triangle of the forest service, the timber industry, and congressional committees, reinforced by a system where 25 percent of receipts from timber sales went to the counties.[24] Multiple use arose partially in response to field managers being encouraged if not forced to overproduce commodities from the national forests and Bureau of Land Management lands—through statute, budget, or headquarters directive—at the expense of environmentalist values. In a context of shifting tides of political power, environmental groups succeeded in counteracting the environmental abuse by enacting laws consonant with multiple use.[25]

The change in philosophy from the 1970s onward evolved in response to the awakening environmental movement and an influx of a large population in the West who were not economically dependent upon timber. Reflecting the shift in popular awareness and values, the 1964 Wilderness Act moved decision making to Congress. These changes also led to increased judicial review and scrutiny of administrative actions, as well as litigation initiated by environmental groups. A critique of the corporate capture of administrative agencies resulted in the expansion of input from different constituencies.[26] In 1976, the National Forest Management Act (NFMA) moved congressional oversight to more environmentally sensitive committees, established a planning process that expanded public participation, and elevated the value of species protection. This act led to a further litigation explosion as well as to the replacement of agency officials with more nonforesters.[27]

The 1970s congressional initiatives in forest management crystallized multiple use. The Renewable Resources Planning Act was passed in 1974, and the National Forest Management Act and Federal Land Policy and Management Act in 1976. These acts directed the Forest Service to engage in large-scale centralized planning. Emphasis was put on resource inventory and the economic balancing of benefits and costs. Interest groups at this time encouraged centralized planning because they saw it as a long-needed point of influence on the Forest Service.[28]

Centrality Rationalized

With the goals of rational planning and economic efficiency, land capabilities and uses are measured, alternative options are defined, and a choice is made. The Forest Service has utilized a computer program called FORPLAN to make tentative land-use allocations that are then adjusted according to additional information and public input. The underlying thinking has been that efficiency can be generated by increased data when subject to proper management.

Nature resource economist Marion Clawson[29] has pointed out a key underlying policy assumption—that information would solve policy issues and that more objective information would bring to light the rational answer that all could agree upon.[30] The NFMA of 1976 was based on the idea that objective planning would solve conflicts over wilderness, clear-cutting, herbicides, below-cost sales, and other national forest issues.[31] Based on traditional planning that espouses the notion of value freedom, technicians would now make decisions based on comprehensive and objective assessments of problems, and their assessments would be provided equally and be accessible to all interested parties. Given this challenge, technical rationality supplanted formal rationality, to use the Weberian terminology. Managers valorized technique at the expense of awareness of the differential outcomes for conflicting social strata.

Increasingly globalized corporate actors and the class most invested in them benefited at the expense of the locally embedded individual. Technique functioned in part to mask outcome; expertise (however inadvertently) served to disinform understandings of policy consequences. The relevant knowledge appeared inaccessible to ordinary individual actors; actual ecological truths more slowly became ascertainable for all. The planning process in time could be recognized as "a procedural black hole which threatens to suck in all the money, manpower, and data which comes near."[32] The number of ordinary citizens today who can penetrate FORPLAN's mysteries without the help of a professional consultant is said to be countable on the fingers of one hand.[33]

The planning effort has pointed in a universalizing rather than a localizing direction, in that national and local interests were asserted to be virtually identical. Its models assign equal weights to national and local interest by subsuming them under criteria such as maximizing net benefits, and they move control of land management agencies from the field to the national offices of the agencies.[34] This process escalates the centralization of decision making in the state and removes the decisions on land use from experienced land managers and hands it over to technical experts—(corporate) lawyers, economists, and politically active special interest groups.

The value of the environment has been moved entirely into the realm of resource, at the risk of losing all sense of environment as commons. The result is centralization and professionalization of the policy making apparatus in Washington, as well as an overemphasis on centralized, statutory solutions to localized management problems. Universalities come to supplant locally detailed knowledges. The results have been questionable and management by budget has become common. The MUSY concept, interpreted and implemented for economic or political expedience in the centralized practice of "predatory pluralism," has seriously degraded resource quality on much federal land.[35] It has also enabled the private use of anything deemed valuable on public lands. In this last respect, MUSY echoes the de facto federal land use policy in operation almost from the beginning of the republic.

Recent gridlock and acrimony in the federal lands arena results from multiple-use policies of the Multiple Use and Sustainable Yield Act of 1960 and Federal Land Policy and Management Act of 1976. It has resulted in coalitions of single-resource users (often corporate) and single-resource professional managers who transform multiple use into an adversarial game of adjacent, single-resource, land-use allocations.[36] Definitions of community interest remain difficult to discern or are poorly articulated.[37]

Forest use problem solving is based on the errant Enlightenment model of rationality and the related assumption that more information on a phenomenon automatically leads to better management. As was the case with colonial reasoning with respect to the new lands, the constitutive role of the decision maker at the top has been minimized. Conclusions have been treated as speaking for themselves, free of the formative influence of the forest manager. The 1976 National Forest Management Act was based on the belief that increased data and models would of themselves give forth correct answers. Practitioners came to (1) seek measurement for measurement's sake, (2) restrict the knowledge claims that would be seriously considered, (3) rely on technical experts, and (4) emphasize analytical technique.[38]

Conservationists, if their rationality is narrowly bounded, can easily misunderstand a problem and incorrectly specify its solution.[39] At the same time, scientific speech can signal an arrogance of technical expertise that fails to accord sufficient legitimacy to its citizen interlocutors. Ecological problems can be complex and multivariate with interactive effects difficult to tap methodologically. Models used can extract a misleading simplicity from holistic interdependencies; they can also transform accuracy for a small niche into inaccuracy regarding a larger bioregion. Such methods sometimes furnish a veneer of clear-cut findings that cover over misleading data and solutions. Once a problem is misunderstood or misdefined, precision and rigor merely compound the initial misunderstanding.[40]

The Forest Ecosystem Management Assessment Team (FEMAT) created by President Clinton to solve the problems of Northwest forests in 1993 was not classed under MUSY policy, but showed important similarities with respect to science. The Northwest forest problems were attributed to MUSY, yet as in many other natural resource planning efforts, the Ecosystem Management Team invested in state-of-the-art science and the latest planning technology. The effort did little to ameliorate the public conflict over forest management. The obvious and rational solution has not arisen from the science. Lawrence, Daniels, and Stankey[41] show that the isolation of the FEMAT project as a largely technical-scientific issue is its most severe shortcoming. A belief in the methods of science underlies the attempt at problem solving, yet in spite of the data gathering, legislative oversight, and planning, a decision could not be reached with which all were satisfied. Social matters of contention resist technical solutions.

Other attempts at moving away from the MUSY policy model have met with similar problems created by the reigning scientific paradigm. Critiques of the Interior Columbia Basin Ecosystem Management Project (ICBEMP) display related lacunae associated with the model of knowledge utilized. The ICBEMP's purpose is to restore and maintain long-term ecosystem health and integrity in the region; to support the economic and social needs of its people, cultures, and communities; and to provide sustainable levels of products and services from agency lands.[42] While scientists say that maintaining the integrity of ecosystems should stand as the overriding concern of the management system of the Columbia Basin, health and integrity are not measurable within the scientific paradigm that justifies its priority[43]

The Yellowstone Park region has been the focus of a similar attempt at ecosystem management. The exercise began in 1985 when the House Subcommittee on Public Lands and National Parks and Recreation examined whether appropriate regionwide, coordinated, interagency management was being carried out. The study culminated in a 1986 report, "Greater Yellowstone Ecosystem: An Analysis of Data Submitted by Federal and State Agencies." Like the Columbia Basin initiative, a major obstacle has been the lack of an understood definition of ecosystem management and thus a lack of shared problem definition.[44] The Greater Yellowstone project seemed to become an effort at agency coordination more than anything else.

The universalizing nature of science as it is ordinarily understood abstracts nature, humans, and their interrelationships from the thickly nuanced, intricately interactive reality. Yet the process of dispute resolution sometimes utilized by the U.S. Forest Service with respect to its citizen interlocutors can lead it in the opposite direction. This approach counteracts the universalizing nature of science. When the service does engage in dispute resolution, agency officials learn to distinguish between prime timber harvest areas and more marginal areas where some harvesting is conducted for other purposes.[45] The dispute resolution procedure engenders more realistic assessments on the part of the USFS. By acknowledging its practical, realistic interests and constraints, the agency is better able to defend and maintain its core program.[46] Such a situation creates an opportunity for meaningful dialogue and consensus building.

As a science-based policy, multiple use sustainable yield is often deceptive, its trappings misleading in ways common to technical expertise everywhere. More locally based, experiential (as opposed to formal, model-based) knowledge could have led to more satisfactory dialogue and to more appropriate stewardship. Locally generated and tested knowledge could lead to more appropriate coexistence with the land. Universalizing cognition based on the goal of controlling nature in order to improve its utility to humans has again and again shown itself a servant of formal rather than substantive rationality. That is, such cognition quite adeptly generates information useful for the objectives of some, at the expense of long-term wisdom regarding the systemic whole. With MUSY, as elsewhere, technical expertise too readily functions less as a resource for democratic, dialogical decision making and more as a rationale for the agendas of corporate and related forms of power. In doing so, it contributes to apathy, withdrawal, and nondemocratic styles of conflict engagement in many of the individuals affected.

Variations on the Theme

Additional initiatives to MUSY have been proposed. Cawley and Freemuth[47] advocate a dominant use assessment that is intended to produce a clearer picture of community interests and then stand for them. This dominant use assessment would indeed move away from viewing citizens as components to be managed, which is typical of scientific management, toward the concept of a public to be consulted. Yet, even a view of the citizens as a consulted public does not necessarily integrate them meaningfully and wholistically into the management process. Consultation is often synonymous with collecting individual comments at public meetings.

R. W. Behan[48] proposes that instead of focusing on uses one should look at the resource systems found in federal forests and rangelands. Part of this change would entail a movement from private, multiple uses of public lands toward emphasizing the public uses of public land. Private uses of public land would gradually recede. Behan articulates a case for the provision of public goods rather than private goods. He envisions a decentralized, constituency-based, multi-resource management system for the transition from a private-goods to a public-goods emphasis.

Another alternative emphasizes a change in property rights. Reidel[49] proposes an intriguing rethinking of public and private cooperation defined as a contract, i.e., a legal relationship. On this view, a more truly social contract involving shared rights and responsibilities and striking a balance between private property and social property is in order. Examples of this approach come from other nation-states. For instance, New Zealand has undergone a divestiture of public lands in the context of a national, integrated land-use planning and environmental protection system.[50] Its multiple-use paradigm has moved toward a dominant use system based on zoned categories of land with public agencies managing reserves, parks, and protected areas, and new land corporations managing all commercial forestry, grazing, and farming areas. Yet, the overarching framework is one of strong local, regional, and national environmental and resource management and planning controls. Of course, the

English definition of a park diverges from the U.S. definition of a park. It is an area of special land that includes a mix of public and private lands but is under strict planning, zoning, and use regulations. For Reidel, organized actions on the part of both nonprofit and government agencies help point the way out of the present situation.

The Problem of a "Public"

Economist Kenneth Boulding[51] has rightly pointed out that a satisfactory resolution of the problem of the environmental commons as posed by Hardin[52] and others necessitates a careful consideration of the matter of the public. The analysis here presumes the work of Boulding and a long line of similar thinkers from the time of Tocqueville and the English pluralists to the current civil society literature, C. W. Mills, Robert Bellah, and others, but draws environmental applications particularly from the work of Margaret Shannon.[53]

None of the above forestry solutions satisfactorily addresses the role of the public in part because Taylorist "scientific management" criteria have been incorporated into the regulation of resource use.[54] Technically trained professionals manage while the citizenship is allowed to have its say. Proponents would exclude lay groups from agency decision making, citing lack of technical expertise and a need to depoliticize public policy. Although the MUSY policy, developed in the 1970s, did institute input from the public in the planning process, the problem of the meaning of the public and the public good remains unresolved. The idea of "right" to be involved in decisions is frequently voiced, but the nature of involvement is seldom discussed.[55] Those within agencies and interest groups frequently experience public participation requirements as constituting a technique for gaining legislative support and political legitimation. Often, support of large numbers of citizens is treated as tantamount to the public interest. The use of survey research may serve similar strategic purposes.[56] The concept of the right of this type of consultation may in fact usurp deeper levels of participation, limiting the public interest to the support of a large number of individuals. The consultation is not integration of the public into decision making. It is the collection of information, a way to reduce tensions, or social therapy—all a far cry from meaningful participation.[57]

The Enlightenment liberal forum language is evident in the concept of the process of hearings. The process often begins with ideas from experts. The noteworthy major players are then notified of the public meeting, which in turn proffers legitimacy as a forum open to the major corporate, environmental, and local interest groups and individuals. An engineered consensus based on economic realities and political practicalities then ensues, but public participation in actual decision making has long ago been relegated to the bureaucracy.

Like much scientific reductionism, political theory has reduced the idea of the public to a set of aggregated individuals available for top-down consultation with managerial representatives of the state apparatus. In this way, public participation is reduced to voting, to the opportunity for individuals to attend meetings, to exposure to public hearings at which administrators inform the audience of their projected initiatives, and to the capacity to write memos to administrators expressing individual opinions regarding the desirability or warrantedness of those plans.[58]

Each of the dominant categories of the idea of the public, as delineated by Shannon, starts from an aggregate of individuals and then relates them to the political life of society. The public can be viewed as market players with preferences. In this case, the state exists for purportedly minimal purposes. Alternately, the public can be portrayed as client—the aggregate of an organized interest group. When the public is mainly characterized as the recipient of the outcomes of policies, it has become a patient, a recipient of top-down therapeutic discourse. The public is conceptually flattened to mere consumer or producer. In none of these perspectives is the public defined as comprising whole persons who share an identity that is superordinate to whatever else divides them.[59] Furthermore, the present concept of the public serves to maintain the corporate forestry stance. As with the devolution from an authentic public to public relations elsewhere,[60] the transformation works to render the economic and political imbalances of participants less visible and more apparently natural. Again, the social contract philosophy of classical liberalism proves to be both misleading and mythically useful for framing relations between the individual, the state, and the hegemonic form of corporate entity. Public input into forestry management decision making is an example of what Alan Wolfe calls alienated politics, "the process by which people's communal, self-governing capacities are absorbed and returned to them in a form that, while falsely pretending to serve universal needs, in fact atomizes their sociality and collective sense, induces their consent to illegitimate hierarchy, and substitutes heteronomous control by the powerful for autonomous self-direction by the people."[61]

This concept of the public masks responsibility for outcomes. Just as the market places no blame on the buyer of products that exploit people and ecosystems, so market models of liberal politics require little accountability from individuals for the consequences of their preferences on the commons. Final choices rest with bureaucratic expertise that in turn is responsive to transnational corporate agendas situated afar. Public relations management is no substitute for public deliberation and meaningful dialogue, whether at the national or local level.

Local communal life and the sense of wholeness that it enhances needs to be restored, thereby generating a relationship-based public. This requires policy framed in terms of human scale rather than that of the distended state apparatus and transnational corporation. Locally embedded policy is called for, not the policy of the oligarchy of the state. A concrete community is one where people's everyday conversation includes political discussion and debate; the populace is organized to make choices about use and control of shared resources and to take responsibility for social control and enforcement. The obvious ingredient requisite for such community is local control over shared resources, which is the element most often missing in federalist government structures.[62] The social and biophysical characteristics of communities today are being abstracted out of context by the universalizing science invoked by technical expertise.

Just as the political tension between individual and polity has long encountered responses of a state-managerial sort, individual self interest (combined with an apparently neutral procedure) surfaces to illuminate the path to resolution. For example, Lawrence, Daniels, and Stankey[63] search for a decision-making procedure that will make participants more satisfied, apart from the outcomes, believing a key weakness within the participation perspective of the federal agencies is that public participation is supposed to bring about a "better" outcome than nonparticipation by the public. These authors thus avoid the issue of value judgement on "better" by trying to focus on satisfaction apart from outcome. They turn to E. A. Lind and T. R. Tyler to help develop an alternative to the outcomes-oriented approach to public participation, combining an individual self-interest model (participant motivation in decision-making processes is to maximize personal gain—optimal decisions are then those that maximize net gain to participants as a whole), and the group-value model (group membership is a significant factor determining attitudes and behaviors). For instance, a procedure that yields necessary data might enable the decision maker to maximize outcome satisfaction. However, if the procedures fail to meet societal standards of fairness, the sense of group/societal membership will have been violated and aggregate satisfaction will be less than if the procedures were perceived as fair. The measures of proposed fairness derive from Leventhal and are invoked so that all parties will be satisfied if the process is seen as "unbiased." Leventhal postulated six rules: (1) consistency across people and time, (2) suppression of bias, (3) basis of good information (informed), (4) correctability of errors, (5) representativeness of groups of affected individuals, and (6) compatibility with moral and ethical values.[64]

The Lawrence, Daniels, and Stankey approach puts too much weight or faith in the formal procedure. It formulates self-interest and then avoids the danger of self-interested parties being unable to satisfactorily engage in moral discourse by relegating the value decisions to (purportedly objective) managerial procedure. Interested parties are represented and consulted and then the well-informed professional will be able to make fair decisions. The mechanism and guidelines proposed are laudable as far as they go, which is within the limit of managerial rather than truly democratic decision making. Aggregated differences involving decisions are given over to an agent of the entity that claims to represent all members of the collectivity, the state. That agent purports not so much to simply choose particular courses of action from among contested alternatives, but rather to eliminate bias and error and consult all representatively so as to generate decisions satisfactory to the entire collectivity. Hobbesian assumptions regularly invite Hobbesian resolutions. The onus for value judgements is relegated to the consultation error-reduction mechanism itself. Apparent satisfaction with the procedure can be made to stand in for satisfaction with the actual outcomes or decisions themselves.

Ecosystem Management

At present, the influential forest management philosophy is ecosystem management (EM). Elements of ecosystem management include an emphasis on ecosystem-based units, sustainability, and an emphasis on interagency coordination and public communication.[65] The single objective for management under EM is forest condition rather than sustainable timber yield. That is, thinking has evolved from a focus on what the forests should produce to what forests should be.[66]

Ecosystem management does not reflect a legislative origin and is not administratively formalized through a legal or managerial process. The writings of Aldo Leopold and the early work of the Ecological Society of America's Committee for the Study of Plant and Animal Communities provides its historical roots. In the 1970s, with the increasing crisis of biodiversity and the growing environmental movement, scholars began to advocate using ecosystems as the basis for public land policy. In the 1980s, a book by Agee and Johnson further developed the philosophy by presenting a theoretical framework that included homo sapiens directly in the equation and began to question the presumed role of science in unraveling ecological problems.[67] The 1990s brought about attempts to implement the emerging philosophy. California management policies tilted toward an EM basis in 1991 and the Forest Service started altering its focus a year later.[68] At the same time, the new management philosophy was articulated in a proclamation of the former chief of USFS, Dale Roberts.[69]

The adoption grew in response to the rising number of court cases and conflict in which the USFS has found itself since the passage of the 1970s laws mandating multiple use.[70] Policy initiatives had failed to slow the biodiversity crisis, while the safety net of environmental law had been stretched to its limits. An increase in administrative and litigation challenge to policies and national forest planning resulted.[71] In the meantime, changes in North Americans' understanding of the relationship between humans and nature added to EM's development, as did increased theoretical and empirical development of conservation biology.

In theory, ecosystem management takes into account the totality of relationships between forest organisms and their environment. Biological considerations take precedent over economic or social factors. Forest condition is the output; other goods are mere byproducts.[72] Ecosystem management shifts from managing total yield of an individual production or use to one of managing systems. It emphasizes maintaining the health and integrity of ecosystems while still providing the goods and services that humans require of them.[73]

The philosophy of EM addresses a growing societal acceptance of the concept of ecosystem integrity for management purposes, wherein the objective of management is to enhance or maintain ecological integrity while providing a sustainable flow of desired goods and services consistent with the capability of the ecosystem.[74] Common themes in EM include a systems perspective that respects ecological boundaries, an emphasis on ecological integrity, the need for more research and data collection, adaptive management that assumes the provisional nature of scientific knowledge, interagency cooperation reflecting changes in the structure of land management agencies, and the placement of people and values in nature.[75]

Ecosystem management strives to integrate scientific knowledge of ecological relationships within a complex sociopolitical and values framework with a goal of protecting native ecosystem integrity over the long term. Ecosystem management's stance on the provisional nature of scientific knowledge and its election for interagency cooperation result in collaborative decision making and socially defined management goals and objectives. In this respect, significant departures from the previous policies have occurred. In the past, public land managers questioned the place of a professional land management agency in such fractious and contentious environments; organizational incentives tended to limit their interaction with public and neighbors.[76] Staff were concerned with the entire forest or district, while citizens were concerned about specific places on the land. Thus citizens could not relate to the plans. Staff were working with a universalizing model of abstracted lands, while the local populace was focusing on knowledge tied to the contextual aspects of a particular place. Formal channels where staff merely acknowledged comments led to use of the courtroom to affect decisions.[77] In other words, EM entails a more promising ecological worldview, but there remains evidence of less productive citizen-forest management relations in practice. Federal relations retain more top-down public relations than open-ended dialogue. If EM is to truly comprise a significant change from MUSY, a new integration must be structured.

Is ecosystem management significantly different from MUSY? R. Edward Grumbine[78] argues that the U.S. Forest Service defines the goals of ecosystem management narrowly within the old resource management paradigm and seeks to operationalize these within a positivistic scientific framework. He claims that EM requires (1) scientists to collect better data at all scales, (2) policymakers to revisit environmental laws, (3) codification of biodiversity, (4) regional economic studies, (5) U.S. society to confront issues of population growth and consumption, (6) managers to hire more conservation biologists, (7) the decision making process to be opened up, and (8) citizens to be literate in ecology and environmental advocacy.[79] Is this so different from the past management philosophies? Grumbine attributes to EM great promise for sustaining nature and integrating culture with nature, but is it a realizable promise as conceptualized? Or is EM a concept, like biodiversity, headed for reification?[80]

Ecosystem management is helpful for such procedures as establishing boundaries, but less so for developing objectives.[81] The problem of determining value and ends still lingers. Ecosystem management remains dependent on natural resource professionals whose approach is antithetical to issues of norms and values. These professionals have typically aimed their energy at educating the public about technical programs in order to gain their support, rather than to identify public goals.[82] Their focus remains on techniques rather than values and citizen participation.

If ecosystem management is to fulfill its perceived promise, it must assimilate itself to an alternative notion of the scholarship-advocacy nexus. The requisite scholarship must transcend narrowly scientistic theories of knowledge. It must accommodate complexity, nonlinearity, and other properties of complex systems,[83] but it must do more than that. A more democratic science-cum-social science (sketched in a subsequent chapter) is needed. The necessary scholarship must wholly engage matters pertaining to "ought" as well as to "is." A more democratic science that supplants that of technical expertise is in order. Such a science would attend more to a pragmatic monitoring of the outcomes of initiatives and less to an (correspondence model of truth) attempt to build universal knowledge for its own sake.

The balance between locally specific knowledge and universalized generalizations would tilt more toward the former. Methodological techniques per se would recede in rhetorical value, and evidence produced by nonspecialists would ascend. Normative questions would be addressed more directly[84] and not be sublimated into empirical, and purportedly neutral, managerial ones.

Ecosystem management does not, to date, exemplify meaningful participation of the public. It remains either a vision of a highly rationalized model of scientific management with no consensus on societal goals, or at best, treats citizens as phenomena to be surveyed and added to the ecosystem framework, but not for inclusion in the goal setting process.[85] The "healthy" state toward which ecosystems are to be managed remains elusive and bounded by individualist assumptions and values that remain subsumed under the rubric of science.[86]

With science understood to refrain from addressing value questions, a common response throughout policy research is to use survey data of the citizenry to assign value. So with respect to forest management, Hetherington, Daniel, and Brown[87] engage value issues empirically by focusing on the readily measurable matter of "What values do people assign to forest ecosystems?" The actual normative question is framed by the researchers but then is redirected to a sample of citizenry in order to display pertinent data for resolving the value questions themselves.

Science often assists the effort to understand what ecosystems are and how they work, but in its current self-understanding cannot tell us what to manage ecosystems for. What exactly is to be sustained? Science does not tell us the answer nor does individualistic public participation build toward a common vision for what specifically is to be sustained at various geographic levels. Economics informs the populace of financial costs of choices, but avoids the direct question as to what is possible or desired. Neither science nor economics acknowledges establishing values, yet values indicate what is desired and guide our choices.[88]

The ability to protect environments, revitalize economies, and enhance and encourage healthy communities starts not with nature preserves, databases, ecological classifications, or any other technological tools, but with human dialogue and vision. Structures that are built on different assumptions about the nature of reality and possibilities either enhance or distract from our ability to build such a vision. The rhetoric enjoins the populace to consensus decision making, but, in actuality, government regulators and the courts responsive to political-economic power and buttressed by nondemocratic science make the calls. Aggregated individuals face off against business corporations and the similarly scaled government bodies responsive to them.

The forest management policies detailed in this chapter are marked by difficulties pertaining to their Enlightenment heritage. Individualist thinking has been shown to underwrite them, with attendant consequences. Social groupings have been treated as aggregates of individuals, social implications and complications have been missed, and the citizenry has been treated as a universalized public. These policies have worked with an individualistic concept of science. They have drawn on technical expertise at the expense of citizen involvement. The science has emphasized technique over and against holistic subtlety. An alternative notion of scholarship does exist, a science that is more democratic and less universalizing. Such scholarship more directly speaks to value commitment questions in ways resisted by the science of forest management and elsewhere. It is our contention that in doing so the work would contribute to a more satisfactory forest management, albeit one less responsive to corporate and other concentrations of wealth and power.

We turn next to a comparison of United States and Canadian forestry. The example will show that communal conceptions of society are not limited to the Third World. The dominant worldview described thus far conceives of a planning and management strategy that involves individuals as abstract aggregates of identical drives and needs.[89] The Canadian comparison will show that it need not be so. In a country with multiple cultures, local cultural traditions have forced the community to be incorporated into societal conceptions and legal structures. The United States could have and can likewise choose alternative structures that enhance communal life and natural resource management.

Notes

1. Gerald Torres, "Environmental Law," in *The Politics of Law*, ed. David Kairys (New York: Basic Books, 1998): 172-89, 185-86.

2. Robert K. Merton, *Social Theory and Social Structure* (Glencoe, Ill.: Free Press, 1957), 197.

3. Frederick H. Buttel, "Environmental Quality and the State," *Research in Political Sociology* 1 (1985): 167-88.

4. Sterling Brubaker, ed., *Rethinking the Federal Lands* (Washington, D.C.: Resource for the Future, 1984), 6-12.

5. Janel M. Curry-Roper and Steven McGuire, "The Individualistic Imagination and Natural Resource Policy," *Society and Natural Resources* 6, no. 3 (1993): 259-72.

6. Alan Randal, "Property Rights and Social Microeconomics," *Natural Resources Journal* 15 (1975): 729-47, 732.

7. Randal, "Property Rights," 746.

8. Roger A. Sedjo, "Toward an Operational Approach to Forest Management," *Journal of Forestry* 94, no. 8 (1996): 24-27, 24.

9. Jeff R. Jones, Roxanne Martin, and E. T. Bartlett, "Ecosystem Management: The U.S. Forest Service's Response to Social Conflict," *Society and Natural Resources* 8, no. 2 (1995): 161-68, 163.

10. Sedjo, "Toward an Operational Approach," 24.

11. Thomas R. Waggener, "Community Stability As a Forest Management Objective," *Journal of Forestry* 75 (1977): 710-14, 710.

12. R. N. Byron, "Community Stability and Forest Policy in British Columbia," *Canadian Journal of Forest Research* 8, (1978): 61-66, 61.

13. Byron, "Community Stability," 61-62.

14. Byron, "Community Stability," 63.

15. Byron, "Community Stability," 65.

16. William S. Prudham, "Timber and Town: Post-War Federal Forest Policy, Industrial Organization, and Rural Change in Oregon's Illinois Valley," *Antipode* 30, no. 2 (1998): 177-96, 184.

17. Prudham, "Timber and Town," 185.

18. Robert G. Lee, "Sustained Yield and Social Order," in *Community and Forestry: Continuities in the Sociology of Natural Resources,* ed. Robert G. Lee, Donald R. Field, and William R. Burch Jr. (Boulder, Colo.: Westview Press, 1990), 83-94, 87.

19. Lee, "Sustained Yield and Social Order," 86.

20. Lee, "Sustained Yield and Social Order," 88.

21. Lee, "Sustained Yield and Social Order," 90.

22. Robert G. Lee, "Community Stability: Symbol or Social Reality?" in *Community Stability in Forest-Based Economies,* ed. Dennis C. Le Master and John H. Beuter (Portland, Ore.: Timber Press, 1989), 36-43.

23. Sedjo, "Toward an Operational Approach," 25.

24. George Hoberg, "From Localism to Legalism: The Transformation of Federal Forest Policy," in *Western Public Lands and Environmental Politics,* ed. Charles Davis (Boulder, Colo.: Westview Press, 1997), 47-73, 49.

25. R. W. Behan, "The Irony of the Multiple Use/Sustained Yield Concept: Nothing Is So Powerful As an Idea Whose Time Has Passed," in *Multiple Use and Sustained Yield: Changing Philosophies for Feudal Land Management,* United States Congressional Research Service, (Washington, D.C.: Government Printing Office, 1993), 95-106, 101.

26. Hoberg, "Localism to Legalism," 50-52.

27. Hoberg, "Localism to Legalism," 52-53.

28. Perry R. Hagenstein, "The Federal Lands Today-Uses and Limits," in *Rethinking the Federal Lands,* ed. Sterling Brubaker (Washington, D.C.: Resources for the Future, 1984), 74-107, 99.

29. Marion Clawson, *The Federal Lands Revisited,* (Washington, D.C.: Resources for the Future, 1983), 115.

30. Clawson, *Federal Lands Revisited,* 116.

31. Randal O'Toole, *Reforming the Forest Service* (Washington, D.C.: Island Press, 1988), 174.

32. O'Toole, *Reforming the Forest Service,* 175.

33. O'Toole, *Reforming the Forest Service,* 178.

34. Hagenstein, "Federal Lands Today," 100.

35. Behan, "Irony of Multiple Use," 98.

36. R. McGreggor Cawley and John Freemuth, "A Critique of the Multiple Use Framework in Public Lands Decision Making," in *Western Public Lands and Environmental Politics,* ed. Charles Davis (Boulder, Colo.: Westview Press, 1997), 32-44, 35.

37. Cawley and Freemuth, "A Critique of the Multiple Use," 38.

38. Gerald M. Allen and Ernest M. Gould, "Complexity, Wickedness, and Public Forests," *Journal of Forestry* 84, no. 4 (1986): 20-23, 22-23.

39. Tim W. Clark, "Creating and Using Knowledge for Species and Ecosystem Conservation: Science, Organizations, and Policy," *Perspectives in Biology and Medicine* 36 (1986): 497-525, 509.

40. Clark, "Creating and Using Knowledge," 515.

41. Rick Lawrence, Steven E. Daniels, and George H. Stankey, "Procedural Justice and Public Involvement in Natural Resource Decision Making," *Society and Natural Resources* 10, no. 2 (1997): 577-89, 578.

42. Larry Hill, "A Summary of SAF's Comments on ICBEMP," *Journal of Forestry* 96, no. 10 (1998): 40-41, 40.

43. Jay O'Laughlin, Bob Maynard, Steve Fitzgerald, Arnie Arneson, and Dan Pittman, "Seven Suggestions for Revising ICBEMP," *Journal of Forestry* 96, no. 10 (1998): 42-45, 42.

44. Pamela Lichtman and Tim W. Clark, "Rethinking the 'Vision' Exercise in the Greater Yellowstone Ecosystem." *Society and Natural Resources* 1 (1994): 459-78, 465.

45. Nancy J. Manring, "Alternative Dispute Resolution and Organizational Incentives in the U.S. Forest Service," *Society and Natural Resources* 11 (1998): 67-80.

46. Manring, "Alternative Dispute Resolution," 75.

47. Cawley and Freemuth, "Public Lands Decision Making."

48. Behan, "Irony of Multiple Use."

49. Carl Reidel, "A Public/Private Cooperative Paradigm for Federal Land Management," in *Multiple Use and Sustained Yield: Changing Philosophies for Federal Land Management,* United States Congressional Research Service (Washington, D.C.: Government Printing Office, 1993), 145-72.

50. Reidel, "A Public/Private Cooperative Paradigm," 155-56.

51. Kenneth Boulding, "Commons and Community," in *Managing the Commons,* ed. Garrett Hardin and John Baden (San Francisco: Freeman, 1977), 280-94.

52. Garrett Hardin, "The Tragedy of the Commons," *Science* 162 (1968): 1243-48.

53. Margaret A. Shannon, "Community Governance: An Enduring Institution of Democracy," in *Multiple Use and Sustained Yield: Changing Philosophies for Federal Land Management* (United States, Congressional Research Service, Washington, D.C.: Government Printing Office, 1993), 219-46.

54. Gerald Torres, "Environmental Law," in *The Politics of Law*, ed. David Kairys (New York: Basic Books, 1998), 172-89.

55. Norman Wengert, "Citizen Participation: Practice in Search of a Theory," *Natural Resources Journal* 16, no. 1 (1976): 23-40, 25.

56. Wengert, "Citizen Participation," 26.

57. Wengert, "Citizen Participation," 26-27.

58. Shannon, "Community Goverance," 223.

59. Shannon, "Community Goverance," 223.

60. Wright C. Mills, *The Power Elite* (New York: Oxford, 1956), 298-324.

61. Karl Klare, "Labor Law and the Liberal Political Imagination," *Socialist Review* 43 (1982): 45-71, 64.

62. Shannon, "Community Goverance," 233.

63. Lawrence, Daniels, and Stankey, "Procedural Justice,"

64. Lawrence, Daniels, and Stankey, "Procedural Justice," 586.

65. Carlos Galindo-Leal and Fred L. Bunnel, "Ecosystem Management: Implications and Opportunities of a New Paradigm," *The Forestry Chronicle* 71, no. 5 (1995): 601-6, 603-4.

66. Sedjo, "Toward an Operational Approach," 25.

67. Edward R. Grumbine, "What Is Ecosystem Management?" *Conservation Biology* 8, no. 1 (1994): 27-38, 28-29.

68. Grumbine, "What Is Ecosystem Management?" 29.
69. Jones, Martin, and Bartlett, "Ecosystem Management," 162.
70. Jones, Martin, and Bartlett, "Ecosystem Management," 162.
71. Grumbine, "What Is Ecosystem Management?" 29.
72. Sedjo, "Toward an Operational Approach," 24-27.
73. Jones, Martin, and Bartlett, "Ecosystem Management," 161-68.
74. Thomas M. Quigley, Richard W. Haynes, Wendel J. Hann, Danny C. Lee, Richard S. Holthausen, and Rebecca A. Gravenmier, "Using an Ecoregion Assessment for Integrated Policy Analysis," *Journal of Forestry* 96, no. 10 (1998): 33-38, 33.
75. Grumbine, "What Is Ecosystem Management?" 30-31.
76. Hanna J. Cortner and Margaret A. Shannon, "Embedding Public Participation in Its Political Context," *Journal of Forestry* 91, no. 7 (1993): 14-16, 14.
77. Cortner and Shannon, "Embedding Public Participation," 15.
78. Grumbine, "What Is Ecosystem Management?"
79. Grumbine, "What Is Ecosystem Management?"32-33.
80. Galindo-Leal and Bunnel, "Ecosystem Management: Implications," 603.
81. Sedjo, "Toward an Operational Approach," 25.
82. Jones, Martin, and Bartlett, "Ecosystem Management," 166.
83. James W. Crossley, "Managing Ecosystems for Integrity: Theoretical Considerations for Resource and Environmental Managers," *Society and Natural Resources* 9 (1996): 465-81, 465.
84. Crossley, "Managing Ecosystems for Integrity," 474.
85. John Freemuth, "The Emergence of Ecosystem Management: Reinterpreting the Gospel?" *Society and Natural Resources* 9 (1996): 411-17, 413.
86. Sedjo, "Toward an Operational Approach," 26.
87. John Hetherington, Terry C. Daniel, and Thomas C. Brown, "Anything Goes Means Everything Stays: The Perils of Uncritical Pluralism in the Study of Ecosystem," *Society and Natural Resources* 7 (1994): 535-46.
88. Hal Salwasser, "'Ecosystem Management': Can It Sustain Diversity and Production?" *Journal of Forestry* 94, no. 8 (1994): 6-10, 9.
89. Robert A. Nisbet, *The Quest for Community* (New York: Oxford University, 1953), 272.

CHAPTER 10

A TALE OF TWO COUNTRIES

To define property is thus to represent boundaries between people; equally, it
is to articulate at least one set of conscious ecological boundaries between
people and things.[1]

William Cronon

CANADA AND THE UNITED STATES share a continent, an economy, and, at least
in the case of the English-speaking majority, a common language and culture.
Both are countries with great geographic and ethnic diversity, and both have
advanced industrial economies with high standards of living. Both have political
systems that are federal and democratic.[2] In spite of all these similarities, the
institutional structures that frame Canadian and U.S. natural resource policy
show subtle but significant differences. These include differences in the
governmental levels of responsibility for policy and management, policy
flexibility, and concepts of rights, as well as different responses to the challenge
of integrating humans into forest systems. A comparison of forest policy in both
countries aids in illuminating these differences as well as the variations in
empowerment of the community forestry movement. The comparison offers
lessons on the societal level on differential structures and their ability to
encourage change.

As illustrated in the previous section, solutions to natural resource
management in the United States have had two foci. Either private individuals
have been seen as the solution to the problem, or the federal government has
been called on to solve the problem. Where the state is perceived as only the
protector of individual interests, it becomes inevitable that centralized state
functions are required to balance the forces of individual interests. Nowhere in
this history have legislators or others articulated a policy that encourages the
moderation of individualistic tendencies or a strong sense of the commons.[3]

Unlike those in the United States, the governments of Canada did not pass
through an era of unregulated forest exploitation, nor did they face a challenge
to their right to retain lands in public ownership. Policy in newly acquired areas

165

was based on the Crown Timber Act adopted by the Union government in 1849. This act established government-extracted revenues from resource exploitation by private sector interests through the use of area-based licenses and volume-based stumpage fees.[4] The Canadian government's goals have been, from the first, the extraction of maximum possible rents from Crown-owned timber, the institution of stumpage and export duties, and the prohibition of the sale or granting of Crown timber lands.[5]

The structure of Canadian natural resource ownership was established in the British North America (BNA) Act of 1867, the same act that established an independent Canada. The BNA Act provides for provincial ownership and control over natural resources by giving the provinces powers of direct taxation; control of the management and sale of public lands, local works, and undertakings; and control over property and civil rights and all matters of a merely local or private nature. Provincial authority is based on more than ownership, since provinces are also permitted control over development. Even where land and mineral rights have been alienated or given over to the private sector, the province still has some basis for regulating resource development. Federal power in the resource area is derived mainly from the peace, order, and good government clause, which gives the federal government authority over trade and commerce and over any mode or system of taxation, as well as authority in areas excepted from those assigned to the provinces.[6]

The main impediment to an expanded federal presence in the forest sector has been the constitutional division of powers that has placed both ownership of the forest resource and the right to legislate in this area in the hands of the provincial governments. The only avenue open to the federal government to accomplish its policy objectives is intergovernmental consultation and cooperation.[7] The federal government of Canada has never given up its attempts to influence the development of provincial forest policies through control over production and pricing and through the exercise of spending power, as in federal-provincial shared-cost programs.[8] Federal interest has been in the viability of the forest industry and the availability of long-term supplies of timber for industrial users.[9] For example, federal expenditures have often taken the form of regional development incentives or modernization subsidies.[10] In 1987, the federal government formed a new Ministry of State for Forests, quadrupled planned federal expenditures, and concluded a series of Forest Resource Development Agreements (FRDAS) with several major producing provinces under the Economic and Regional Development Agreement (ERDA) umbrella.[11] Thus, much of the federal government's involvement has been through the establishment of forest sector industrial strategies.[12] In addition, many joint reforestation projects have been initiated, such as the 1979 Alberta Federal-Provincial joint reforestation project.[13]

The Canadian Forest Service has never equaled the importance of the United States Forest Service. After the loss of the balance of its lands to provincial control in 1930 it was reduced to a modest research organization. Since then it has engaged in research, administered programs of federal-provincial agreements such as forest inventories, and, by invitation, cooperated with the provinces in various studies and projects.[14]

One of the results of the BNA Act is that provinces have created an exceedingly diverse system of rights for users of natural resources, ranging from freehold titles to temporary licenses and permits.[15] At present, the general move is toward long-term licenses often referred to as evergreen agreements.[16] This system of granting extensive area-based licenses, carrying responsibility for planning and silviculture with them, is now in place in all Canadian provinces that have significant industrial forest activity.[17] Much of the best forestland has fallen under the guidelines of these long-term lease programs. Companies must provide long-term management plans for their leased territory that must be approved and inspected by provincial government authorities.[18]

United States forestry has been typified by its struggle between the rights of individuals to exploit the commons or claim rights of usage, which has resulted in increasing federal control. Science has largely replaced meaningful discourse with the courts as the battleground. The solution to the need for involvement of the public has been reduced to either the collection of individual comments or the balancing of interest group desires. Ecosystem Management, the newest attempt to resolve the internal conflicts within the country over management, remains within the positivist framework, attempting to integrate humans into a scientifically yet-to-be-defined concept of ecosystem health. Sociocultural factors are among the many aspects to be considered within the scientific framework.

Canadian forestry has from its beginning focused almost exclusively on economic outputs and development of the resource. Provincial control of resources has left the federal government with a marginal role in forestry within the country. Furthermore, the growth of the system of long-term leases that are individually negotiated with minimal legislative oversight, has led to a clientele-provincial system that takes into account few larger environmental issues such as biodiversity. A major inquiry into the state of forest management in 1978 reported that the situation in Canada compared very unfavorably with the United States.[19] Attempts on the part of policy community members to bring about a paradigm shift in which the overriding objective of forest management becomes ecological sustainability, rather than sustainable levels of fiber production, have largely failed.[20]

While the United States' response to the crisis of authority and public input has been the growth of more federal control and laws, increased judicial intervention, as well as growth in the use of Ecosystem Management as the newest "neutral" scientific tool, the Canadian response has been very different. In Canada, the concept of community forestry has grown in response. The science-driven Ecosystem Management paradigm has not come to terms with the socioeconomic dimension of forestry, which is at the core of Canadian institutions. Canada has long known a rural, populist movement aimed at local control of natural resources and targeted at big government and business alike. In northern Ontario and the interior of British Columbia, this movement has fueled demands for community forests and local resource boards whose management practices will be based on the needs of the regional economy and the local knowledge of practitioners. This movement is very different from, and potentially hostile to, a science-based drive for Ecosystem Management.[21] Yet it provides an alternative to the system that has led to the increasing power of large licensees, because it redistributes licenses to smaller, community-based operations and restores aboriginal rights.[22]

A community forest can take many different forms, yet it must incorporate a setting where the people of a community have some sense of place, common interests, and goals, and where they are willing to cooperate to achieve those goals. The term "community forest" is uncommon in the literature in the United States. The few examples would include the county forests of tax-forfeited land in the Great Lakes and New England, and the Menominee Tribe forest in Wisconsin. Yet, community forest thinking is pervasive in British Columbia, is growing in Ontario,[23] and has a long history in Canada as a whole.

Newfoundland has a history of community forestry. The use of the forests was closely linked to fisheries, and the principle developed that the coastal forest resources would be reserved for the use of those in the inshore fishery and would be treated as a common property resource. These principles were later maintained through a policy of not issuing licenses or leases within a three-mile limit of the coast, a practice that was generally, but not always, followed. A community-based sawmill sector, dependent on the timber from the three-mile limit, developed largely to meet local needs.[24] In 1979, the government incorporated almost all of the three-mile limit under forest management units, requiring cutting permits for use, restricting the amount of the cut, and restricting cutting to designated areas.[25] Roy reported on one community-based project that involved public education, identified locations where people could cut, and gave priority to the protection of healthy growing stock. The community forestry project, as part of an overall attempt to control cutting, was quite successful until a government cutback of funding undermined its continuity.[26]

In 1993, the National Assembly of Quebec passed a bill authorizing local municipalities to sign forest management agreements with the government. A 1994 Government of Quebec agreement with the Abitibi-Temiscaming Development Council empowered some eighty municipalities to control Crown land within their boundaries, thus initiating a major decentralization experiment in forest management.[27] This move is a return to an older tradition in Quebec. Community forestry was attempted early in the century as cantonal forest reserves, but in most cases open-access behavior was rampant and the system was dismantled. In the 1930s, another attempt was made with the residents of the Gaspé region, an endeavor that provided a starting point for the emergence of a cooperative movement in forestry. In Quebec, community forestry was instrumental in making room for local people in a tenure system tailored to fit the requirements of corporate forestry.[28]

An example of local forest tenure in Quebec is the Girardville Co-op in the Lake Saint John area. The co-op benefited from the proximity of an old and untouched cantonal reserve, and achieved stunning results at stopping population outflow and diversifying the local economy. The Girardville story is not unique. Aboriginal communities are also involved in managing forests according to their traditions in Wisconsin.[29]

Ontario is also looking at alternative models of forest tenure. In Ontario, 84 percent of the productive forestland is owned by the province and is organized into thirty forest-management units. All of the Forest Management Agreement (FMA) holders are either single forest-products companies or consortia of smaller forest-products companies. The FMAs are twenty-year, evergreen agreement contracts, which confer timber-harvest rights and forest-management responsibilities upon the holders.

A key weakness of current FMAs is that a multiple-use approach that considers nontimber values is imposed on the timber management contracts and is conflict-ridden and counterproductive in too many cases.[30] In addition, FMAs exclude the local community people from meaningful levels of involvement in forest-management decision-making, since control remains under industry and the provincial government.[31] The alternative is to offer communities their own forest tenures.[32] Community forestry is a shift from this traditional tenure system to one where public lands are managed and utilized by the local public. The management might take the form of FMAs, which would grant exclusive rights to communities to manage for both timber and nontimber values. Under FMAs in Ontario, the Ontario Ministry of Natural Resources assumes the role of the final authority, rather than having an implementation role, which ensures that community forestry activities operate under forest management guidelines, as well as under fishery and wildlife guidelines. Under ideal circumstances, these guidelines would be designed together by the community and the provincial government.[33]

Success of a community forestry program is favored by the existence of a number of institutions relevant to community forestry planning and execution. Such institutions include cooperatives, trusts, local governments, first nations councils, economic development corporations, and chambers of commerce.[34]

In 1991, the Ontario Minister of Natural Resources initiated a community forestry project as part of the province's sustainable forestry program. Several associations and towns had been lobbying for such an initiative for some time.[35] Themes surrounding the initiative included self-determination, wealth retention, resource stewardship, and decentralization.[36] Several pilot projects, one with the community of Geraldton and another involving a first nation, have led to some lessons to be learned.[37] The pilot program pointed out the need for both a fair degree of consensus within each community and high credibility among the lead agencies. The program must also have a clearly articulated mission, a meaningful delegation of authority between agency and community, meaningful forest tenure granted, sufficient revenue sources, autonomy to meet objectives, and a high degree of financial independence. The success of the program is dependent on the inclusion of relevant interests and reliance on existing structures, such as a municipality or Indian band.[38] This initial project has evolved into larger studies and pilot projects.[39]

Several examples of such community forests already in place in Canada are found in British Columbia. The Mission Municipal Forest operates with a Tree Farm License (TFL) and does not enjoy any preferential community tenure status. The forest is governed by the same forest laws and regulations as other companies and is managed as a department within the District of Mission structure. The Forestry Department is directly responsible to the elected Council via the Municipal Administrator.[40] The North Cowichan Forest was acquired through nonpayment of taxes during the 1930s and 1940s. In this case, the forest land base is owned by the municipality and its management is overseen by a Forest Advisory Committee that reports to the Municipal Council.[41]

Why has the solution to forestry management issues taken such different turns in the United States and Canada? We believe the answer lies in the cultural and institutional frameworks of these two countries. The Canadian institutional and legal context shows much more influence of the concept of subsidiarity than does the United States. In Canada, the test for the level of responsibility of many natural resource management issues is whether the whole problem is one that can be solved within a province. If it could be, and the federal Parliament attempted to regulate it, the courts would decide against it. If the question is of urgent national concern, there is federal jurisdiction. This is the doctrine on which the Canada Water Act is based.[42]

Provinces have primary responsibility for public lands and timber and can manage these as they choose. The Maritimes disposed of their forestlands extensively. Other provinces kept their forests. Furthermore, by virtue not only of their extensive proprietary rights but also on account of their legislative jurisdiction under the BNA Act, the provinces have been enabled to extensively alter the common law concepts of rights in property.[43] This delegation of authority means that a range of acceptable policies is initiated rather than the imposition of narrow standards for the entire nation.

This general institutional allowance of a range of policies has created a structure in which flexibility was allowed in the negotiating of forestry leases and agreements between companies and government. While some would say that this flexibility and lack of clear legislative guidelines led to the corporate-provincial oligarchy, this same structure allows for the development of community forestry.

Canada has not been wedded to the use of science as a neutral mediator to the same extent as the United States. Canadian forestry management has always been strongly connected to social goals and these have always included cultural sustainability. Simeon describes contrasting frameworks that can depict the differences between the United States and Canada.[44] In the United States, the constitutional structure puts resources in the realm of belonging to the country as a whole rather than to any subnational province or region. Attempts to capture their benefits for a particular state have been very limited. Moreover, policies are made according to the principle of majority rule at the federal level, so national majorities prevail over regional majorities.[45] The emphasis is on the free flow of goods and services throughout the national territory, with the federal government playing a major role in guaranteeing a free market and economy.

The province-building model, on the other hand, seems to describe Canada, with the stress put on the primacy of the provincial community. Canada is a collection of provincial communities with a compact among them. These communities have rights, such as ownership of natural resources, which cannot be taken away by any national majority. Provincial governments are the juridical equals of the federal government.[46] National interests must emerge from the interaction of eleven governments, rather than through the majority rules of a collection of individuals.[47] Furthermore, the province-building model put forth by Simeon points out that such a view of society includes the elements of provinces' securing the future for themselves as distinct societies.[48]

An example of the differences arising out of these two variant models is the use of public enterprises or corporations. In comparison to the United States, provincial governments have used public enterprises, or Crown Corporations, to a much greater extent. They are used to intervene in the economy in order to foster economic development, to redistribute economic benefits and power, and to further nationalism or provincialism.[49] A public enterprise established to realize nationalistic objectives is used to enhance provincial interests at the expense of interests outside the province, especially in the case of Quebec.[50]

The concept of rights and their meaning across the two countries is also essential for understanding the evolution of their forestry policies. The United State's historical emphasis on individual rights plays itself out in forestry policy through the struggle between the individual's rights to forest resources and the necessitating of growth of federal control to mediate among individuals claiming these rights. In Canada, the lack of a revolutionary tradition means that the charter values of the nation have been less clear.[51] The structure of the Canadian confederation arose out of the fear that a national government with representation by population would give control to one group—the English majority. This danger could be minimized if the principal matters of French Canadian concern were assigned to the legislative jurisdiction of the provinces, where they could not be threatened by the national English majority and thus embedding the concept of group rights into the structure.[52] In Canada, the charter groups were constitutionally permitted to retain their identities.[53] In contrast, in the United States the federal union was primarily a political and economic one, with relatively little direct ethnic import or cultural implications.[54] The United States is often described as being oriented toward egalitarianism and the opportunity to achieve.[55]

The traditional role of the judiciary in Canada has also allowed more flexibility and room for mediating structures. The nature of Canadian federalism apparently has contributed to conditions in which the national government has found that it is not in its interests to guarantee substantive equality.[56] The Canadian Supreme Court does consider the intent of Parliament, but it generally has not applied any tests similar to the U.S. Supreme Court's requirement that legislative classifications have a rational basis. The result of asking whether a law is within the legislature's authority, and not whether the act accomplishes a justifiable state objective, is that the Court has been able to avoid many policy considerations.[57] This has created much more space within the institutional structure for different policies for different situations and places.

Early in the history of the United States, the Supreme Court laid the groundwork for strong central government. The British Judicial Committee, which played the role equivalent to the United States Supreme Court, moved Canada in the opposite direction, conferring many more powers on the provinces.[58] Appeals to the Judicial Committee were abolished by the Supreme Court Act of 1949, and the Canadian Court took over its role. Yet the federal aspects of the Canadian constitution have come to be less what the courts say they are than what the federal and provincial cabinets and bureaucracies in a continuous series of formal and informal relations have determined them to be.[59]

The Canadian structure requires dialogue, and this may mark the greatest difference between the United States and Canada. The structure of Canadian policy requires much more negotiation than that in the United States. Though it fragments decision-making and thus renders national resource planning difficult, it also creates a climate where policies can only be determined by bargaining between autonomous yet interdependent governments.[60] Executive federalism denotes a seemingly endless series of conferences, often at ministerial levels, between officials of federal and provincial governments. These conferences feature negotiations in which the making of national policy in areas of common interest is attempted and sometimes realized.[61]

These differences in political cultures reflect two types of approaches and rhetorics to forest community stability as defined by Robert Lee: idealism and social reality.[62] The function of an idealistic sense of community is to organize or mobilize mass populations in order to achieve purposes advocated by agents for the state on private interests.[63] The measure of stability for such communities is the public opinion poll.[64] The interest group politics of making forestry policy in the United States fits well with the model of an idealistic sense of community.

The alternative, social-realist view of community connects individuals, groups, and the larger society in an integrated whole. This approach recognizes the enormous disparity among forest-dependent communities in their ability to cope with change and thus demands different approaches.[65] Particular communities maintain stability differently. Economic or environmental conditions are concrete means for sustaining both human relationships and personal enjoyment in everyday living. Community takes the concrete form of a style of life, and stability refers to the perpetuation of that culture with its network of social relationships.[66]

Manring points out that the process of dispute resolution, required to a greater extent in Canada than in the United States, involves dialogue and negotiations among equal parties. Such dialogue and negotiations force natural resource agencies to make clearer distinctions, acknowledging its on-the-ground reality.[67] The absence of such ground-level reality allows the public and the issues to remain abstract, conceptualized within the universalizing paradigm of reductionism science.

The Canadian example illustrates the potential for different institutional structures within the same legal tradition. In the United States, community-based forestry has had to circumvent normal government management channels to find expression. Its future lies in its ability to overcome the legal challenges of interest-group politics based on an individualist paradigm. Within Canada, the institutional structure has left room for the tradition and growth of community forestry. The Canadian system is not a panacea, but it is a step in the right direction. The emphases on cultural sustainability, flexibility in policy choices that are not thwarted by the legal system, and dialogue, create a different and more open context for the growth of nuanced, community-based management systems.

Fikret Berkes points out that such communal property management makes more sense because ecosystems are not divisible. Communal property is marked by a connectivity that is missing in private property regimes and higher-level government regimes.[68] This is a connectivity not only among natural systems but also among natural systems and human social life and economies. Private property is recent in origin and came with a worldview as portrayed in earlier chapters. As long as we subscribe to the ethics and philosophy of Cartesian rationalism, positivism and reductionism, and a mechanistic view of nature, communal property systems will always look fragile. However, if we begin to see things differently and build on the realities of the Canadian community forestry movement, then a new reality emerges.[69] The vision put forth by Berkes is one where, given the limited ability of centralized governments to respond to local needs and to act for the common good, devolution will become the norm, and communities and citizens' groups will share decision-making powers. Institutional structures will allow for a great diversity of power-sharing arrangements, reflecting the complexities and ambiguities in the linked social-ecological system. These co-management institutions will use market mechanisms and old-fashioned government regulation, but above all, local participation.[70] This local participation, built on consensus, local knowledge, and trust will not only change our relationship with nature but also our relationship with the people with whom we live and share space. This change involves recovering skills that were once available and affirming the fundamentally relational nature of humanity.

Notes

1. William Cronon, *Changes in the Land: Indians, Colonists, and the Ecology of New England* (New York: Hill and Wang, 1983), 58.

2. Roger Gibbins, *Regionalism: Territorial Politics in Canada and the United States* (Toronto: Harcourt Brace and Company Canada, Ltd., 1994), 2.

3. Janel M. Curry-Roper and Steve McGuire, "The Individualistic Imagination and Natural Resource Policy," *Society and Natural Resources* 6 (1993): 259-72.

4. Michael Howlett, "Forest Policies in Canada: Resource Constraints and Political Conflicts in the Canadian Forest Sector" (Ph.D. thesis, Queen's University, Kingston Ontario, 1988), 123.

5. Howlett, " Forest Policies in Canada," 114.

6. Marsha A. Chandler, "The Politics of Provincial Resource Policy," in *The Politics of Canadian Public Policy*, ed. Michael M. Atkinson and Marsha A. Chandler (Toronto: University of Toronto Press, 1983), 43-67, 45.

7. Michael Howlett, "The 1987 National Forest Sector Strategy and the Search for a Federal Role in Canadian Forest Policy," *Canadian Public Administration* 32, no. 4 (1989): 545-63, 561-63.

8. Howlett, "Forest Policies in Canada," 128-29.

9. Howlett, "Forest Policies in Canada," 131-32.

10. Howlett, "1987 National Forest Sector Strategy," 557-58.

11. Howlett, "1987 National Forest Sector Strategy," 548.

12. Howlett, "Forest Policies in Canada," 134.

13. Howlett, "Forest Policies in Canada," 285.

14. Frances Wetton, "Evolution of Forest Policies in Canada," *Journal of Forestry* 76, no. 9 (1978): 563-66, 565.

15. Peter H. Pearse, "Property Rights and the Development of Natural Resource Policies in Canada," *Canadian Public Policy* 14 (1988): 307-20, 307.

16. Monique M. Ross, *Forest Management in Canada with Contributions from Michael Howlett, Jeremy Rayner, and Martin K. Luckert* (Calgary, Alberta: Canadian Institute of Resource Law, University of Calgary, 1995), 74.

17. Ross, *Forest Management in Canada*, 87.

18. Howlett, "Forest Policies in Canada," 217.

19. Wetton, "Evolution of Forest Policies," 565.

20. Ross, *Forest Management in Canada*, 95.

21. Ross, *Forest Management in Canada*, 105.

22. Ross, *Forest Management in Canada*, 10.

23. P. N. Duinker, P. W. Matakala, Florence Chege, and Luc Bouthiller, "Community Forests in Canada: An Overview," *Forest Chronicle* 70, no. 6 (1994): 711-20, 712-15.

24. John A. Gray, *The Trees behind the Shore: The Forests and Forest Industries in Newfoundland and Labrador* (Ottawa: Economic Council of Canada, 1981), 17, 74.

25. Gray, *The Trees behind the Shore*, 18.

26. M. A. Roy, "Guided Change through Community Forestry: A Case Study in Forest Management Unit 17-Newfoundland," *Forestry Chronicle* 65 (1989): 344-47.

27. Duinker et al., "Community Forests," 715.

28. Duinker et al., "Community Forests," 715.

29. Duinker et al., "Community Forests," 715-16.

30. Peter N. Duinker, "Public Forests in Ontario, Canada: Improving the Management Partnerships," Proceedings of the 10th World Forestry Congress, Paris 20.2 (1991): 300-306, 302.

31. Duinker et al., "Public Forests in Ontario," 304.

32. Duinker et al., "Public Forests in Ontario," 304.

33. P. W. Matakala and P. N. Duinker, "Community Forestry As a Forest-Land Management Option in Ontario," in *Forest Dependent Communities: Challenges and Opportunities*, ed. David Bruce and Margaret Whitla (Sackville, New Brunswick: Mount Allison University Rural and Small Town Research and Studies Programme, 1993), 26-58, 34.

34. Matakala and Duinker, "Community Forestry," 42.

35. Stephen Harvey and Brian Hillier, "Community Forestry in Ontario," *Forestry Chronicle* 70, no. 6 (1994): 725-30, 726.

36. Harvey and Hillier, "Community Forestry in Ontario," 727

37. Harvey and Hillier, "Community Forestry in Ontario," 727-28.

38. Harvey and Hillier, "Community Forestry in Ontario," 729.

39. Stephen Harvey, *Ontario Community Forestry Pilot Project: Lessons Learned 1991-1994. Taking Stock of Ontario's Community Forestry Experience, Community Forestry Group* (Sault Ste. Marie, Ontario: Ministry of Natural Resources, 1995); Julian A. Dunster, *Establishing the Geraldton Community Forest Phase I: Concepts and Background Information* (A report prepared by Dunster and Associates, Geulph, Ontario, 1989); Anthony J. Usher, *Partnerships for Community Involvement in Forestry: A Comparative Analysis of Community Involvement in Natural Resource Management, Community Forestry Project* (Sault Ste. Marie, Ontario: Ontario Ministry of Natural Resources, 1994).

40. Kim Allen and Darrel Frank, "Community Forests in British Columbia: Models That Work," *The Forestry Chronicle* 70, no. 6 (1994): 721-24, 722.

41. Allen and Frank, "Community Forests in British Columbia," 723.

42. Gerard V. La Forest, "Jurisdiction over Natural Resources: Provincial and Federal," in *Natural Resource Development in Canada: Multi-Disciplinary Seminar*, eds. Philippe Crabbe and Irene M. Spry (Ottawa: University of Ottawa Press, 1973), 211-16, 215.

43. Leslie D. Shaw, "Property, Possession, and Ownership: Changing Concepts," in *Natural Resource Development in Canada: Multi-Disciplinary Seminar*, ed. Philippe Crabbe and Irene M. Spry (Ottawa: University of Ottawa Press, 1973), 245-74, 253.

44. Richard Simeon, "Natural Resource Revenues and Canadian Federalism: A Survey of the Issues," *Canadian Public Policy* 6, (1980): 182-91.

45. Simeon, "Natural Resource Revenues," 185.

46. Simeon, "Natural Resource Revenues," 185.

47. Simeon, "Natural Resource Revenues," 185.

48. Simeon, "Natural Resource Revenues," 186.

49. Chandler, "Politics of Provincial Resource Policy," 51.

50. Chandler, "Politics of Provincial Resource Policy," 52.

51. William V. Monopoli, "'Equality before the Law' and 'Equal Protection of the Law,'" in *Cross-National Perspectives: United States and Canada*, ed. Robert Presthus (Leiden: Brill, 1977), 102-26, 103.

52. Gibbins, *Regionalism*, 26.

53. Monopoli, "Equality before the Law," 104-5.

54. Monopoli, "Equality before the Law," 105.

55. Monopoli, "Equality before the Law," 104.

56. Monopoli, "Equality before the Law," 114.

57. Monopoli, "Equality before the Law," 115.

58. Gibbins, *Regionalism*, 35.

59. Gibbins, *Regionalism*, 36.

60. Wetton, "Evolution of Forest Policies," 566.

61. Howard Cody, "The Evolution of Federal-Provincial Relations in Canada: Some Reflections," *The American Review of Canadian Studies* 7, no. 1 (1977): 55-83, 56.

62. Robert G. Lee, "Community Stability: Symbol or Social Reality?" in *Community Stability in Forest-Based Economies*, ed. Dennis C. Le Master and John H. Beuter (Portland, Ore.: Timber Press, 1989), 36-43, 38.

63. Lee, "Community Stability," 40.

64. Lee, "Community Stability," 41.

65. Lee, "Community Stability," 39.

66. Lee, "Community Stability," 41.

67. Nancy J. Manring, "Alternative Dispute Resolution and Organizational Incentives in the U.S. Forest Service," *Society and Natural Resources* 11 (1998): 67-80, 75.

68. Fikret Berkes, "Dialogues of the Commons: Emerging Directions for Jointly Used Natural Resources," *The Common Property Digest*, no. 46 (1998): 17-20, 19.

69. Berkes, "Dialogues of the Commons," 20.

70. Berkes, "Dialogues of the Commons," 20.

PART III

RE-MEDIATION OPTIC

CHAPTER 11

IN THOUGHT

It is not enough to think in terms of two-level relationships, with the individual at one level and the state at another.[1]

Vernon Van Dyke

[I]t is arbitrary to assume that groups can and should gain status and rights only by becoming states. Groups in fact have status and rights at an intermediate level between the individual and the state. . . . Somehow the social contract theory in its dominant form neglects the obvious.[2]

Vernon Van Dyke

'Think globally, act locally' is a good slogan, but sometimes is better reversed.[3]

C. Douglas Lummis

IN THE LAST SECTION we dwelt on interrelated difficulties in connection with community's relationship to the land. We have held that extant land and oceans management policy solutions will fail because they are individualistic and fail to recognize the existence of community. The culture and its legal discourse proceed primarily in terms of the individual or corporation and/or the state. Forestry, agricultural, rangeland, and fisheries problems have been framed and addressed through assumptions that are traced back to Locke, Hobbes, Descartes, and others. Policies fail to empower community entities between the individual and the state, and that is a large part of the reason why they are unsuccessful. In failing to empower community groups, these policies rely on universalizing science instead of meaningful negotiation and dialogue. Decisions are made according to a scientific management model.

In detailing the problem, we have shown how the history of community and land are inherently intertwined. The tapestry of problems we have presented requires a tapestry of proffered solutions. Multifaceted social problems cannot be distilled into simple lawlike resolutions, and simplification through reduction would inevitably lead to less democratic and contextually sensitive solutions.

Thus the positive alternatives presented in this final section attempt to recognize the intertwined nature of community, the law, and knowledge itself.

Community

We presume the "self" to be socially embedded rather than atomistically autonomous. Humans start out in families and communities. Only academic practice leads a few of us to come to think that our nature is otherwise. We hold that the healthy self defines itself by inclusion within particular groups rather than exclusion from particular groups.[4]

Our understanding of community, broadly construed, is inseparable from our perception of the human person. Personhood is defined by personal individuality. But alternatively, individual personhood blossoms through membership in a community and atrophies if detached from the community. A community is a group with whom one regularly interacts and shares space. Community is something we are; it is a property of our personhood. A community is a human organism constituted by the shared life of a number of persons.[5]

From the turn-of-the-century writings of Emile Durkheim and Georg Simmel onward, social scientists have appreciated that collectives of human beings embody more than the aggregated qualities of their constituent individuals. Social groupings generate "emergent" qualities not reducible to their individual component parts. Bands, tribes, and ethnic groups establish their own cultures. Such cultures display complicated multiple and reciprocal causalities. Groups are "real."[6] Upon formation, they take on emergent traits of their own. In this connection, the organic metaphors of community utilized a millennium ago were more useful than the mechanical ones that replaced them. By their very nature, humans experience wholeness in social relations.

Philosophers of justice such as John Rawls and Michael Sandel use several concepts of community. An instrumental community is one in which individuals cooperate only to achieve their own ends. A sentimental community views cooperation as good in and of itself. A third concept is that of the notion of a constitutive community.[7] The latter understands the individual to constitute his or her identity through the community and is the closest of the three to the model we are invoking.

The human person finds self-fulfillment only as life is directed toward a source of meaning beyond the self, whether as individual or as communal self. This inclusive wholeness is expressed in human society in a rich diversity of communal types, with no single type dominating. Thus, rather than saying that a human person is an individual, it is preferable to say that the human person embodies individuality and a quality of communality, both of which belong to all human persons.[8]

Some psychologists support the claim that human growth does not involve a movement from dependence to independence but rather involves learning more and more sophisticated modes of relating, with a movement from immature dependencies to more mature dependencies and attachments.[9] Philosopher Elizabeth Wolgast bases her work on this alternative view of humanity. She states that the present model, born out of the scientific paradigm and Enlightenment philosophy, as reflected in our views of property rights,

> leads to the conceptual neglect of families and groups bound together by motives other than the combined self-interests of the members. It assumes that people always associate in a basically competitive way, each with his interests defined independently of the interests of others, and so assumes that society has its justification in the egoistic terms appropriate to an individual. To this one may object that we have no clear understanding of what an individual is apart from a human, social context.[10]

The concept of covenant offers an instructive alternative to the social contract view of the individual and the view of collective life as fictions of rationalized interests.[11] The covenant is a relationship between parties which, unlike the parties in the Lockean contract, have a prior relation. The covenant is not a limited relation based on self-interest, but an unlimited commitment based on loyalty, trust, and relationship.[12] Yet some liberal theorists claim that such a covenant order is a suspect institution because it is familized and gendered. Ironically, as our earlier analysis showed, social contract is itself gendered in such a way as to render women invisible and fundamentally subordinate. Communities change, and we would argue that "covenant" can be made to invoke a fully empowered community more readily than "social contract" can. Community is not inevitably oppressive, as legal reasoning assumes; it involves obligations to each other that transcend self-interest, while promising a deeper sense of self-fulfillment through participation.[13]

The healthy community is hard to talk about because human community is no more or less healthy, of its nature, than is the human condition. In this current cultural context of romanticizing community, we need to reiterate the obvious. When closely examined, communities regularly display a negative side, as do individuals. Just as individuals are endemically capable of the full palette of human emotions and behaviors, so, too, are communities ordinarily exemplary of the full range of possibilities.

Healthy community is coterminous with the full panoply of voluntary associations and other mediating social institutions. We have called upon Tocqueville and the English Pluralists to demonstrate the value of mediating institutions between individual and society as a whole. De Tocqueville particularly was writing at a time when some preferred to have a direct line of authority from state to individual. But we concur with him on the value of mediating institutions in checking the power of the state, and even more so their value in constituting community.

Healthy community overlaps substantially with a democracy of everyday life. Political structures are not the only structures that can be examined for their democracy quotient. Social organizations of all sorts can be studied for the degree to which they operate democratically or oligarchically. The same can be said for political parties, workplaces, and collective living arrangements.

Our contention is that the more a community lacks a communal, covenantal sense of itself, the less healthy it is. Exceptions likely abound, but not enough so as to undo the generality of this statement. In this case, some aspects of leadership can be found among the rural areas of the South or the Two-Thirds World.[14] The danger, of course, lies in thinking that only the current forms are possible; to laud the value of certain aspects of current two-thirds world communities is to risk being taken to advocate "going back" in time. However, it is not a matter of going back in time, but a matter of noticing what sorts of positive elements do exist, identifying certain commonalties among them, and inviting discussion on the most promising.

We are not attempting to specify a grand theory of healthy community, but rather advocating the value of the locally embedded form of life. We have suggested throughout that this form of life more closely matches the notion of human scale. As we have seen, globalization not only has the potential for further reducing the mediating structures of societies, but also for moving power to higher levels in order to manage transnational relations.[15] The promising solution lies in locality. For example, industrial restructuring is now taking place that involves both small enterprises and regional economics, and is described under the labels of post-Fordism or flexible specialization.[16] In some instances, the industrialized world is presently changing from large, vertically integrated corporations—dinosaurs that are unable to compete in a postindustrial—world, to firms that need more flexible forms of work and interfirm interaction. This has led to the emergence of networks of mostly small, linked, but generally loosely coupled, spatially clustered manufacturing companies that form industrial districts where each small firm specializes in one or a few phases of a complete production process. Small, flexible firms will often cooperate with one another, sharing tools, information, and even skilled personnel, only to compete fiercely for a share of the next new contract or market opportunity. They use small-scale, stand-alone, computerized automation, allowing for flexibility and rapid reconfiguration. Efficiencies are found at the district level rather than the firm level.[17]

Communities are important in this trend toward the dispersal of productive activity in growing new industrial districts.[18] Theory that explains this restructuring emphasizes the interdependence of firms, the flexibility of firm boundaries, cooperative competition, and the importance of trust in reproducing sustained collaboration among economic actors within the districts.[19] Their success is not based on a society of atomistic competitors, aware of each other only through the market. These trends have not yet been felt in agriculture, which continues down the path of the Fordist, or mass production, industrial mode.[20]

The bifurcation of society into the individual and the state has created what have been called institutional blanks. Institutional blanks are social spaces that lack an implementing and integrating institution to meet a new purpose.[21] As with the industrial districts, new institutions are being created to fill those blanks. Creating institutions at the community level to manage resources is not easy, however. Policies often undermine our communal natural resource management abilities. For example, in Canada in 1968, the "Davis Plan" for fisheries was initiated, which sold transferable fishing licenses. The group of fisheries, for whom long-term conservation really did make sense, was divorced from the management rights of the resource. The number of fishers and vessels declined, but the size and capacity of remaining vessels increased.[22] Individuals with long-term commitments to the industry upgraded their vessels and gear, though individual fishers were on record as fearing a decline in the resource. Collectively, however, they had no means of taking responsibility and were obligated to accept government regulation.[23] Far from mismanaging a common property, they were not permitted to manage the fishery at all.[24]

One facet of the import of human scale is the capacity of communities to meet the need for a dynamic of trust. The atomized view and the role-defined view of human actions fail to include the concept of trust amongst individuals, as philosophers of democracy and students of social capital have recently noticed. Trust implies relational embeddedness that is chosen and developed over time, leading back to an alternative concept of freedom that arises from such long-standing relationships. Institutional arrangements have been increasingly proposed as substitutes for trust in an attempt to make individuals behave within certain accepted norms. The societal transformations outlined earlier dissipated informal social control and conflict resolution and marked the establishment of more formalized controls in their stead. But embeddedness in personal relations itself discourages misbehavior far more strongly than more formalized, institutional control. Anthony Giddens and many others in the last one hundred years have made it clear that one of the results of the process of modernization has been the disembedding of individuals from the trust of personal relations with those with whom one shares time and space.[25]

Rationalized organizations and specialists have replaced this type of trust. This thesis, put forth by Giddens and others, has been so central to social science as to generate a huge literature arguing the degree and the conditions under which it holds. Suffice it to say that while evolutionary before/after contrasts are oversimplified in several ways, the claim that trust declines in face of modernity still holds. But in many contexts, the features depicted for the preindustrial world have persevered. Mark Granovetter identifies such trust in the developed world as well.[26] Less willing to accept the idea that space-time embeddedness of social relations is lost, Granovetter utilizes examples that illustrate the kind of embeddedness that best reflects societal workings. If problems arise between individuals who have made a contract, those prior detailed agreements are often not referred to and solutions are negotiated as if there had never been a contract.[27] Similarly, today general contractors usually employ only two to three subcontractors in a given trade area, no matter the number of projects. This is due in part to the benefit from the investment of learning to work together and the pleasure derived from sustained social interaction. Such pleasure and benefit could not be obtained if a different subcontractor were used on each project.[28]

Trust and embeddedness require physical proximity—place and community. Only within the context of treating space as place do we recognize the freedom such embeddedness can provide. The physical proximity of place implies human scale, and human scale facilitates "strong democracy."[29] It facilitates shared knowledge, trust, local identification, and a sense of civic connection.

Community proximity and relationships are important in the prosperous new industrial districts. Their existence is not explicable by conventional neoclassical economics, but rather their growth comes from the emergence of informal ties based on trust, mutuality, and intimacy.[30] In the standard urban economic models, which are space-based, proximity facilitates the exchange of information on which individual, atomistic decision-makers may then act. The place-based argument offered by the industrial district theorists—that proximity promotes the digestion of experience, which leads to trust, which promotes recontracting, and ultimately enhances regional growth—is built on a different logic. Trust is an expression of embeddedness—entrepreneurs see one another regularly in social clubs, in churches, and on the advisory boards of local cooperatives and regional government agencies. Proximity leads to experience, to trust, to collaboration, and to enhanced regional economic growth, thus entwining economic relations into a deeper social fabric.[31] Arendt would describe the attractiveness of such places as being rooted in the human condition of social embeddedness—a necessary condition for people to live as whole people.

Economic globalization, in contrast, involves the integration of national economic activities and the growth of enterprises that target the global market or conduct part of their production activities outside national boundaries. This extended market reduces the self-protection side of the equation because states find it difficult to exert effective control over economic and social relations.[32] Furthermore, constraints are placed on member states on national and subnational policies.[33]

An interconnection exists between communal concepts of society and agricultural systems as well. The assumptions of neoclassical economics have also had their impact on our concept of agriculture and have underlain many of the changes in U.S. agriculture of the past one hundred years. Those who support conventional agriculture production emphasize individual farm profitability. Connections of individual farm enterprises to community and environment are left out of the formula.[34] On the other hand, proponents of sustainable agriculture articulate flaws in the neoclassical approach to farming that parallel the misconceptions articulated above. Sustainable agriculture supporters argue for the reality of embeddedness within the natural environment and particular social contexts and emphasize living with nature and within a rural community.[35] The conventional agriculture paradigm emphasizes farming as a business with specialization, capital inputs, efficiency, reduced labor, large-scale processing, and global markets. The sustainable agriculture paradigm emphasizes farming as a way of life embedded in nature and community with diversification, environmental sustainability, decentralized markets, and processing.[36]

Lyson and Welsh found that increases in expenditures for equipment and machinery, the prevalence of corporate farms, higher rates of tenancy, and the prevalence of larger farms are all associated with less diversity in the crops grown.[37] Conversely, a greater diversity of crops is grown in counties where farm labor expenditures are higher, where there are more medium-size farms, and where there is a prevalence of farmers who derive most of their income from farming. They conclude that the range of crops grown in a county is an indicator that can distinguish conventional agricultural systems from sustainable agricultural systems, the latter being more oriented toward the inherent link between production, society, and the environment. Lyson and Welsh claim that counties that have farmers who structure their operations to remain flexible and better able to grow a variety of crops as markets dictate do not conform to the organizational assumptions of the neoclassical economic paradigm. As described above, the emphasis on competition in the global market is associated with monocropping and a disembedding from the local, shifting the locus of control from local place to far-off centers of economic power. The post-World War II work of Walter Goldschmidt, which showed the association between corporate farming and a lack of community-level health, still holds. Sustainable agriculture reiterates the diversity lost to the globalizing history. Extending the application of Granovetter's findings, we predict more pressure for vertical integration in a market where such social embeddedness is missing. Where a stable network of social relations exists, the pressures for vertical integration should be less.

Optimal self embeds in optimal community. The embedded community has struck chords of unease in many quarters. Community, like family, can stifle. It is something of a sociological staple that community can stifle nonconformity and freedom, while the cosmopolitan modern city engenders a good, open-minded, healthy diversity of thought. But much of the lost freedom is a freedom from "compliance with obligations that enhance the well-being of one's family, neighbors, and friends."[38] Such consideration can be seen as positive rather than negative.

The idea that living in places leads to a lack of freedom permeates the culture. While it is clearly the case that places can be oppressive, it is also the case that families can be oppressive and dysfunctional as well. This does not lead us to conclude that we need to do away with families. Healthy families, like healthy places, at their best produce healthy and mature individuals. The point is to clarify that which is healthy; such a clarification requires an appreciation of the rootedness of humanity in place.

Just as the Hobbesian social contract becomes inappropriate for portraying the relation between mother and child, legal discourse fails to appreciate the essence of personhood. All persons stand grounded in community and place. The abstract concepts of legal personhood, ideally unconstrained by place and freely moving across space, insufficiently calibrate the actual practices of people. People do not want to move freely in space but want to be able to choose particular places.

America's image as the land of freedom depicts freedom as independence. The counterargument is that not only do individuals gain true understanding of physical systems such as agricultural systems in particular places, but also only through the development of a rooted existence in family, spiritual community, and beyond. We become individuals through the development of personal attachments to, and care for, a place. The result is the growing recognition that we must treat geographical place as a contributing factor to personhood and that human freedom is most meaningful and fulfilling in community.[39] Our values are formed and grounded in the context of a community that is place-bound.

Curry-Roper presents an extended case study with reference to these considerations.[40] In a discussion with a group of farmers in Hull, Iowa, she presented a story of a situation where a farmer was faced with selling his farm due to development pressures. However, he knew that if he did so, the whole community would follow because he was the largest farmer who rented and worked the acreage of others, thus helping to sustain the community. His tremendous turmoil over the decision focuses on the knowledge that, as the largest landowner, he will affect the entire community by his decision. He is strongly embedded in community and place. The Hull group's response to the narrative focused on the community as a whole. Participants spoke of the similar desire of people in Hull to stay in the community. They spoke critically about the heirs of this farmer, who would probably value money over the preservation of the community. Discussants also referred to the respect this farmer surely must have enjoyed in the community for putting the community's needs first. This communal vision of life arose throughout discussions in this community.

The origins of this communal vision pertain to fundamental spiritual commitment. How does this worldview contribute to the physical making of a place? In the Hull case, the Dutch Reformed community has historically utilized farms of smaller size than seven other groups studied in Iowa, including two in the same part of the state. The 1960s and 1970s brought dramatic changes in farm size to the Midwest. A representative Dutch Reformed township near Hull strongly resisted the trend toward extensive expansion of farm holdings. Their largest increases in farm size were in the 1960s—27 percent—only to slow in the 1970s to 10 percent, leaving them with the smallest farms of eight Iowa groups studied. Between 1982 and 1992, Sioux County farm size increases continued at the relatively low rate of about 10 percent. Likewise, Sioux County saw the lowest decreases in farm population of all the study areas during the 1980s (19 percent). The area is known for its intense competition for land and expanding Dutch settlement boundaries, both the result of the desire of many to stay in the community. The physical landscape with its dense settlement pattern is the visible reflection of the underlying worldview that sees life through communal eyes.

Legal Alternatives

The foregoing pages press the case for embeddedness in local place. But we have seen earlier that legal discourse operates myopically with respect to collective entities between individual and state. We have the lone rights bearer and something like the omnipresent state, but anemic corporate bodies lie in between, except for the business corporation. Only corporate bodies, other than the business corporation, can bring balance. What changes would move us in this direction?

Christopher Stone argues for clarification of "nonperson rights," by which he means animal rights, the assignation of rights to environmental interests such as trees, as well as the rights of corporations.[41] Today, the law wrongly treats the corporation as "just another person who happens to be especially large and powerful."[42] Stone suggests legal changes that would limit those entitled to hold corporate office, establish "limited public directors," and require an appropriate information system that would highlight corporate malfeasance.[43] Stone chooses to avoid the constitutional issue of lack of federal chartering of corporations, indicating that such federal oversight would bring minimal gains.[44] The proponents of federal chartering, Ralph Nader, Mark Green, and Joel Seligman, opt for targeting more fundamental matters, as does Lappe.[45]

Important actions have already been initiated.[46] A recent attorney general successfully revoked the charter of a tobacco corporation front group. Several states disallow corporate farming. States and communities are attempting to establish three-strikes laws or ordinances preventing corporations with a history of corporate crime from entering their communities or states. Point Arena, California, has passed a resolution holding that corporations are not a person, and California's Supreme Court held in 1982 that Oakland might use its power of eminent domain to keep the Oakland Raiders from moving to Los Angeles.[47] Corporate rights are also being restricted by shifting the vocabulary of rights, such as the right against self-incrimination, so that they are described as "human rights" rather than personal rights.[48] The same holds for initiatives within the United Nations that are seeking to make transnational corporations more accountable.[49]

Staughton Lynd has traced the logic of a community right to industrial property.[50] The then-mayor of Youngstown asked United States Steel to donate a former mill site to the city, and upon refusal threatened to use eminent domain and verbalized the only thinkable right of community to industrial property. Does not a community have any right to force an emigrating industrial corporation to sell its property to the community rather than dispose of it in a less socially responsible way? The affected corporations responded that it was their legal duty to stockholders to maximize profits. Youngstown activists sued on grounds that U.S. Steel was in breach of promise while employees had lived up to their part of the contract. They also invoked the aforementioned community property right. The judge eventually ruled that no statutory or legal precedent had yet established such a property right. However, eminent domain has been invoked to acquire industrial property. In another example, nine city councils in the region of Pittsburgh took the legal steps necessary for final incorporation of a local authority to acquire and reopen a U.S. Steel facility. The same use of eminent domain has since been successfully utilized by the city of Bedford, Massachusetts.

The noteworthy character of the experiences of Youngstown and Pittsburgh taken together is that they offer community control of corporate malfeasance without recourse to the centralized bureaucratic state. They place an intermediate entity on the table between individuals and the state. Federal investment is involved but eminent domain is the primary instrument used to establish local and public ownership. However, these cases are limited to acquiring operations where owners have failed to use them for the common good. In spite of this limitation, the strategy has shown itself politically desirable and practicable to ordinary "middle Americans."

Workplace democracy, worker ownership, and control of companies have been available and economically successful. Clusters of employees buy out and rehabilitate struggling businesses often enough, just as groups form successful new worker-owner cooperatives.

> This recasting of the rationale for community ownership of industrial property avoids a dichotomous choice between the public world of the state and a nonpublic world based on the exclusive private ownership and management of property. . . . Public ownership can coexist with the virtues of voluntarism, spontaneity, and popular participation usually associated with private ordering.[51]

Related social movements seek to protect the environment. Legal reasoning in domains that are otherwise disparate, such as labor law and environmental law, may forge inclusive concepts and precedents capable of eliciting widespread support. If the problems of community and land have been irretrievably paired, so might the solutions.

Community Rights

We have looked at one kind of alteration in legal thought, that of reining in the business corporation for community and/or environmental interests. What would it look like to take the opposite angle, that of enabling community rights? The notion of group rights can seem strange in today's context but this need not be the case. The business corporation sprang from the same well as the corporate body of the municipality, the church, and the like. Early corporate bodies were accorded group rights to create and operate common domains like canals and tollways. These group rights that have receded in the West stand closer to the thinking and functioning of pre-Westernized peoples than individual rights do. One of the features that earmarks the Western tradition of human rights is the extent that individuals are the objects, the units to which human rights norms are fulfilled to the exclusion of collective rights.[52] For example, the right to education means individual access to public schools, not the right of a group to institutionalize its own education. Even when individual members of a disadvantaged native group procure legal redress on the basis of human rights, they do so mainly as individuals rather than as a group. Thus, "the state would tend not to like group rights standing in the way of the nation-building enterprise, preferring direct lines of command to the social atoms, the individuals."[53]

The 1948 Universal Declaration of Human Rights states in part that rights go to every individual. Such a concept bespeaks the Western ideology that universalizes itself.[54] The individualist "human rights" as normally discussed in the North and exemplified in this document are indeed a universalizing Western construct at variance with more community-based concepts around the planet.[55] The West dominated the conference that initiated the United Nations, and the Universal Declaration was formulated while most countries were still colonies. The document functions to replace traditional concepts of rights that deserve more reflection than they are usually accorded.

Pre-European Africans valued consensus more than their colonizers.[56] Much current African thought then, finds less need than Western thought to protect the individual against the group. In turn, traditional African thought gives precedent to "the reality of the communal world over the reality of individual life histories."[57] "Human" is defined by reference to the environing individual, in contradistinction to Western concepts of the lone individual. The individual sees self as human only through rootedness in an ongoing community. In biology and in language-based thought, the one is constituted out of the many. The lone rights bearer would in such a world be a mere dangler, not fully incorporated into community, and, hence, not fully a person. In this sense, African traditions reach for a maximal designation of the person, rather than the minimal one exemplified by Western philosophy. In this experience, community is more than an additive, aggregated "mere collection of self-interested persons." The African "we" is a fundamentally, thoroughly fused "we."[58] If Africans were the sole authors of the Universal Declaration of Human Rights, they might have ranked the rights of communities above those of individuals.[59] An appreciation and incorporation of both aspects would have reflected the more complex reality of personhood.

At the same time, African legal culture held a different, more context-based notion of norms.[60] Africans focused more on contextual particulars than on abstracted universals. In conflict resolution, conflicts were better handled by the consideration of as much local details as were relevant, rather than by reduction to universal maxims. Other non-Western legal cultures have been more informal and locally based as well.

Native Americans held a similar perspective. Their reference point was not the individual but the whole.[61] While Hobbesian thought requires a leviathan to protect society against brutish self-interest, Native Americans conceived individual self-interest and tribal survival as intertwined and nearly identical. The Western culture of individualist, competitive, self-interested man supplanted cultures with a sense of the person defined in terms of spiritual unity, consensus, cooperation, and self-denial.[62] Creation-based customs worked well enough that written law was not required. Similarly, Indian tribes exemplified unified "nations," rather than "states" based upon centralized bureaucratic authority. Canadian First Nation leaders have testified that Western rights documents such as the Canadian Charter of Rights and Freedoms (which attempts to accord rights to aboriginal peoples) by their worldview and structure serve to unravel the Indian way of life.[63]

Such notions might be relegated to the venerable precolonial past of prelegal nations long since incorporated into modern states with their individualistic legal structures. Have not modern states entirely unraveled such communal spiritual compacts? The Islamic states present an obvious counterexample, and is one often simplified and misunderstood by the universalizing West.[64] Those who think deeply about the rationales for human rights find communalist complications in a number of locales, and not just in Africa or on Native American reservations.[65] To use social science terms, the basic unit of analysis is often the clan or tribe or local community rather than the individual. Western discourse presumes that the communal unit for engaging collective matters is the state.

Recently, in such places as Greece, Spain, and Portugal, human rights have been thought to emanate from the state itself rather than from the individual.[66] European states furnish more collective rights than does the United States. As one travels away from Europe, the metaphysical differences increase. China embodies an example by which a prominent current state still works with some vestiges of what might be called the covenantal alternative of Native American and African precontact peoples. Confucianism addressed a world of cosmic harmony ordered by custom-based rules of behavior. Even after Western contact, such thinking has influenced Chinese law, so that many disputes are accorded the auspices of conciliation in keeping with ethical principles and customs rather than being relegated to the law.[67] The Confucian natural order is one featuring a range of social institutions and relationships between the individual and the state. To be sure, other influences counteracted the Confucian influence on the law, but its role remains evident. Similar customs and institutions mark current Japanese law.

Some of the most interesting exemplifications of group rights come from areas formerly under European colonization, cases that could have treated all citizens as equal individuals, but have proceeded in terms of groups. In New Zealand, Maoris are permitted to register separately on electoral rolls. The country is also divided into general and Maori electoral districts, with Maoris guaranteed 6 seats of the 120. Fijians have three voting rolls, one for indigenous Fijians, one for those descended from India, and one for Europeans and others. Each group is assured a certain proportion in Parliament, much as their colonizers' House of Commons allocates seats on a quota basis to the English, Scots, Welsh, and Irish. The British also reserved approximately 83 percent of the land for Fijians, specifically on behalf of 6,600 communal land-owning units. Such an arrangement could be said to interfere with the rights of individuals, but in this case the preservation of the group's culture takes precedence.

Indigenous Malays are accorded similar group rights in Malaysia. The head of state is assured always to be a Malay, and certain subnational offices and civil service are reserved for them as well. Nicaragua's constitution of the late 1980s furnishes a more recent illustration of group rights ensconced in the legal apparatus. A full section of the constitution pertains to the rights of the Atlantic Coast groups, and establishes a constitutional claim for those peoples' right "to choose their own forms of social organization, and to administer local affairs in conformity with their traditions."[68] Lebanon, for most of its modern history, thrived under a political system that allocated power among various ethnic-religious groups. Only the destabilizing force of Palestinian refugees and Israeli cross-border attacks unraveled this "Switzerland" of the Middle East.

Europe itself does provide instances of formalized group rights in a setting that might be thought closer to home. The Belgian cabinet must be comprised of an equal number of French- and Dutch-speaking ministers, with the possible exception of the prime minister. The ministers are not purported to represent their linguistic communities, but, in effect, each group is able to resist domination by the other. The same principle holds in civil service, above a certain grade. Legislation has also established protections for the different language groups in such a way as to preserve Flemish. The language communities are corporate entities with collective legal rights. Switzerland grants the right of territorial integrity to its linguistic communities, as well as their representation in the Federal Council.

These examples might still be held inapplicable to the U.S. government, except that they mirror processes already formally placed under its auspices. The constitution of American Samoa protects persons of Samoan ancestry against "alienation of their lands and the destruction of the Samoan way of life and language contrary to their best interests."[69] Native Americans and Amish exemplify group rights provisions within the continental United States. They are dealt with not just as individuals but as a group.[70]

From the above discussion, it should be evident that rights need not be limited to the individual. Between the individual and the state there regularly exists the nation, the language group, the ethnic group, and many other corporate entities. The dynamics of collective organization "take on a life of their own. The conception that groups should have only those rights possessed by their constituent members is a fiction."[71]

The notion of group rights is controversial due to concerns about protecting the individual against the tyranny of the majority.[72] Several philosophical and practical issues also arise, but only because their development has been neglected.[73] The time has come to explore such notions because of their deep connection with environmental concerns. Environmental matters pertain to bioregions that do not correspond to political boundaries of the interstate system and such matters within states are not being satisfactorily resolved by those states. As Van Dyke states:

> I assume that groups and communities can exist in the same sense that corporations exist, it being understood that a corporation is an entity that has rights and obligations distinct from those of individual stockholders. The rights of the corporation are of course created by human decision, but they do

not derive from the rights of individuals and cannot be reduced to the rights of individuals. They are original to the corporation, and disappear when the corporations disappear.[74]

As Van Dyke's statement indicates, group rights appear more realistic when compared to the rights of corporations, which have been shown to exert a remarkable legal influence.

We have seen that law's body at present has forgotten its roots in community and responsibility to the whole. But law is beginning to feel a bit less subservient to the corporate form. And the need to live within the limits of land and environment may be the force that is initiating the change.

Science in Thought

In the preceding section, we pointed to a direction that might be taken by people who are concerned about community—addressing theory before practice. Part of the difficulty regarding community on land today pertain to the dominance of a particular type of science, in particular, its preeminent status as a way of knowing and controlling human affairs. In earlier chapters, we pointed to a number of connections between the tradition of Descartes, Hume, and empiricist social science on the one side and environmental and community problems on the other. As an alternative, we spoke to the matter of commitment and the value of local knowledge.

Our position is that nonfoundationalist approaches to knowledge do exist, most notably in postmodernism and in pragmatist philosophy. The two schools of thought mentioned provide an impetus for articulating a more communal understanding of knowledge building. We do not believe that all foundational enterprises are inadmissible nor do we argue that empirical scientific work is by its nature irreparably flawed. Quite the contrary, we find much empirical research to be quite helpful when it comes to generating knowledge about society and nature.

However, a less remote, less disembodied alternative model of knowledge is available. Rather than as a body of content absorbed by its own inner logic, knowledge can be generated more as an outcome of engagement, collectively ascertained. Pragmatist stances toward truth such as ours more readily acknowledge the implications of building on its everyday knowledge. In contrast, corresponding stances act as if nothing is known except that which is accredited by the relevant demarcating community, such as that of science. The empiricist model shows strength in the logical calibration of disembodied ideas. The pragmatist model works with more embodied action. A good pragmatist stance, we would argue, necessarily incorporates something like an interest in accuracy, but within a notably different framework. Richard Rorty would say that no essence of science or scientific procedure demarcates it from other such knowledge structures.[75] Methodological guidelines are worth following, but provide no particular key to a totally authentic knowledge structure.

Would an end to discussion about community and land—generated by compelling empirical work settling all the questions—be desirable? Such a goal of "capturing" the subject matter works hand in glove with that of controlling it. From the time of Bacon onward, many have looked to science for help in improving nature. Such intent meshed well with colonialism and colonizer Enlightenment's elevated understanding of itself. Encountered lands and peoples were recurrently made objects of control rather than coexistence, just as later the various academic disciplines have come to seek control. The more communal, less individualist alternative to the dominant scientific paradigm takes authentic dialogue itself as the goal. As such, the dialogue will not and should not end, and indeed it shows no sign of stopping with the "crucial experiment" or other attempts to put matters beyond discussion.

Empiricist social science's idea of value commitment is a point for departure. A tension exists between that which has been demonstrated to be true beyond doubt and that which is interesting. A parallel tension exists between the former and that which is important, and it carries moral resonance. The more interesting the scholarship, the more it embodies value implications. The great works are regularly expressed in a manner that begins to speak to matters of value commitment in a non-technocratic way.

The most basic commitment identifies the heart of any conceptual perspective. The fundament of what is important and what is good and how knowledge is done—this source animates and orders the rest. Empire-based empiricism would have it that social scientific practitioners approach sensory data open enough so that the data transcends differences in worldview. Fundamental assumptions fall in the face of data, rather than structuring practitioners' assessments of the value of the data. Values govern the doing of the work, but only those values belonging to science. Extrascientific values are set aside or subordinated to the values of scientific study.

Kuhn, Feyerabend, Polanyi, and others since, have shown innumerable examples by which the fundamental assumptions have transcended and shaped practitioners' readings of empirical data. Societal scholarship arises from and exemplifies ultimate commitment.[76] Such ultimate commitment embodies a stance toward some concept of the good. Commitment is constitutive rather than arbitrary and peripheral and from it, worldviews are developed. They only arise within the context of a community or a tradition. These traditions deeply shape which beliefs within a given collectivity are plausible to its members and which are not. "Communities of commitment," as Bellah calls these worldview communities, take on perspectives of their own.[77]

Empiricist scholarship would like to make contributions to the questions of where to go from here, but finds it can only provide information rather than speak directly to the question. Empiricism works to provide the neutral findings with which citizens can make their value decisions. But such projects unwittingly and unacknowledgedly speak with value stands that are taken for granted and thus not perceived as such. Sometimes under the canopy of technical expertise they make value decisions but accord the onus of decisions to the data rather than to the decision-maker. Responsibility is sometimes deflected away from personal choice and toward the facts themselves. "Determinate models of judgments . . . relieve individuals of the responsibility for the judgments they make."[78] We would argue that by dodging or veiling—rather than directly speaking to—the question of where to go from here, empiricists have presumed conventional value judgments as if they were something else:

> The ideology of modern science, along with its undeniable success, carries within it its own form of projection: the projection of disinterest, of autonomy, of alienation . . . the dream of a completely objective science. . . . The objectivist illusion reflects back an image of self as autonomous and objectified: an image of individuals unto themselves, severed from the outside world of other objects and simultaneously from their own subjectivity. It is the investment in impersonality, the claim to have escaped the influence of desires, wishes, and beliefs—perhaps even more than the sense of actual accomplishment—that constitutes the special arrogance, even bravura, of modern man, and at the same time reveals his peculiar subjectivity.[79]

Science in "Place"

Local knowledge exemplifies our more pragmatist stance to science because it is more interested in immediate, concrete applications as opposed to more abstract, universalizing generalities. Somewhat as policy science has been differentiated from disciplinary science, local knowledge is concrete and oriented to practical application. Pragmatist knowledge calls up a wider evidentiary base than empiricist science, and speaks more directly to value questions. In establishing its measures of certitude, local knowledge embodies a distinct rigor and value of its own that should be appreciated in more universalizing quarters.

Local knowledge moves us toward an understanding of ourselves as ecologically embedded. The ethical relationship of humans with nature, Jim Cheney shows, is also best grounded in places where "an understanding of self and community is an understanding of the place in which life is lived out and in which an understanding of place is an understanding of self and community."[80] In contrast:

> The modern specialist and/or industrialist in his modern house can probably have no very clear sense of where he is. . . . Geography is defined for him by his house, his office, his commuting route, and the interiors of shopping centers . . . and places of amusement—which is to say that his geography is artificial; he could be anywhere, and he usually is.[81]

Too often the science specialist parallels other expertise, in that she or he could be anywhere. The unrooted universalizer seeks to control rather than to live within. The Hanford Nuclear Reservation in eastern Washington state is typical of a denuded "earth alienation" (Hannah Arendt's term) scientific practice.

> Nakao [Hajime] said, "Take a good look, everybody, this is atomic culture." In the middle of the beautiful and awesome expanse of the eastern Washington desert was a town that had absolutely no relation to the place on which it had been built. . . . Richland could almost as well have been underground or in outer space as in eastern Washington.[82]

Earth alienation science has chalked up an enormity of productivity toward the end of human control over nature. "Noplaceness threatens to become characteristic of everyplace."[83] While we don't wish to jettison all the accomplishments of a universalistic science, current emphasis on space rather than place, and the pursuit of universalistic knowledge, appears unable to produce a locally meaningful land ethic.

Any reorientation of human relationship to nature will be a response to the ecological experience of environmental degradation in the daily lives of the citizenry, not a kind of abstract knowledge about environmental problems.[84] Precisely because humans are themselves embedded in nature and its process, an experiential basis underlies environmental knowledge and wisdom. Through experiences that lead to knowledge, humans begin to identify with nature, not by seeing all of nature as one's self (universalizing), but by experiencing, in a place, one's self as dependent on and part of nature.

Christopher Lasch has shown the parallel for family relationships.[85] He holds that the capacity for loyalty is stretched too thin when it tries to attach itself to something as universal as the whole human race. Its loyalties must be attached to specific people and places, not abstract ideals. Such universalized ideals rest on the fiction that men and women are all alike and, as a result, concern and loyalty cannot be maintained when differences are discovered. Flesh-and-blood love, on the other hand—the love of particular women and men, not of humanity in general—is based on complementary differences, not on sameness, and can only flourish by embeddedness in a place.

As in the above articulation of Locke, Mill, and others, universality not infrequently shows itself to be a rhetorical move concerned with obliterating difference. Universality elevates itself over and above its other. It speaks of abstract ideals when it would withhold them from those encountered as different. Concrete work at building a human relationship requires a utilization of the full contextual knowledge relevant to each party in the relationship, far more so than a dual commitment to a universal ideal. As we have argued earlier, a healthy communal pluralism invokes a situated management of difference rather than a search for or attribution of similarity.

Keith Basso, in *Wisdom Sits in Places*, reveals the concrete nature of the relationship that can exist between place and ethics. Among the Apache, places and their names remind the people of associated stories, which in turn have morals. Seeing these places daily reminds Apache of the place-names, the stories, and the morals, creating an ethical system that physically surrounds them. The place-names are used in conversations to gently make points of morality. The path to wisdom in the culture is tied to one's ability to use place-names and their associations in making ethical judgments, thus the title, *Wisdom Sits in Places*.[86] The absence of the places would lead to the demise of an ethical system. Perhaps in a similar, but less concrete way, the nature of the physical landscapes of communities becomes part of the ethical system of boundaries. The absence or presence of wild birds tells of obedience or disobedience to the sacred order; the density of the farmsteads tells of commitment to community. Wendell Berry says:

> This generalized sense of worldly whereabouts is a reflection of another kind of bewilderment; this modern person does not know where he is morally either. He assumes . . . that there is nothing that he *can* use that he should not use. His "success" . . . is that he has escaped any order that might imply restraints or impose limits. . . . This mentality has been long in the making, and its rise evidently parallels the exploitation of the New World.[87]

The unrooted modern person feels insufficient connection and moral responsibility. Knowledge tied to local place leads more clearly to an ethic of connection to creation and a responsibility for place and those within the collective web. The rationalized world focuses on what will work to the exclusion of value issues. We put forth for examination the thesis that a turn in the direction of local knowledge will function to bring environmental ethics more into play, as it will for moral questions overall.

Local knowledge requires forms of organizing or practice that provide space for new kinds of ideas and relationships.[88] For example, quite complex systems of local grazing systems demand skill, flexibility, ingenuity, and profound attention to detail. The process of observation and interpretation of the dynamic system required to make decisions about when pastures need to be grazed, leads to improved ways of experiencing the land. Practitioners transcend the conceptualization of the atomized variables and acquire a wisdom that allows them to sense the subtler impacts of the interrelationships of those variables, the weighted average of the forces at work. This wisdom is a crucial component of healthy farming. Such intimate knowledge leads some grass farmers to question the need for chemicals and to break out of corporate paradigms in modern commercial farming.

Local knowledge requires farmers to think for themselves, though along with others who are doing the same. Together, new ways of thinking about farming arise. Local knowledge and the practical become intertwined with the cosmological, with how one sees the world.[89] We are less interested in analytically categorizing areas, showing both influences as either corporate or local, than in understanding the value of the latter in the context of the effect of individualism on the land.

A distinctive conceptualization of human relationships with nature has been made with the development of the concept of community-based agriculture and "foodsheds." Harriet Friedmann has characterized the principal elements of the world food economy as being distance and durability, as opposed to the particularities of time and place.[90] The objective of those involved in the extant globalized food system is to recreate the world into a featureless plain, free of physical or social obstacles, with a free flow of money and agricultural commodities. If the attempt to overcome the distance introduced by the societal transformations of the last few hundred years is the central challenge of our modern, global food system, then greater attention to proximity—that which is relatively near—should be an appropriate response.[91]

What does this attention to place entail? If economic concentration results from the absence of an embeddedness based on proximity, the vision of

202 • CHAPTER 11

community-based agriculture lies in small and mid-sized enterprises—mediating institutions in accord with human scale. Such institutions are far more capable of responding affirmatively to the opportunities and responsibilities of an emergent commensal community. In this vision, agriculture extends community—eating together. A second element of the vision of food-sheds and community-based agriculture is an emphasis on local knowledge that is sensitive to the "expectations of the land" and replaces the universalizing perspectives of agricultural science that treat all places the same.[92]

This vision is founded on respect for the integrity of particular sociogeographic places. In contrast to practices of the transnational corporation, the landscape is treated as a place intricately interwoven with an individual community and with human activity conforming to the natural characteristics of that place. The vision is based on the concept of once again becoming native to a place. The moral economy of the food-shed will not be based on individuals with unrestrained freedom to pursue their own self-interest, but will be shaped and expressed in communities that attempt to build sustainable relationships amongst themselves and with the land.[93] Wise ethical systems are, in their living out, place-based.[94]

In this chapter, we began to go beyond a negative social commentary toward advocacy of positives. We first addressed alternative ways of thinking. We now turn to alternative ways of acting, or a practice that exemplifies our notion of where to go from here.

Notes

1. Vernon Van Dyke, "The Individual, the State, and Ethnic Communities in Political Theory," *World Politics* 29 (1977): 343-69, 343.

2. Vernon Van Dyke, "Justice as Fairness, for Groups?" *American Political Science Review* 69 (1975): 607-14, 614.

3. Douglas Lummis, *Radical Democracy* (Cornell, N.Y.: Cornell University Press, 1996), 140.

4. Frances Moore Lappe and Paul Martin Du Bois, *The Quickening of America* (San Francisco: Jossey Bass, 1994), 287-95.

5. Stuart Fowler, "Communities, Organizations, and People," *Pro Rege* (June 1993): 20-32, 26.

6. Susan Wheelan, *Group Processes: A Developmental Perspective* (Boston: Allyn and Bacon, 1994).

7. Joel F. Handler, *Law and the Search for Community* (Philadelphia: University of Philadelphia Press, 1990), 94-95.

8. Fowler, "Communities, Organizations, and People," 22-24; Herman Dooyeweerd, *A Christian Theory of Social Institutions,* trans. Magnus Verbrugge, ed. John Witte Jr. (La Jolla, Calif.: The Herman Dooyeweerd Foundation, 1986).

9. Bonnie J. Miller-McLemore, *Also a Mother: Work and Family as a Theological Dilemma* (Nashville: Abingdon Press, 1994), 185.

10. Elizabeth H. Wolgast, *Equality and the Rights of Women* (Ithaca, N.Y.: Cornell University Press, 1980), 154.

11. John O'Neill, *The Missing Child in Liberal Theory: Towards a Covenant Theory of Family, Community Welfare, and the Civic State* (Toronto: University of Toronto Press, 1994), 39.

12. Janel Curry-Roper, "Embeddedness of Place: Its Role in the Sustainability of a Rural Farm Community in Iowa," *Space and Culture* 4, no. 5 (2000): 204-22, 206.

13. Robert N. Bellah, "The Church in Tension with a Lockean Culture," *New Oxford Review* 57, no. 10 (1990): 10-16, 11.

14. Lummis, *Radical Democracy*; Ivan Illich, "Silence Is a Commons," *CoEvolution Quarterly* 40 (1983): 5-9.

15. Luc Julliet, Jeffrey Roy, and Francesca Scala, "Sustainable Agriculture and Global Institutions: Emerging Institutions and Mixed Incentives," *Society and Natural Resources* 10, no. 3 (1997): 309-18, 311.

16. Harriet Friedman, "After Midas's Feast: Alternative Food Regimes for the Future," in *Food for the Future,* ed. Patricia Allen (New York: John Wiley, 1993), 213-33, 228.

17. Bennet Harrison, "Industrial Districts: Old Wine in New Bottles?" *Regional Studies* 26 (1992): 469-83, 471.

18. Harrison, "Industrial Districts," 470.

19. Harrison, "Industrial Districts," 470-71.

20. John Fraser Hart, "The Industrialization of Livestock Production in the United States," *Southeastern Geographer* 38, no. 1 (1998): 58-78.

21. Wade H. Andrews, "Social Inventions for Environmental Solutions and Filling Institutional Blanks," *Society and Natural Resources* 10, no. 5 (1997): 501-5, 502.

22. Patricia M. Marchak, "What Happens When Common Property Becomes Uncommon," *BC Studies* 80 (1988-1989): 3-23, 14.

23. Marchak, "What Happens When Common Property Becomes Uncommon," 15.

24. Marchak, "What Happens When Common Property Becomes Uncommon," 18.

25. Anthony Giddens, *The Consequences of Modernity* (Stanford, Calif.: Stanford University Press, 1990), 20-21.

26. Mark Granovetter, "Economic Action and Social Structure: The Problem of Embeddness," *American Journal of Sociology* 91 (1985): 481-510.

27. Granovetter, "Economic Action," 497.

28. Granovetter, "Economic Action," 498.

29. Benjamin Barber, *Strong Democracy: Participatory Politics for a New Age* (Berkeley: University of California Press, 1984), 245-51; Nicholas Blomley, *Law, Space and the Geographies of Power* (New York: Guilford, 1994); Kirkpatrick Sale, *Human Scale* (New York: Putnam, 1980).

30. Harrison, "Industrial Districts," 471.

31. Harrison, "Industrial Districts," 478.

32. Julliet, Roy, and Scala, "Sustainable Agriculture," 310.

33. Julliet, Roy, and Scala, "Sustainable Agriculture," 311.

34. Thomas Lyson and Rick Welsh, "The Production Function, Crop Diversity, and the Debate between Conventional and Sustainable Agriculture, *Rural Sociology* 58, no. 3 (1993): 424-39, 424.

35. Curtis E. Beus and Riley E. Dunlap, "Conventional Versus Alternative Agriculture: The Paradigmatic Roots of the Debate," *Rural Sociology* 55, no. 4 (1990): 590-616.

36. Beus and Dunlap, "Conventional Versus Alternative Agriculture," 590-616.

37. Lyson and Welsh, "The Production Function," 433.

38. Lummis, *Radical Democracy*, 61.

39. James Campbell, "Personhood and the Land," *Agriculture and Human Values* 7, no. 1 (1990): 39-43; J. Peter Cordella, "Reconciliation and the Mutualist Model of Community," in *Criminology As Peacemaking*, ed. Harold E. Pepinsky and Richard Quinney (Bloomington: Indiana University Press, 1991), 30-45; Fowler, "Communities, Organizations, and People," 20-32.

40. Janel M. Curry, "Community Worldview and Rural Systems: A Study of Five Communities in Iowa," *Annals of the Association of American Geographers* 90, no. 4 (2000): 693-712; Janel M. Curry-Roper,"Dutch Reformed Worldview and Agricultural Communities in the Midwest," *The Dutch-American Experience: Essays in Honor of Robert P. Swierenga*, ed. Hans Krabbendam and Larry Wagenaar, VU-Studies in Protestant History 5 (Amsterdam: VU University Press, 2000), 71-89; id., "Embeddedness in Place: Its Role in the Sustainability of a Rural Farm Community in Iowa, *Space and Culture* 4, no. 5 (2000): 204-22; id., "Worldview and Agriculture: A Study of Two Reformed Communities in Iowa," in *Reformed Vitality: Continuity and Change in the Face of Modernity*, ed. Donald Luidens, Corwin Smidt, and Hijme Stoffels (Lanham, Md.: University Press of America, 1998), 17-32; id., "Community-Level Worldviews and the Sustainability of Agriculture," in *Agricultural Restructuring and Sustainability: A Geographical Perspective*, ed. Tim Rickard, Brian Ilbery, and Quentin Chiotti (Wallingford, UK: CAB International, 1997), 101-15.

41. Christopher Stone, *Earth and Other Ethics* (New York: Harper & Row, 1987); id., *Should Trees Have Standing?* (New York: Avon Books, 1975); id., *Stalking the Wild Corporation* (Cambridge, Mass.: Cambridge Policy Studies Institute, 1976).

42. Stone, *Stalking the Wild Corporation*, 87.

43. Stone, *Stalking the Wild Corporation*, 87.

44. Stone, *Stalking the Wild Corporation*, 18.

45. Ralph Nader, Mark Green, and Joel Seligman, *Taming the Giant Corporation* (New York: Norton, 1976); Frances Moore Lappe, *Rediscovering America's Values* (New York: Ballantine, 1989).

46. Russell Mokhiber and Robert Weissman, *Corporate Predators* (Monroe, Maine: Common Courage Press, 1999); "Turning the Tables on Pennsylvania Agri-Corporations," *By What Authority* 3, no. 2 (2001): 5-7.

47. Mokhiber and Weissman, *Corporate Predators* 5-7; "Turning the Tables."

48. Suzanne Corcoran, "Does a Corporation Have a Sex?" in *Sexing the Subject of Law*, eds. Ngaire Naffine and Rosemary J. Owens (London: Sweet and Maxwell, 1997), 215-32.

49. Raymond J. Michalowski and Ronald C. Kramer, "The Space between Laws," in *Deviant Behavior and Human Rights*, ed. John F. Galliher (Englewood Cliffs, N.J.: Prentice Hall, 1991), 256-73.

50. Staughton Lynd, "The Genesis of the Idea of a Community Right to Industrial Property in Youngstown and Pittsburgh, 1977-1987," *Journal of American History* 74 (1987): 926-55; id., "Towards a Not-For-Profit Economy: Public Development Authorities for Acquisition and Use of Industrial Property," *Harvard Civil-Rights Liberties Law Review* 22 (1987): 13-39.

51. Lynd, "The Gensis of the Idea," 958.

52. Johan Galtung, *Human Rights in Another Key* (Cambridge, Mass.: Polity Press, 1994), 16.

53. Galtung, *Human Rights*, 17.

54. Menno Boldt and J. Anthony Long, "Tribal Philosophies and the Canadian Charter of Rights and Freedoms," *Ethnic and Racial Studies* 7, no. 4 (1984): 478-93.

55. Adamantia Pollis and Peter Schwab, "Human Rights: A Western Construct with Limited Applicability," in *Human Rights*, eds Adamantia Pollis and Peter Schwab (New York: Praeger, 1979), 1-18.

56. Rhoda E. Howard, *Human Rights and the Search for Community* (Boulder, Colo.: Westview Press, 1995).

57. Ifeanyi A. Menkiti, "Person and Community in African Traditional Thought," in *African Philosophy*, ed. Richard A. Wright (Lanham, Md: University Press of America, 1984), 171.

58. Menkiti, "Person and Community," 179; Fowler, "Communities, Organizations, and People," 20-32.

59. Koo VanderWal, "Collective Human Rights: A Western View," in *Human Rights in a Pluralist World,* eds. Jan Berting, Peter R. Baehr, J. Herman Burgers, Cees Flinterman, Barbara de Klerk, Rob Kores, Cornelius A. van Minneu, and Koo VanderWal (Westport, Conn.: Meckler, 1990), 83-98.

60. A. St. Hannigan, "The Imposition of Western Law Forms upon Primitive Societies" *Comparative Studies in Society and History* 4 (Nov 1961): 1-9, 1.

61. Menno Boldt and J. Anthony Long, "Tribal Traditions and European-Western Politicial Ideologies: The Dilemma of Canada's Native Indians," *Canadian Journal of Political Science* 27, no. 3 (1984): 537-52; id., "Tribal Philosophies and the Canadian Charter of Rights and Freedoms," *Ethnic and Racial Studies* 7, no. 4 (1984): 478-93.

62. Boldt and Long, "Tribal Philosophies," 480.

63. Boldt and Long, "Tribal Philosophies," 480.

64. Howard, *Human Rights and the Search.*

65. See, for example, Jan Berting, *Human Rights in a Pluralist World* (London: Westport, 1990).

66. Pollis and Schwab, "Human Rights," 1-18.

67. Michael Bogdan, *Comparative Law* (Cambridge, Mass.: Kluwer, 1994), 210-15; Konrad Zweigert and Hein Kotz, *An Introduction to Comparative Law,* vol. 1: *The Framework,* trans. Tony Weir (New York: North-Holland Publishing Company, 1977), 353-63.

68. David M. Speak and G. Lane Van Tassell, "The Notion of Group Rights in the Nicaraguan Constitutions," in *Rights, Justice, and Community,* eds. Creighton Peden and John K. Roth (Lewiston, Maine: Edwin Mellen Press, 1992), 411-23, 421.

69. Vernon Van Dyke, *Human Rights, Ethnicity, and Discrimination* (Westport: Greenwood Press, 1985), 94.

70. Van Dyke, *Human Rights,* 1994.

71. Michael Freeden, *Rights* (Minneapolis: University of Minnesota Press, 1991), 68.

72. Jack Donnelly, "Human Rights and Human Dignity: An Analytic Critique of Non-Western Conceptions of Human Rights," *American Political Science Review* 76 (1982): 303-15; id., *Universal Human Rights in Theory and Practice* (Ithaca, N.Y.: Cornell University Press, 1989).

73. Mary Ann Glendon, *Rights Talk: The Impoverishment of Political Discourse* (New York: Free Press, 1991), 137; Thomas A. Cowan, "Group Interests," in *The Sociology of Law,* ed. William M. Evan (New York: Free Press, 1958), 82-90.

74. Van Dyke, *Human Rights,* 207-8.

75. Richard Rorty, "Method, Social Science, and Social Hope," *Canadian Journal of Philosophy* 11, no. 4 (1981): 569-88.

76. Alan F. Blum, *Theorizing* (London: Hienemann, 1974); Alan F. Blum, "Positive Thinking," *Theory and Society* 1, no. 3 (1974), 245-69.

77. Robert N. Bellah, Richard Madsen, William M. Sullivan, Ann Swidler, and Steven M. Tipton, *Habits of the Heart* (Berkeley: University of California, 1985).

78. Mark E.Warren, "Nonfoundationalism and Democratic Judgement," *Current Perspectives in Social Theory* 14 (1994): 151-82, 164.

79. Evelyn Fox Keller, *Reflections on Gender and Science* (New Haven, Conn.: Yale University Press, 1985), 70.

80. Jim Cheney, "Postmodern Environmental Ethics: Ethics As Bioregional Narrative," *Environmental Ethics* 11, no. 1 (1989): 117-33, 131.

81. Wendell Berry, *The Unsettling of America* (New York: Avon, 1977), 53.

82. Lummis, *Radical Democracy*, 88-90.

83. Lummis, *Radical Democracy*, 90.

84. Raymond Murphy, *Rationality and Nature: A Sociological Inquiry into a Changing Relationship* (Boulder, Colo.: Westview Press, 1994), 244-48.

85. Christopher Lasch, *The True and Only Heaven: Progress and Its Critics* (New York: W.W. Norton and Company, 1991), 36.

86. Keith H. Basso, *Wisdom Sits in Places* (Albuquerque, N.M.: University of New Mexico Press, 1996).

87. Berry, *The Unsettling of America*, 53, emphasis in original.

88. Neva Hassanein and Jack R. Kloppenburg, Jr. "Where the Grass Grows Again: Knowledge Exchange in the Sustainable Agriculture Movement," *Rural Sociology* 60, no. 4 (1995): 721-40, 723-25.

89. Hassanein and Kloppenburg, "Where the Grass Grows," 736.

90. Harriet Friedman, "After Midas' Feast: Alternative Food Regimes for the Future," in *Food for the Future*, ed. Patricia Allen (New York: John Wiley, 1993), 213-33.

91. Martha Crouch, "Eating Our Teachers: Local Food, Local Knowledge," *Raise the Stakes* (Winter 1993), 5-6; Jack Kloppenburg Jr., J. Hendrickson, and G. W. Stevenson, "Coming in to the Foodshed," in *Rooted in the Land: Essays on Community and Place,* eds. W. Vitek and Wes Jackson (New Haven, Conn.: Yale University Press, 1997), 113-23.

92. Kloppenburg, Hendrickson, and Stevenson, "Coming in to the Foodshed."

93. Kloppenburg, Hendrickson, and Stevenson, "Coming in to the Foodshed."

94. Tom Kitwood, "What Does 'Having Values' Mean?" *Journal of Moral Education* 6, no. 2 (1977): 81-89, 85-86.

CHAPTER 12

TOWARD COMMUNITY ON LAND

Monroe would have dismissed such beliefs as superstition, folklore. But Ada, increasingly covetous of Ruby's learning in the ways living things inhabited this particular place, chose to view the signs as metaphoric. They were, as Ada saw them, an expression of stewardship, a means of taking care, a discipline. They provided a ritual of concern for the patterns and tendencies of the material world where it might be seen to intersect with some other world. Ultimately, she decided, the signs were a way of being alert, and under those terms she could honor them.[1]

Charles Frazier, *Cold Mountain: A Novel*

Although responsible use may be defined, advocated, and to some extent required by organizations, it cannot be implemented or enacted by them. . . The use of the world is finally a personal matter. . . .Organizations may promote this sort of forbearance and care, but they cannot provide it.[2]

Wendell Berry

THE NARRATIVE WE HAVE TOLD thus far has at times appeared, rightly so, as many intertwined short stories. Colonization connected with the rise of the business corporation. The corporation's ascendancy paralleled and contributed to the demise of other corporate bodies and related to the development of the Enlightenment view of personhood in the form of the so-called autonomous person. Science built on the reductionism of Enlightenment philosophy and replaced meaningful discourse with supposed rational neutrality. These interrelated stories had their impact on nature. The commons became commodity and was managed by the tools of science from afar. But it is the creation, or land, that offers the way back to a deeper understanding of personhood, of community, and of what it means to live in a place. To face environmental problems is to be forced to look at the rest of the story. Materials regarding community give shape to community on land, and attentiveness to land leads human societies back toward community.

As common lands nearby became enclosed, the Diggers embodied an alternative. As the rising corporate form undercut the economic power of the craft worker, Rochedale Pioneers and Luddites reiterated an alternative. Prairie populists in the 1880s resisted the economic forms that threatened them with cooperative movements that suggested an alternative by which concentrations of power and wealth could be leveled. A clear continuity exists to date, in a myriad of social movements and mediating institutions.

Our reading of the social landscape today beholds a plethora of social groupings in sympathy with both community empowerment and environmental stewardship. One leads inevitably to the other and vice versa. Lappe and Du Bois list many such stories, the accumulation of which led to their work on the democratic self.[3] Harry Boyte provides a full volume of examples of mediating groups that resonate well with the concerns we have outlined.[4] Bill Berkowitz has limned a similar vision of local community empowerment or what might be called embedded social capital, much of which has been enacted in practice.[5] Many of the groups about which these authors write illustrate a growing model of the politics of local place.[6] This model is more about what might be called the radical democracy of local daily life than it is about the national political apparatus. The cooperative movement is locally based and displays serious attempts at democracy and decentralized local self-management. Such groups are distinctly democratic in their functioning in action and not just in rhetoric. Their politics entails bringing citizens into the decision-making process in contradistinction to the experiences of many natural resource policy approaches dominated by state and corporate interests with the aid of science. The deeply democratic aspect of such groups is crucial for ecologically and community-based resource use.[7]

We advocate a resuscitation of community in various ways: (1) return to community control over business corporations; (2) develop and work with legal rights for groups, communities, and bioregions; (3) reinvigorate certain group-based worldviews and increase appreciation for non-Western cultural systems and practices in resource management. A less universalistic, more place-based legal culture is yet another way to constitute reinvigoration of local community. The literature on government regulation of such bodies as the Environmental Protection Agency, for example, furnishes a useful contrast that clarifies the increasing value being attributed to informal justice practices. This literature contrasts two styles: a "command and control" adversarial formal legal style and an often more informal style concerned with conciliation and prevention more than punishment.[8] Liberalism favors the former for its universalized, visible, equitable treatment, but the more flexible informal and conciliatory aspect is always present and is of late being held in much higher accord than it was two generations ago. The latter is seen to work best where there is an ongoing relationship that must be restored when the conflict is settled; the former, where there is no basis for continuing relationship. The latter naturally extends local embeddedness while the former better fits more disconnected, if not globalized, concerns. While the former may be more vulnerable in this context to "agency capture," i.e., corporate control of a regulatory agency, the distinction between the two styles remains useful.

Natural Resource Management

An earlier chapter briefly pointed out that communal property regimes not only have long existed, but continue to exist in contradistinction to the notion of the Tragedy of the Commons. Many academicians and others appear to think that individualist notions of land ownership have supplanted communal ones and that the inexorable direction of history is away from communal property schemes. The reality is far more complicated. Many different kinds of common property regimes have long existed and coexisted.

Private ownership has always existed but many societies have been able to mix private with communal, "allocating distinct use rights to individual owners and defining those rights in ways peculiarly suited to the needs of the community."[9] The variations on individual ownership include land trusts, cooperatives, and condominiums. To show that concrete examples of the more communal type of alternatives do exist, consider the Menominee Tribe in Wisconsin. They practice sustained yield management of their forestland. Economists consider their management inefficient, but efficiency is deliberately sacrificed for other cultural values—the desire to maintain their culture on this particular piece of land, the desire to protect the forest, and the desire to provide jobs for the community.[10] The goal of a self-sustaining economic base is directly tied to their survival as a people—an allowance of true pluralism. The apparent reduction of efficiency in terms of cost-effectiveness has contributed to a social system in which the state plays a less prominent role in overseeing marginal individuals. The limits of mobility and resources force the community into an alternative economic model. The provision of jobs over economic efficiency enables its members to remain in place, benefiting the whole through employment rather than through business net income. The same commitment to a place also forces a different type of relationship with the forest.

One of the basic norms for policy initiatives should be the building up of a plurality of mediating social institutions and communal conflict resolution. If we assume a pluralism of worldviews among groups in our society rather than the reducibility of all problems to the rational, we must also assume the appropriateness of a plurality of approaches to natural resource problems. Support of private property rights can lead to individualism and attendant problems, as in the case of the Conservation Reserve Program described earlier. In this program, individual farmers who gained the rewards were those who had been practicing poor soil conservation by plowing up more marginal lands, thus showing the least social responsibility. But the program need not do so. For example, Alaska attempted to deal with overfishing the commons by implementing a system that awarded a limited number of fishing permits for specific fisheries to individuals, based on a complex and long-negotiated formula that attempted to balance various interests. These permits are freely transferable. Fishermen's bargaining positions and prices have improved, since big processors can no longer refuse to deal with fishermen who demand higher prices. The limited entry protects profit margins by eliminating overcrowding. Moreover, fishermen have been willing to assess themselves collectively for contributions to expand hatcheries in the state.[11]

The sort of pluralism we are sketching here requires a rethinking of the political. It will not do to advocate a community in which everyone agrees and/or perceives the common interest. Nor, in acknowledging the fractured diversity, should we abandon the development of a common morality. These contentions are not contradictory but rather paradoxical in the sense that neither diversity nor common morality would be sacrificed for the other; both can be accommodated. The "moral optic" need not be as fractured as the tradition of the Enlightenment has assumed.

We recommend further the value of a movement beyond the rights of life, liberty, and the pursuit of property. Rights should not be limited to individuals, nor should individual rights be presumed more fundamental than communal ones. Institutions also deserve rights, which the state must protect. John Neville Figgis argued that groups within society, like church, union, and family, had tangible personalities, including wills of their own. From this he concluded that just as individuals were given room for self-development, so also association should be afforded that freedom for the cause of true social liberty.[12] From the individualist framework, "justice" is government protection of individual freedoms and property. Consider an alternative by which "justice" implies nonproperty owners, indeed all living things,[13] as well as a stewardship over the inanimate. Such a concept of justice would accord rights to future generations (e.g., future users of the resources) and indeed past ones (e.g., respecting memorials, burial grounds, and other places held sacred). Rights and responsibilities for property would be accorded to various entities on the basis of justice for all times and for all of life.

Community and Natural Resource Management

What natural resource management regimes would reflect a healthier paradigm? Attempts at community management have usually amounted to mere consultation, which does not always bring the knowledge, interests, and the will of resource users to the fore. Cooperative management, on the other hand, involves the delegation of some authority from the centralized government to local-level institutions, with the state setting the overall framework.[14] One factor that has weakened the ability of local institutions to effectively take advantage of the delegated management is the lack of ability among resource users to speak with one voice. This lack of a single voice can be due to the fragmentation of advisory bodies, especially when regulatory bodies cut across local communities.[15] The result is a lack of representation of community interests. The lack of attention to community configuration in turn undermines any attempt at building local institutional capacities, which results in rent-seeking behavior and interest-group politics.

In addition, McCay and Jentoft point out that what is clearly absent from management models (for fisheries management in their survey) was the involvement of families and communities of people dependent on the resource.[16] By focusing on interest groups as participants in management, interest group self-interest becomes the self-fulfilling prophecy. In contrast, community interests force cooperation across natural constituencies.

The fragmentation of groups via the management system, illustrated with the forest management philosophy, allows the notion that first and foremost the process should be science-based and that this serves the public and user group interests. The public becomes an abstract concept, one more element to add to a technical question, allowing the expert to remain above the fray.[17] Through the process of more informal dispute resolution, a natural resource agency is forced to make clearer distinctions, acknowledging its on-the-ground reality.[18] The absence of such ground-level concepts allows the public and the issues to remain abstract, conceptualized within the universalizing paradigm of science and empiricist reductionism.

Though it might be ideal to match ecosystem boundaries with management systems, this is not always possible. McCay and Jentoft then propose, and we support, using the concept of subsidiarity. This is a normative principle for institutional design proclaiming that decisions affecting people's lives should be made by the lowest capable social organization. The principle has been adopted by the European Union with the Maastricht Treaty that laid out the framework for further European integration. Under the subsidiarity principle, the higher authority bears the burden of proof about the need for centralization. The higher authority holds an obligation to exhaust the possibilities of realizing the principle by strengthening the capacity of the local-level institutions to retain or acquire management responsibilities. Implicit is the belief that the local-level institutions should not be fully controlled by higher authorities, and thus it involves the delegation of authority rather than decentralization.[19]

Local autonomy provides direct feedback on social choices, which leads to effective communications. An understanding of environmental degradation arises out of first-hand experiences of the degradation, thereby stimulating a more adaptive orientation toward nature.[20] The reality of ecological systems is that their long-term stability requires models that integrate nonlinearity, complexity, flexibility, quick feedback, and change.[21] Delegation of authority leads to systems that may be more adaptable and flexible in situations where contingency and change are paramount and learning is critical.[22]

We contend that law must become embedded in communities and so must the economy. Just like the force of the abstract language of law, the language of the economy has taken on an inevitable, abstract quality that gives it power over society as if society must be shaped to its needs.[23] The self-regulating market system has forced land and labor into the mode of commodities, while other social movements have struggled for self-protection from commodification.[24] This need not be so.

Alternatives Arising

In the past ten years, new and creative responses have arisen out of the context of failed environmental and resource management initiatives and growing discontent at the local level. These movements are largely local in character and are built on a renewed sense of what it means to live with others in a particular environmental context. They are not limited to one type of natural setting. They arise out of fishing communities, and those that depend on the grasslands of the west, as well as forest-dependent communities. These movements share common elements with Third World development experiences: (1) community empowerment by governmental agency; (2) an emphasis on local initiative, trust-building, and accountability; (3) encouragement of dialogue amongst those who share a place rather than among interest groups; (4) a commitment to consensus; and (5) attention to real-life settings and visible change rather than to policy that is abstracted out of the local context. These strategies are not limited to those groups that share tribal or religious identity, as our examples will illustrate.

Fisheries

Community management strategies of a variety of types have been initiated in the management of fisheries. Command and control regulatory approaches have not worked. Furthermore, regional fisheries management councils have tended to reflect vested interests and thus emphasize short-term gains over the long-term health of fisheries.[25] Alternative strategies for fisheries management come from around the world. These new management schemes have the goal of the fishery's health through the empowerment of the local community. Davis and Bailey claim that fishing is often treated as a hunting activity in which the knowledge and wiles of the individual fishers are pitched against the sea. In reality, fishing people utilize various local rules and practices that establish claims of access to fishing grounds, ensure equity among rightful participants, govern conduct, and levy sanctions against violators.[26]

Community management strategies have arisen around the globe. In each instance, the government provides legitimacy and accountability, while management moves to a more participatory model. Beginning in the 1960s, the Philippines began the journey in this direction on San Salvador Island. The government began to build institutional capabilities in order to develop marine resource management plans that strengthened local responsibility for the management and income-generating projects. As part of this development, the government established coral reef fish sanctuaries and marine reserves.[27]

The municipal government played a crucial role in the development of community-based management. It passed the necessary enabling legislation, mediated conflicts, and provided funds for the initial patrolling of the reserve. In essence, it provided the political environment for the development of institutional capacity.[28] Law enforcement has grown to be a collective responsibility of the government, fishers' organization, and the village police, which results in village fishers adhering to nondestructive fishing practices and to the overall improvement in the condition of living coral cover.[29]

The characteristics of success seen on San Salvador Island in the Philippines are not limited to the Third World. The Hobbesian worldview of the developed world creates different challenges, however. Ethnographic studies, particularly in Atlantic Canada, show how fishermen, through informal arrangements, have been locally regulating their fishing by controlling access and monitoring each other. In reality, local fisheries do not operate as a Hobbesian anarchy or as a Tragedy of the Commons. Increasing capitalization, however, has tended to undermine such informal norms and has intensified competition among boats and among groups of fishermen.[30] In Norway, the principle that, by law, fishermen have the authority to determine fish prices, is generally accepted today (under the Raw Fish Act of 1938). Even the fish processors' association has given up fighting it. This arrangement is unique and is an example of organizing horizontally to affect fishermen's income distribution and increase their power. The same could be done vertically by establishing producer cooperatives.[31]

Norway has a history of legal empowerment of local management of fisheries. The most important cod fishery, the Lofoten fishery, has been regulated by fishermen of the fishery since the Lofoten Act of the 1890s. Before every season, the fishermen elect their representatives to the committees responsible for updating the regulations and for policing their enforcement. The management is successful because user rights are backed by a government act, the Lofoten Act.[32]

The fishing industry needs collective solutions, yet state involvement has not been a successful example of one. The alternative is a strategy that is built on cooperative management at a decentralized level with the backing of state authority. In the case of both San Salvador Island of the Philippines and the Lofoten fishery of Norway, this cooperative approach encourages a fair distribution of incomes, better coordination among interdependent actors, institutional capacity for regulation, entrepreneurship, and innovation.[33]

Such cooperation leads to less secrecy and more cooperation among fishermen and processors in the planning process, thus preventing excess capacity. This is the alternative to the destabilizing effects of periodic declines and federal or regional government-level decisions on which individuals should be allowed to invest—how much, where, and when.[34] As in the Norwegian and Philippines cases, communities rather than individuals need to be empowered.

The same strategies that show success in Norway and the Philippines can be applied to coastal problems in general. Environment Canada has replaced its basic management model with a more flexible approach in its development of its Atlantic Coastal Action Program (ACAP). The program stresses community involvement in dealing with coastal problems.[35] It funds a coordinator for each of thirteen areas and a local management committee, conceived as a roundtable, is made up of representatives of particular stakeholder groups and makes decisions based on consensus.[36] Community involvement goes beyond participation to what are referred to as community-based initiatives.[37] The role of Environment Canada has changed to allow for local ownership of decision-making and actions. In the case of the ACAP, environmental monitoring activities are often done by unpaid volunteers because government funding is not sufficient.[38] Yet government agencies still need to empower the local community, support their initiatives, and provide some funding.[39] Another important role for government agencies is the provision of the detailed information needed to make decisions. Common characteristics underlie the success of these initiatives. Stakeholders and the government must recognize the existence of the resource problems, and this serves as an impetus for all to enter into joint management arrangements. Local institutional capacity must exist or be built. User rights must be clearly defined and enforcement must be effective through the provision of legal and policy support. The objects of the management scheme must be clear with tangible results. In the end, the combination of these characteristics leads to positive attitudes toward both rules and collective action, rather than their being undermined.[40]

Willapa Bay

Willapa Bay, along Washington's Pacific Coast near the Columbia River's mouth, has become the focus of an experiment in innovative resource management that began in 1992. The Bay's watershed is isolated from the Columbia basin, is home to six major undammed rivers, and is largely made up of privately held tree farms. The watershed has been cutover to such an extent that each square mile averages about five miles of logging roads. In spite of the rich resources of the area, per capita income remains well below the average for Washington State.[41] Within this context, the Willapa Bay Alliance, a loosely connected network of individuals and groups, is attempting to get the community to think of planning in terms of a thousand years, and through this vision focus on the long-term restoration of ecosystems and the building of sustainable economies.[42] The restoration and preservation of the ecosystem is thought to lie in strengthening such economic activities as salmon fishing, oyster growing, cranberry farming, and small-scale logging.[43]

The Alliance wants to bring this vision to reality through the avoidance of lawsuits and confrontation.[44] Alliance founders include the Weyerhaeuser Company, which sees itself in Willapa Bay for the long haul. Since most of the land is in private hands, the Alliance realized from the beginning that it had to succeed within that context. Usually found on the opposite side from lumber companies, environmentalists committed to the Alliance have learned that opposing companies like Weyerhauser rather than working with them does not always lead to productive ends. So, while laws like the Endangered Species Act could be applied here to save the salmon, environmentalists are not using it and are choosing to build consensus instead.[45]

The Willapa Bay Ecosystem project has been a model among attempts at community management centered on the salmon resource. The project was developed on the principles of community-based sustainable development, which suggest that landscape resources should be available for the use and appreciation of all members of the community—including future generations—and that decisions about resource use should include all stakeholders.[46] Ecosystem boundaries were used to define the management unit for the comprehensive plan, and process was considered as important as outcome with consensus and cooperative action as key elements. Adaptive management is also part of the strategy wherein information is gathered throughout the implementation of the plan and the plan is modified as appropriate.[47] The actual plan was developed and implemented by a large policy-level team made up of key parties involved in Willapa fisheries management. Smaller technical teams are selected by the policy team that did data collection, analysis, and interpretation. Multidisciplinary groups of some policy team members and others provide expertise.[48]

The Alliance has attempted to contextualize science. The strategy is to procure as much agreement as possible while avoiding absolutes. Actions are identified on some stretches of some streams, out in front of everybody, so everyone can see the results, and they become part of the community's information.[49] Accepted wisdom is that the history of exploitation has created vested interests and a situation too complicated for scientific consensus. The alternative put forth by the Alliance is that the local committee must gather the best information and then act. The results of that action become in turn the information base for the next action. The commitment is not to some "objective" science but to a pragmatist engagement with a place and with others who depend on and inhabit that place. Such engagement in Willapa Bay requires that loggers, gillnetters and biologists literally wade the same stream together and squeeze the same fish.[50]

The Willapa Bay Alliance includes economic health and sustainability in its vision. Ecotrust, an organization out of Portland that has been involved with the Willapa Alliance, has developed a set of conservation-based principles that it uses to screen businesses for participation in its regional economic development program. These principles, contained in the Willapa Business Development Plan, relate to the impact of business activity on ecosystem integrity and diversity, their use of nonrenewable resources, and their contribution to the quality of human life. Businesses whose operations are consistent with the principles will become eligible for special financing, marketing, and other technical assistance.[51]

Shorebank Corporation, a development bank based in Chicago, has teamed up with Ecotrust to promote sustainable development in the Willapa Bay area and eventually other Northwest rural communities. Shorebank helps finance new and existing businesses that meet the sustainable development principles that were tried originally in cooperation with Willapa Alliance. The joint venture will attempt to develop a national market for Willapa products based on their reputation for quality and their contribution to the area's economic and ecological sustainability.[52]

Community Rangeland Initiatives

Federal rangeland management—the great holdout of individualism—has also been forced into new ways of thinking of late. The Federal Land Policy and Management Act (FLPMA) moved in the direction of replacing rancher-only Grazing Advisory Boards of the federal Bureau of Land Management with a more broadly representative institution—the District Advisory Council. This move was meant to make the public land grazing policies more broadly based and involve a broader range of interests. Similarly, Coordinated Resource Management Planning (CRMP) has developed over the last forty years. In northeast California and northwest Nevada, representatives of agencies, organizations, and associations having a direct interest in land management of the area were included as equal participants to operate the program.[53]

In December 1993, Governor Romer of Colorado brought together diverse groups in an attempt to reach consensus.[54] Modeled after the Colorado initiative, Secretary of Interior Bruce Babbitt verbalized a commitment to new regulations that ensured this type of balanced representation of diverse groups and interests.[55] His vision utilized broadly based councils that would operate by consensus to the maximum extent feasible with the authority to be more than mere advice providers.[56]

Steens Mountain in eastern Oregon is an example of this change in a conceptual framework that goes one step beyond broadly based councils. Many environmentalists and recreationalists would like to develop a national park here, requiring the thirty-five ranchers who own land within the area and hold federal grazing leases to be bought out. Babbitt had a different vision. He wanted to preserve ranching and inholdings while simultaneously improving stewardship and providing recreational opportunities.[57] Babbitt asked the Bureau of Land Management's (BLM) Oregon Resource Advisory Council, a diverse group that represents many interests, to come up with an overall plan that included wilderness protection and grazing management for the Steens National Conservation Area.[58] Babbitt said conflict could be avoided by giving locals a chance to chart the future of the Steens.[59] Giving the locals a chance also affirms the work of some ranchers who already initiated action to protect streambanks from overgrazing through independent action or through signed conservation agreements with the U.S. Fish and Wildlife Service to protect redband trout.[60]

Government action alone does not capture the fundamental changes taking place in rangeland areas. Outside old committee structures, an entirely new form of rangeland policy making is taking root—groups of ranchers, environmentalists, and interested citizens meeting over coffee and kitchen tables to reach some consensus and develop mutual confidence[61]—reinventing the idea of local participation to fit the new realities of the American West.[62] The Trout Creek Mountains of southeast Oregon are home to one of these groups, the Trout Creek Mountain Working Group. In spite of federally protected species on the area's public grazing allotments, sensitive riparian zones, and numerous federal wilderness study areas, ranchers on Trout Creek Mountain have negotiated some of the most secure grazing rights in the West. They have done it by joining with government and conservationists to develop new grazing methods that maintain grazing while simultaneously preserving a healthy habitat for fish and wildlife.[63]

By the late 1980s, the Trout Creek Mountain was in poor condition and the trout in the stream were in danger of extinction. The reality was that if things did not change, grazing would soon not be taking place on the mountain. Into this crisis situation came Doc and Connie Hatfield, innovative ranchers from an adjacent area, along with a BLM riparian specialist. The working group arose out of a meeting of locals with Hatfield and the BLM, with the breakthrough being a role-playing exercise that forced everyone to articulate the opposing side's viewpoint.[64]

The goal of the working group is to see improvements in land health. The BLM is invited to attend their meetings, not the other way around, and consensus is the rule. Where the BLM sees consensus at work, it responds positively. So when the working group developed a long-term grazing strategy, the BLM shaped it into a long-term grazing plan.[65] The strategy is similar to the Willapa Bay experiment in that consensus is agreeing not to agree on many things but agreeing to work on those things you can agree upon. The successes are visible signs of a direction and provide local knowledge for future action.

The characteristics of the successful grassroots management initiatives are similar. Krueger has summed them up in his description of a similar group, the Oregon Watershed Improvement Coalition (OWIC), established in 1986 and consisting of three industry and six environmental groups. He says that we must start with the belief that resources are generally abundant and that with proper management, enough exists to meet everyone's needs. This requires that we think of resources not as something that can be measured and bounded, but as a rich environmental context that is in relation with the particular group of people who inhabit that place. Thus, if we focus on meeting the needs of the land, we will meet the needs of resource users as a natural outcome of a healthy functioning ecosystem. Principles of operation to arise from this perspective are: (1) to focus on the potential of the watershed; (2) to work toward common goals and common understanding; (3) to set aside areas of difference while working on areas where common solutions seem probable; (4) to be sensitive to personalities; (5) to recognize that resource damage was and is not intentional; (6) to reach consensus; (7) to spend substantial time on site; and (8) to focus on specific, constructive programs that work, not on general environmental problems that need to be solved.[66] As with Willapa Bay and Trout Creek Mountain, OWIC meetings include significant time in the field, which provides the basis for understanding. Trust and respect within the membership, arising out of the overall principles of operation, is the major bedrock on which change is built.[67]

Forestry

As we saw in earlier discussions, institutional structures of rights and policy create the framework within which community resource management develops, is maintained, or is frustrated. Liz Wily has illustrated this in a study of forestry in Duru-Haitemba, Tanzania. At one point in time, the state eliminated the local sense of proprietorship over forests by creating government forests.[68] The government did try to involve the community in management decisions by trying to assess local needs in order to permit local users some share of the forest products. However, government-community roles were clearly defined as that of provider-receiver, resulting in ever-increasing demands upon the government for a bigger and bigger share of forest products.[69] This system added costs to issue permits and to regulate, supervise, and protect the forest.[70] With increasing costs, the state finally agreed to let the forest-adjacent communities try to manage the forests with the only condition being success, which would result in secure community tenure in the forest.[71] Within a year, the community of Duru-Haitemba had obtained such tenure.[72] The community banned damaging activities, including those they insisted were essential when the forest was under government control. The nuanced range of regulations increased along with heavy fines. The basis for these aggressive protective measures was that the state could no longer be blamed if the forest disappeared.[73]

Similar attempts to build local accountability have grown within the institutional contexts of both the United States and Canada. Within the United States, the Northwest has seen a growing number of initiatives aimed at reconciling the goals of economic vitality and environmental stewardship in rural forest-dependent communities. Rural community leaders consider environmental stewardship to be an important part of community sustainability. Increasingly environmental organizations recognize that they can only achieve their goals by working cooperatively with affected communities and landowners.[74] Similar to the community management arising among fishery, range, and urban areas discussed in the previous chapter, these communities use the tool of nonadversarial, facilitated dialogue aimed at integrating economic, community, and environmental goals. They seek to further build trust through broadening the range of participants and keeping the full complexity of the issues clearly on the table.[75] In many cases, the government apparatus must be circumvented in order to bring the process into being.

For example, within the area of the Bob Marshall Wilderness in northwest Montana, the Swan Valley Citizens' Ad Hoc Committee formed in the early 1990s. Established as a creative response to a series of confrontational community meetings, the committee's work focuses on what can be agreed upon. Information is gathered and work proceeds toward common definitions of the problem. Collaborative decision making is the basis for actions with the goal of achieving consensus without sacrificing individual principles.[76] An industry-wide effort illustrates another type of cooperative action. WoodNet, a wood products network, based in Port Angeles, Washington, was founded in 1991. Members bid jointly on contracts no single firm could handle and share the costs of participating in trade shows. The network also encourages the increased use of "waste" wood.[77]

These two examples point out that what has been is not what must be. Policymakers can encourage existing community-based initiatives and assist in the development of these new institutions. Management structures need to address the mismatch that can exist between natural resource ownership and management patterns and the needs of a rural community. Far-off agencies or corporations need not make resource management decisions and resources need not be exported with little value added.[78]

Effective bottom-up management must include meaningful involvement. As has been seen in U.S. forest policy history, public involvement has meant the "synthesized, coded, counted, considered too late, and taken out of context comments that have had little impact on decision-making."[79] What do community-based approaches call for? They call for knowledge that comes from being "of" a place and involves a variety of perspectives, just as a community is made up of a variety of interests. The approach calls for the inclusion of local science knowledge with that of outside experts and an ongoing dialogue with agency resource managers.[80] In this context, ecosystem and community values are no longer undervalued. For example, of all the economic benefits of the Sierra Nevada ecosystem, more than half relate to water and nearly all are captured by downstream users for irrigation, municipal water, and hydropower. None of the value of these benefits goes back to the Sierras to restore ecosystems or support rural communities. If local knowledge and community empowerment were part of the management system, this might not be the case.[81]

Trust is achieved through verification and verification is achieved through monitoring. Monitoring is one of the great unfunded mandates within the United States. Yet to learn from our successes and failures there must be monitoring of ecological, biological, social, and economic conditions. Such monitoring is embedded in local community initiatives because it is essential for building trust, for discussion, and for knowing if actions have led to desired objectives.[82] All-party monitoring shields an ecosystem from any single interest while recognizing the legitimacy of local, national, even international interests. This involves various parties with different backgrounds and different interests who share in the responsibility for monitoring and assessing what they deem vital.[83] Collaboration is a process, not an outcome, just as monitoring is a continuous process. Restoration helps reunite communities and reconnect people to the health of the land that sustains them.[84]

The Quincy Library Group

Within the United States, a community-based forestry movement is growing. Members of this movement are attempting to reclaim their communities and through that process, redefine their relationships with each other, with the trees they depend upon, with the streams that flow through the forests, and with the government agencies that manage the forests.[85] The goal of community-based forestry is to provide jobs while preserving the long-term health of the forest. As with many of the other community-management initiatives, the process involves working closely with neighbors, often overcoming years of hostilities to cultivate trust based on a shared commitment to their communities. Lessons have had to be taken from the experiences of the developing world.[86]

The community-based forestry movement has arisen out of the need to address the effects of national forest policy of the past few decades on the economic, environmental, and social health of rural resource-dependent communities. The 1990 decision to protect the habitat of the Northern Spotted Owl, compounded with automation and resulting mill closures and unemployment, have stressed the social fabric of many communities to their limits. Out of these increasing economic problems and polarization at the local level, grassroots movements began to build new commitments around the land and their communities. The first task has been to rebuild trust that had been shattered by the national polarity over forest management.[87]

The best known of community-based forestry groups is the Quincy Library Group of Quincy, California. The conflicts of the 1980s over jobs versus trees had led to an atmosphere of total hostility, polarizing the population.[88] Bill Coates, local business owner and member of the county board of supervisors concluded that the social cost was too great for the status quo to continue: "It was killing the town, this choosing up sides. It's one thing to attack your opponents on a national level. You don't have to deal with them in the social sphere. In a small town, you meet the people on the other side every day. You run into them at the shopping center, or the Little League games, or at church. Your kids are in school together. They're your neighbors."[89] Coates began to meet with his main opponent, local environmentalist and lawyer, Michael Jackson.[90] They added more people to their meetings over time and eventually settled on the library as a neutral space in which to continue the dialogue; thus giving the group a name. The library setting also forced participants to keep their voices down. The U.S. Forest Service was left out of those first meetings. Later they were invited to attend, but were never given a vote. By August of 1993, they finished a formal three-page Community Stability Proposal. The long-term goal was to restore the forest to its state of one hundred years previous. The proposal set aside one-half million acres that was off limits to logging. Clear-cutting was to be replaced by group selection, with large trees left standing and smaller trees harvested around them. This practice was meant to protect owl habitat. In addition, buffer zones along streams were required, local mills were to be given preference, and total harvest was to be limited. Thirty-six citizens signed the proposal, and four years later no one had broken the promise.[91]

The first test of the local agreement came in 1995. Congress, not recognizing the validity of a local agreement over national forests, passed the Salvage Rider, a measure allowing loggers to salvage dead and dying trees in certain national forests. Within the area under the Quincy Library Group agreement, no timber companies submitted bids on lands that had been declared off-limits. The Forest Service asked for bids a second time, even inviting loggers from outside the area. Still no bids came in. Eventually, the Forest Service withdrew the offer after the Quincy Library Group complained to Washington via its congressional representatives.[92]

The Quincy Library Group caught the U.S. Forest Service off guard and thus illuminated the structural problems associated with U.S. federal forest policy. The Forest Service did not have the authority or ability to respond to the Quincy Library Group proposal. It was used to managing the forests to meet federal budgets and timer quotas, whereas the Quincy Library Group's plan organized management by watershed,[93] with all experimental work closely monitored as a basis for future management decisions. Instead of simultaneous planning on as many as six different timber sales scattered all over the forest, the Quincy Library Group's plan concentrates on a single watershed at a time.[94] It required a more grounded science and one based on local knowledge of the circumstances of the local ecology. The Forest Service officials also did not know how to respond to a coalition of traditional enemies who were now supporting a single concept.[95] Interest group politics had been the main force in the past. In October of 1998, Congress passed the Quincy Library Group plan as a five-year, $12-million, locally drafted pilot project for three national forests around Quincy, allowing limited logging while protecting many envi-ronmentally sensitive areas.[96] The Forest Service had to be circumvented to implement the plan and national environmental groups did not like the precedent set by this circumvention.[97] National environmental groups regard community forestry with suspicion because of timber corporations' involvement and the fear that local initiatives on national forests will exclude nonlocal residents from decision making.[98] The Quincy Library Group is now concentrating on monitoring the program. Trust among the group is backed by verification.[99]

The full impact of the Quincy Library Group has yet to be seen. It remains uncertain whether the societal paradigm and its resulting natural resource policy regime in the United States can adjust to these new initiatives and ways of seeing the world. The Forest Service remains a huge stumbling block to groups like the Quincy Library Group. If the Forest Service continues to be centralized and unresponsive to local needs, the agency will not be able to manage the forest on a watershed-by-watershed basis.[100] If the structure of federal policy and the societal emphasis on individualistic concepts of society continue, the Forest Service will continue to find it difficult to break out of its paradigm. A consortium of ten local groups, called the Lead Partnership Group, has formed to model the alternative. They work at helping groups resolve conflict by pioneering procedures that have helped break down roadblocks within other collaborative groups and between communities and federal land management agencies, particularly the U.S. Forest Service. The focus of the Lead Partnership Group is all-party monitoring, assessing the condition of a watershed by drawing on the information and expertise of everyone—individual or organization, local or not. Partnership members are developing other on-the-ground strategies to help agencies, industry, and community stewards understand the challenges.[101] As a Quincy environmental attorney stated: "Once we assume responsibility for the national forests in our own backyards, neither they nor we will ever be the same."[102] No one involved expects the road to be easy.[103]

Where Is This All Leading?

In many of the U.S. cases, it is the Endangered Species Act that has created the crisis that moves communities to action. This has forced us to think about living within limits, forcing us back to issues of community and stewardship. This in turn forces us to look once again at the complexity of nature and resources. Relationship to nature is intertwined with human society. While we thought we had overcome the limitations of nature by bounding its resources via private property, we thought we could ignore the nurturance of the human community as well. But as soon as the limits were reached, we were forced into different relationships with each other and with nature, and were forced to ask deeper questions on issues of how we want to live and what we truly value. Environmental rights or restrictions then became intertwined with a renewal of our relationship with each other and with nature. Recently, a Montana constitutional duty "to maintain and improve a clean and healthful environment" was tested and upheld, putting such a duty on par with other rights.[104]

If we did start to work within the limits of nature, recognizing ecological health as a precondition for public and market relations, how would we construct human space? Recent developments in San Diego and Seattle, both influenced by the potential restrictions imposed by the Endangered Species Act, illustrate possible directions.

The Endangered Species Act was passed in 1973. Authorization expired at the end of fiscal year 1992, but it has limped along since then without full authorization. Courts have moved in the direction of affirming that government agencies can restrict activities on private property in order to prevent harm to an endangered species, including protecting its habitat.[105] In spite of the lack of full reauthorization, there is a growing perception that it makes more sense to think of species as parts of ecosystems rather than as isolated entities. Large-scale habitat conservation plans currently being developed and executed in many parts of the country seek to accommodate both conservation and development interests on private land despite the fact that the current law has no real guidelines for how to design and assess such plans—multispecies proposals.[106] The reduction in focusing on one species is being replaced with multispecies proposals that go around the law, but which are based on larger visions of building cities that incorporate habitat, greenspace, and wildlife corridors into their plans.

The premier example of an attempt to implement such a plan on a large scale is San Diego's Multiple Species Conservation Plan (MSCP). The San Diego City Council unanimously voted for the plan in March of 1997 to make a 172,000-acre preserve amid urban sprawl that would concentrate on saving the best habitats for eighty-five covered species. Present city lands would make up 29 percent of the preserve. Additional lands would come from developers and landowners through exchange for development rights elsewhere. Over thirty years, 27,000 acres will be purchased, with federal and state governments paying for half of these acres. In exchange, the development permit process is streamlined and the entire framework could aid in the avoidance of a crisis-to-crisis approach.[107] By August 1997, 62,940 acres of unincorporated areas were acquired or designated for acquisition, and developers were making exchanges. In October of 1997, the San Diego County Board of Supervisors passed the plan, and in 1998, the city of Chula Vista followed suit. Santee is the last government unit needed to make the plan complete.[108]

This is the first such plan in the nation and may allow builders to start building again. If totally implemented, the land values would continue to rise, not only because of the lack of land on which to build, but also because of the amenities of the preserve.[109] The result could be a better place to live.

In March of 1999, federal officials listed several species of Northwest U.S. salmon under the Endangered Species Act (ESA). The Puget Sound chinook were the first ESA listing focused on an urban area.[110] The listings are different from others in the Northwest because of their being closer to the home of most of the population. Past environmental battles were in resource-dependent communities where urban conservationists could support and encourage environmental standards from afar.[111] The salmon is the symbol for the region's valuation of clean water and proximity to the great outdoors.[112] Because saving the salmon is linked to maintaining the values of the region, the ESA listing has not created the same fierce opposition that others have. The threatened salmon are interpreted as sending messages about water quality, the effectiveness of environmental laws, and the effectiveness of regional land-use planning. Saving the salmon of Puget Sound is connected to creating healthy places for humans as well.[113] The constraints resulting from this listing force closer analysis of lifestyle choices, the problems of urban sprawl and design, and the pricing of energy and water-related resources. But the goal is to make sure that the chinook life-cycle is woven into land-use planning decisions and decisions on stream-flow allocation, effectively leading to the conservation of multiple species.[114]

The overall rethinking of how we live, based on the signals sent by endangered species, has been formulated as opportunity. Community leaders are starting to see a match between open space and endangered species protection. Rather than site-by-site conflicts, people are beginning to see the connections among the health of their communities and lives and those of nature.[115] This creativity arises from the local level, continues to be built on attempts to make decisions by consensus, and includes taking responsibility for what is at hand.

Community activist Maria Mondragon-Valdez has captured many of the examples described here. She stated that environmental management problems and their relationship to local communities are "symptomatic of a system where land is an expendable commodity. When resources and land are not tied to survival and have no historical bond, they are easily exploited and traded in a market that places little value on the rights of those who depend on the surrounding habitat for existence." To learn to live with the land again, to relearn lost skills, requires time, planning, and education.[116]

Relearning communitarian skills provides for the possibility of social change. Merry, in her article on legal pluralism, argued that alternative institutions, like those associated with these new movements that work toward consensus, community responsibility, and a contextualized science, interact with status quo structures in a dialectical way such that both the alternative system and the status quo order are vulnerable to incremental reformulations.[117] In this way, communitarian groups are likely to interject communitarian elements into society as long as they are not totally marginal or separated from that society. The impacts of communitarian organizations may be greater than both marginal collectives and individualistic interest groups.[118] The great amount of associational involvement done by individuals, even those with strong civic values, may be less likely to create social change and revitalize society and instead reinforce status quo perspectives. Thus individualistic, or interest group activity, by itself, whether local or national, does not lead us toward healthful social change. "Communities of commitment," with their respective societal visions out of which broad-based consensus, accountability, and trust arise, should be the place where we begin the search for answers on how to construct a healthy society that lives in the context of nature.

We argue that while cases can be found of environmental degradation of commons, many cases exist that demonstrate the opposite conclusion.[119] The commons need not be individualized, nor even given over to the centralized state. The state itself, by its distending of human scale, can contribute to degradation tragedies.[120] Some who doubt the viability of the commons may be confusing communal property with open access, when it is the legally backed ability of communities to impose restrictions that help underwrite the viability of the commons that function today. Open access can result in environmental degradation, but many of these cases were ones of colonial imposition of open access that destroyed the existing communal land-tenure systems. Communal property more often than not entails the exclusion of noncommunity members. Exclusion is not the only tool in use for such cases. Abundant evidence exists, contrary to Hardin, on the ability of community groups to design, use, and adapt ingenious mechanisms to allocate use rights among members.[121] Local communities are quite capable of maintaining the commons—from everything from our forests to our soils to our children—without recourse to *homo economicus* exploitation.

Notes

1. Charles Frazier, *Cold Mountain: A Novel* (New York: Vintage Books, 1997), 134.

2. Wendell Berry, *The Unsettling of America* (New York: Avon, 1977), 26.

3. Frances Moore Lappe and Paul Martin Du Bois, *The Quickening of America* (San Francisco: Jossey Bas, 1994).

4. Harry C. Boyte, *The Backyard Revolution* (Philadelphia: Temple, 1980).

5. Bill Berkowitz, *Community Dreams* (San Luis Obispo, Calif.: Impact Publishers, 1984).

6. Karl Hess, "The Politics of Place," *CoEvolution Quarterly* 30 (Summer 1981): 4-16.

7. William A. Shutkin, *The Land That Could Be* (Cambridge: MIT, 2000); Scott Kuhn, "Expanding Public Participation Is Essential to Environmental Justice and the Democratic Decision Making Process," *Ecology Law Quarterly* 25, no. 4 (1999): 647-58.

8. Joel F. Handler, *Law and the Search for Community* (Philadelphia: University of Pennsylvania Press, 1990), 40.

9. Eric J. Freyfogle, "Ethics, Community, and Private Land," *Ecology Law Quarterly* 23, no. 4 (1996): 631-61, 635.

10. Duncan A. Harkin, "The Significance of the Menominee Experience in the Forest History of the Great Lakes Region," in *The Great Lakes Forest: An Environmental and Social History*, ed. Susan L. Flader (Minneapolis: University of Minnesota Press, 1983), 96-112, 110.

11. Robert Repetto, *World Enough and Time: Successful Strategies for Resource Management* (New Haven, Conn.: Yale University Press, 1986), 28-29.

12. Rockne McCarthy, "Liberal Democracy and the Rights of Institution," *Pro Rege* 8, no. 4 (1980): 4-11, 9.

13. For example, Christopher Stone, *Should Trees Have Standing?* (Los Altos, Calif.: Wm. Kaufman, 1999).

14. Bonnie J. McCay and Svein Jentoft, "From the Bottom Up: Participatory Issues in Fisheries Management," *Society and Natural Resources* 9 (1996): 237-250, 239.

15. McCay and Jentoft, "From the Bottom Up," 241.

16. McCay and Jentoft, "From the Bottom Up," 242.

17. McCay and Jentoft, "From the Bottom Up," 243.

18. Nancy J. Manring, "Alternative Dispute Resolution and Organizational Incentives in the U.S. Forest Service," *Society and Natural Resources* 11 (1998): 67-80, 75.

19. McCay and Jentoft, "From the Bottom Up," 244.

20. Raymond Murphy, *Rationality and Nature: A Sociological Inquiry into a Changing Relationship* (Boulder, Colo.: Westview Press, 1994), 244, 248.

21. James W. Crossley, "Managing Ecosystems for Integrity: Theoretical Considerations for Resource and Envronmental Managers," *Society and Natural Resources* 9 (1996): 465-81, 465.

22. McCay and Jentoft, "From the Bottom Up," 247.

23. Harriet Friedman, "After Midas's Feast: Alternative Food Regimes for the Future," in *Food for the Future*, ed. Patricia Allen (New York: John Wiley and Sons, 1993), 213-33, 217.

24. Friedman, "After Midas's Feast," 218.

25. "Rights-Based Fishing: Transition to a New Industry," *Resources for the Future* no. 124 (Summer 1996): 14-17.

26. Anthony Davis and Conner Bailey, "Common in Custom, Uncommon in Advantage: Common Property, Local Elites, and Alternative Approaches to Fisheries Management," *Society and Natural Resources* 9 (1996): 2501-265, 2255.

27. Brenda M. Katon, Robert S. Pomeroy, Len R. Garces, and Albert M. Salamanca, "Fisheries Management of San Salvador Island, Philippines: A Shared Responsibility," *Society and Natural Resources* 12 (1999): 777-95, 782.

28. Katon et al., "Fisheries Management," 783.

29. Katon et al., "Fisheries Management, 784-85.

30. Svein Jentoft, "Models of Fishery Development: The Cooperative Approach," *Marine Policy* 9 (1985): 322-31, 327-28.

31. Jentoft, "Models of Fishery Development," 324.

32. Jentoft, "Models of Fishery Development," 328.

33. Jentoft, "Models of Fishery Development," 323.

34. Jentoft, "Models of Fishery Development," 328.

35. G. M. Robinson, "Theory and Practice in Community-Based Environmental Management in Atlantic Canada," (Paper presented at the International Rural Geography Symposium, St. Mary's University, Halifax, Nova Scotia, 1999), 1.

36. Robinson, "Theory and Practice in Community-Based Environmental Management," 2.

37. Robinson, "Theory and Practice in Community-Based Environmental Management," 3.

38. Robinson, "Theory and Practice in Community-Based Environmental Management," 3.

39. Robinson, "Theory and Practice in Community-Based Environmental Management," 5.

40. Katon, Pomeroy, Garces, and Salamanca, "Fisheries Management of San Salvador," 792-93.

41. Richard Manning, "Working the Watershed," *High Country News* 29, no. 5 (March 1997): 1, 8-12, 8.

42. Manning, "Working the Watershed," 1.

43. Manning, "Working the Watershed," 8.

44. Manning, "Working the Watershed," 1.

45. Manning, "Working the Watershed," 9.

46. Rachel A. Nugent, Katharine F. Wellman, and Allen Lebovitz, "Developing Sustainable Salmon Management in Willapa Bay, Washington," *Society and Natural Resources* 9 (1996): 317-25, 317.

47. Nugent, et al., "Developing Sustainable Salmon Management," 321.

48. Nugent, et al., "Developing Sustainable Salmon Management," 322.

49. Manning, "Working the Watershed," 12.

50. Manning, "Working the Watershed," 12.

51. Kirk Johnson, *Beyond Polarization: Emerging Strategies for Reconciling Community and the Environment* (University of Washington Graduate School of Public Affairs, Northwest Policy Center, 1993), 20.

52. Johnson, *Beyond Polarization*, 21.

53. Michael M. Borman and Douglas E. Johnson, "Evolution of Grazing and Land Tenure Policies on Public Lands," *Rangelands* 12, no. 4 (1990): 203-6, 205.

54. Bruce Babbitt, "Remarks to the Society of Range Management," *Land and Water Law Review* 29, no. 2 (1994): 399-406, 402.

55. Babbitt, "Remarks to the Society," 403.

56. Babbitt, "Remarks to the Society," 404.

57. Stephen Steubner, "Go Tell It on the Mountain," *High Country News* 31, no. 22 (1999): 1, 8-9, 11-12.

58. Steubner, "Go Tell It on the Mountain," 9.

59. Steubner, "Go Tell It on the Mountain," 12.

60. Steubner, "Go Tell It on the Mountain," 11.

61. Babbitt, "Remarks to the Society," 401.

62. Babbitt, "Remarks to the Society," 402

63. Tom Knudson, "The Ranch Restored: An Overworked Land Comes Back to Life," *High Country News* 31, no. 4 (1999): 13-16, 13.

64. Knudson, "The Ranch Restored," 14.

65. Knudson, "The Ranch Restored," 14-15.

66. William C. Kreuger, "Managing Coalition Groups Effectively," *Journal of Forestry* 92 (1994): 8.

67. William C. Krueger, "Building Consensus for Rangeland Uses," *Rangelands* 14, no. 1 (1992): 38-41, 40.

68. Liz Wily, "Moving Forward in African Community Forestry: Trading Power, Not Use Rights," *Society and Natural Resources* 12 (1999): 49-61, 54.

69. Wily, "Moving Forward," 54.

70. Wily, "Moving Forward," 54.

71. Wily, "Moving Forward," 55.

72. Wily, "Moving Forward," 55.

73. Wily, "Moving Forward," 56.

74. Kirk Johnson, "Reconciling Rural Communities and Resource Conservation," *Environment* 35, no. 9 (1993): 16-33, 18.

75. Johnson, "Reconciling Rural Communities," 19.

76. Johnson, "Reconciling Rural Communities," 20.

77. Johnson, "Reconciling Rural Communities," 28.

78. Johnson, "Reconciling Rural Communities," 31.

79. Gerry Gray and Jonathan Kusel, "Changing the Rules," *American Forests* 103, no. 4 (1998): 27-30, 28.

80. Gray and Kusel, "Changing the Rules," 28.

81. Gray and Kusel, "Changing the Rules," 29.

82. Gray and Kusel, "Changing the Rules," 29-30.

83. Gray and Kusel, "Changing the Rules," 30.

84. Michael P. Dombeck, Christopher A. Wood, and Jack E. Williams, "Focus: Restoring Watersheds, Rebuilding Communities," *American Forests* 103, no. 4 (1998): 26.

85. Jane Braxton Little, "The Woods: Reclaiming the Neighborhood," *American Forests* 103, no. 4 (1998): 12-13, 39-41, 12.

86. Little, "The Woods," 13.

87. Little, "The Woods," 13.

88. Edwin Kiester, Jr., "A Town Buries the Axe," *Smithsonian* 30, no. 4 (1999): 70-79, 75.

89. Kiester, "A Town Buries the Axe," 75.

90. Kiester, "A Town Buries the Axe," 75.

91. Kiester, "A Town Buries the Axe," 77.

92. Kiester, "A Town Buries the Axe," 78.

93. Jane Braxton Little, "Ecosystem Management: The Quincy Library Group," *American Forests* 101, nos. 1-2 (1995): 22-24, 56, 24.

94. Little, "Ecosystem Management," 56.

95. Little, "Ecosystem Management," 24.

96. Kiester, "Town Buries the Axe," 72.

97. Kiester, "Town Buries the Axe," 79.

98. Little, "The Woods," 40.

99. Kiester, "Town Buries the Axe," 79.

100. Little, "Ecosystem Management," 56.

101. Little, "The Woods," 40.

102. Little, "Ecosystem Management," 22.

103. Little, "The Woods," 40.

104. Andrea Barnett, "Court Reads the Environment Its Rights," *High Country News* 31, no. 23 (1999): 4.

105. Daniel Sneider, "Species Act Survives Challenge—For Now," *Christian Science Monitor,* 21 February 1997, 3.

106. Amy W. Ando, "Ecosystems, Interest Groups, and the Endangered Species Act," *Resources for the Future* no. 130 (Winter 1998): 7-9.

107. Terry Rogers, "City Affirms Plan to Save Area Wildlife," *San Diego Union-Tribune,* 19 March 1997: A1, A17.

108. Steve La Rue, "Habitat Preservation Plan Taking Shape," *San Diego Union-Tribune,* 2 December 1997: B1, B3.

109. Brian Curry, personal communication with San Diego Land Appraiser, 1998.

110. Ross Anderson, "Salmon Hit Endangered List Today," *The Seattle Times,* 16 March 1999, Local News (http://archives.Seattletimes.com).

111. "Spending, Sacrificing to Save Salmon at Home," *The Seattle Times*, 16 March 1999, Opinions/Editorials (http://archives.Seattletimes.com).

112. Salmon Primer, *The Seattle Times*, 14 March 1999, A13-A16.

113. "Spending," *The Seattle Times*.

114. Sarah DeWeerdt, "Salmon and Suburbs Struggle over a Washington River," *High Country News* 31, no. 16 (August 1999): 8-9, 9.

115. Michelle Nijhuis, "The Secretary Speaks," *High Country News* 31, no. 16 (August 1999): 9.

116. Maria Mondragon-Valdez, "Let's Not Heap Injustice upon Injustice," *High Country News* 26, no. 4 (7 March 1994): 14.

117. Sally Engle Merry, "Legal Pluralism," *Law and Society Review* 22, no. 5 (1988): 869-96, 884.

118. Merry, "Legal Pluralism," 884.

119. Bonnie J. McCay and James M. Acheson, eds. *The Question of the Commons* (Tucson: University of Arizona Press, 1987).

120. Bonnie J. McCay and James M. Acheson, "Human Ecology of the Commons," in *The Question of the Commons*, eds. Bonnie J. McCay and James M. Acheson (Tucson: University of Arizona Press, 1987), 1-34.

121. David Feeny, Fikret Berkes, Bonnie J. McCay, and James M. Acheson, "The Tragedy of the Commons: Twenty-two Years Later," in *Green Planet Blues: Environmental Politics from Stockholm to Rio*, eds. Ken Conca, Michael Alberty and Geoffrey D. Dableko (Boulder, Colo.: Westview, 1995), 53-62; Fikret Berkes and David Feeny, "Paradigms Lost: Changing Views on the Use of Common Property Resources," *Alternatives* 17, no. 2 (1990): 48-55; Daniel W. Bromley, ed. *Making the Commons Work* (San Francisco: Institute for Contemporary Studies, 1992); National Academy of Science, Panel on Common Property Resource Management, *Proceedings of the Conference on Common Property Resource Management* (Washington, D.C.: National Academy Press, 1986).

CONCLUSION:
THE ROAD TO A PLACE

There is a day
When the road neither
Comes nor goes, and the way
Is not a way but a place.[1]

Wendell Berry

IN THIS BOOK we have traced the rise of our society's individualistic imagination, the corollary rise of the corporation, and their combined affect on the land. Predominant natural resource policies of the day reflect the individualism of legal discourse and of the culture as a whole, with discomfiting consequences. Such policies look alternately to the state or to the individual, as has social and political thought in the West since the time of Hobbes and Locke. The state is treated as the neutral arbiter of self-interested individuals, though most responsive to concentrations of power and wealth. Interactions between citizenry and state take on a managerial, administrative format much closer to "alienated politics" than deep democracy.

There has also been a growth in legal conceptions of society that both emphasize the individual and are responsive to market imperatives. They focus on the individual and blur the commons. The individual's history—raised in a family and in a community—is bracketed or minimized in favor of the relations of social contract. The lofty political social contract and the everyday utilitarian economic one become indistinguishable. Covenantal relationship is forgotten. In tandem, the substantive law shows a theme of preoccupation with the individual's right to exploit the environment. Land is a commodity and individual rights take precedence over public or community rights. The rights of intermediate institutions, those that exist between the individual and the state, have been neglected. Yet this lower level institution is more likely to be committed to particular places and consequently more likely to be committed to the long-term sustenance of the land.

235

With irony, the business corporation, the one intermediate group between individual and state, has accrued legal rights. The corporation began as an entity chartered by the sovereign and granted certain privileges in order to operate for the greater good. Europe's colonial expansion necessitated the raising of capital and resources on an ever increasing scale. The corporation filled the bill. The subsequent destruction of land and community in the colonies was an early harbinger of processes that would eventually develop on the home front. In time, legislatures chartered domestic corporations but assigned severe restrictions to counterbalance the monopolistic privileges. Their charters could be and were revoked, and many limitations were placed on their operations throughout the last half of the eighteenth and first half of the nineteenth centuries. Amid much controversy, corporations were accorded limited liability and other freedoms because they were perceived to be the carrier of progress and the conveyer of wealth for the larger population. Limited liability and other mechanisms gave power to a few investors, minimizing their accountability for their actions to the citizenry.

The corporation came to be understood as a kind of fictional person, similar to an individual who might hire neighbors for employment. The courts feared the collective power of a group of employees acting against an employer. That presumption remained even as corporate persons became much more powerful than their collective employees. The corporation was free to hire and fire at will, but groups of "combinations" or unionizing employees were severely restricted from interfering with the former's right to freely conduct business.

In the latter half of the nineteenth century, communities and state governments in the United States that wished to benefit from canals and railroads, provided corporations with many freedoms and much operating capital. Individual businessmen took the opportunity to consolidate their enterprises into entities that transcended the economic power of the states. But control over railroads meant control over the conditions by which others accessed the market. The scale of economic and governmental operations was greatly enlarged. Populists and others challenged the legal rights of corporations and passed many laws limiting them or favoring their employees. But the Supreme Court and the lower courts regularly found in favor of the corporate person, the preeminence of which was largely settled by the turn of the century. Corporations were able to free themselves from their social obligation to serve the public good.

During this time, land increasingly became a market commodity rather than a sacred ground of community. The federal government quickly moved resources into the hands of individuals with the belief that individual private ownership would bring about its best use. Government natural resource policy encouraged the utilitarian use of resources by individual entrepreneurs through subsidy and through upholding the dominance of the free market. The turn-of-the-century conservation movement encouraged government ownership of such resources as forestlands, but still operated within the dominant paradigm. State ownership was necessary only as a counterbalance to the individual, and the state management of resources emphasized a form of rationalized, scientific management. Community-based conceptions were missing.

Environmental gains have been very mixed. Accepted environmental policies regularly subsume community interests under an abstract calculus of benefits and costs. As part of this calculus, policies use a technocratic model of science that reinforces a Taylorized, alienated politics of centralized state administration. Usually formulated at the national level, such resource management strategies abstract land and community out of its context while further disempowering the local community by targeting individual resource users rather than building up local systems of management. Informal community controls of fisheries are lost. Soil conservation programs benefit individuals who are poor stewards of the land, outside any community's knowledge and understanding of a place.

While we have analyzed the historical evolution of our present dilemma, we have not stopped there. Models exist and are in operation that offer alternative directions to our historic precedent. The commons remains more widespread in human experience than the social contract. Communities continue to respond to the need to preserve land and life. The Willapa Bay community looks for ways to preserve forests, fisheries, and economic health. The Quincy Library Group initiated a process of both community reconciliation and resource planning that by necessity circumvents the U.S. Forest Service's scientific management model. The fishers of the Lofoton Fisheries of Norway continue to manage their resources in a sustainable fashion. Canadian forestry and other examples show that communities can and do act to preserve commons, sometimes with less involvement of the centralized state than might be thought necessary by modern society. All such community-based management initiatives have similar characteristics. The community is given authority and empowered by a governmental agency to implement a management strategy that incorporates local accountability. This local accountability is built on dialogue amongst those who share a place, rather than among interest groups, and on a consensus-based decision-making process. The knowledge on which decisions are made pays attention to real-life settings and visible change rather than being abstracted out of the local context.

These communities work with assumptions that are counter to those of our prevailing societal paradigm. The most fundamental assumption of these community models is that human nature is profoundly relational. The implications of this view of humanity are multifaceted. First, it leads us to conclude that rights should be calibrated more in the direction of group rights. This strategy is the most promising one for placing communities on equal footing with corporations, forcing their accountability to the local community. For much of human history and in much of the world, group rights have held more sway than the notion of the "lone rights bearer." Current governments, in both northern and southern hemispheres continue to accord group rights to various ethnic, religious, and linguistic groups, thereby showing one avenue for the establishment of group rights between individual and state. Membership in political and nonpolitical mediating associations and social movements remains substantial. A solid presence of citizenry looking away from the state and toward the collectivity can be found in the north and even more so in the less-developed regions.

We advocate a resuscitation of community through a variety of means. Basic goals for policy should include both the building up of a plurality of mediating social institutions and the development of communal conflict resolution skills. Rights should not be limited to individuals, nor should individual rights be presumed more fundamental than communal ones. Community and land have suffered from the lack of legal recognition of mediating institutions.

Revitalizing the communal aspect of society would lead to further embedding of law and economy in communities. Local rules and practices governing natural resource management would be recognized. Perhaps we could further develop and apply the concept of subsidiarity. This is a normative principle for institutional design proclaiming that decisions affecting people's lives should be made by the lowest capable social organization. Local resource users would be empowered to ensure equity among rightful participants, govern conduct, and levy sanctions against violators. Higher levels of government would provide legitimacy and accountability, but management would take on a more participatory model. Consensus-based decision making and local ownership of decision making and actions would build trust and force local communities to take responsibility for their actions. The issues of societal conceptions of the person, legal conceptions of the corporation, scientific paradigms, and attentiveness to nature are all interwoven with changing our structure of rights. Thus it is insufficient to focus on group rights as a single causal variable. Taken alone, we acknowledge the limitations of this one strategy for change.

A relational view of humans requires a different view of knowledge. The dominant view of knowledge, born out of the history we have presented, must be changed to incorporate an increased understanding and attentiveness to local complexity and replace the reductionism of universality. Universality inevitably cannot incorporate attachment or the relational aspect of reality into its methods and conceptual framework. Enhancement and perfection of ecological and social "fit" must replace the universalistic goal of translocality of knowledge. Discovery and attention to what is there (husbandry) must take priority over attention to the details of a technical system. Discovery of what is there moves us toward relationships, while universalistic reductionism moves us away from relationships with others whether these others are humans or nature.

Changes in our conception of humans demand new research methodologies and theories. It also requires changes in our natural resource and environmental policies. We have briefly sketched a less universalistic and technocratic alternative understanding of science, one emphasizing local knowledge and value commitment. Science must become contextualized. Loggers, gillnetters, and biologists need to develop common understandings of the workings of a stream by walking the stream together. Local scientific knowledge must be included with that of outside experts and an ongoing dialogue between local communities and agency resource managers must be part of that search for knowledge. Trust must be included, or the relational element of reality is missed. Trust is achieved through meaningful involvement in knowledge production and verification. Verification is achieved through monitoring and local accountability.

Finally, the boundary between morality and politics, born out of Enlightenment notions of personhood, must be breached. If this wall were broken down, questions of community health, ecological fit, generational sustainability and stability, attachment, and engrossment and connection, could become issues of public policy. Once the wall between morality and politics is breached, no longer would government be perceived to be the "neutral" distributor of rights and resources. Government's role would be to promote healthy relations among people and between people and nature. Research and policy could include the question of which natural resource systems and structures promote healthy relations and which do not. Issues of social class could become questions of policy because they involve judgements on whether we are moving toward healthy relations or whether we are moving toward social conflict.

We should not see the government's role as distributor of resources among individuals, but as enabler and enhancer of community relations and environmental well-being. Successful communities use the tool of nonadversarial, facilitated dialogue aimed at integrating economic, community, and environmental goals. They seek to further build trust through broadening the range of participants and keeping the full complexity of the issues clearly on the table. Collaborative decision making is the basis for actions with the goal of achieving consensus without sacrificing individual principles. The process involves working closely with neighbors, often overcoming years of hostilities, to cultivate trust based on a shared commitment to their communities.

The Vision

In the introduction to this book, we spoke of our desire to breach the long-established wall between social science and social advocacy. This is where we end. If one starts with a different view of human nature then the boundary between morality and politics is gone. This in turn breaks the boundary between objective social science and advocacy. We are thus freed to include a sense of the ends of human life, virtue, or a moral sense in our social science.[2] This holistic view of social science recognizes and calls forth human judgement across a wide range of fact and feeling, and allows for situations and conditions in which judgement should be set aside in favor of faith and commitment.[3] The rational-objective mode of thinking can then be put in the service of enhancing relationships and caring for others and nature. But this requires that we turn away from the abstract at the right moments toward and back to the concrete. The rational-objective mode must continually be re-established and redirected from a fresh base of commitment. This is what is involved in living in community on land embedded in social relationships and in relationship with nature.[4]

This alternative way of looking at the world requires us to not pursue answers so much as questions. The process might look like something suggested as an alternative to the interest group politics of discussion on subsidies and policies. When people gather around a difficult question in homes and fellowship halls, a new, powerful sense of community emerges. Employees of corporate farms and farm families, for example, see one another as human beings rather than as representatives of vested interests or the unfortunate victims of market forces. Talk about differences among people from opposing sides subsides as they learn that their children sit in the same classroom and play in the same soccer league.[5] Moral problems are then transformed from intellectual problems to be solved by abstract reasoning to concrete human problems to be lived and to be solved in living.[6] Patricia Hill Collins calls this model of theorizing "visionary pragmatism." Visionary pragmatism emphasizes the necessity of linking relationships and theoretical vision with informed practical struggle, visionary thinking, and pragmatic action.[7] Visionary pragmatism more closely approximates a creative tension symbolized by an ongoing journey. Arriving at some predetermined destination remains less important than struggling for some ethical end.[8] It points to a vision, but doesn't prescribe a fixed end point of universal truth. One never arrives but constantly strives. At the same time, by stressing the pragmatic, it reveals how current actions are part of some larger, more meaningful struggle.[9]

The search for "what should be," the goal of the struggle, builds on the memory of our own best moments of being in community, of being cared for, and of caring for others and nature.[10] Our best picture of ourselves caring and being cared for is both constrained and attainable. It is limited by what we have already done and by what we are capable of, and it does not idealize the impossible so that we may escape into ideal abstraction.[11] In this way, conceptions of human nature generate a picture of the good life and in this way inform morality.[12]

Our best memories of being in community require us to see ecological soundness and social responsibility as positive goals rather than negative constraints. The economic, ecological, and social dimensions of life are part of an inseparable whole.[13] Our policies have not matched the realities of what we experience as wholeness.

People are embedded in connections of care and our self-identity is, in large part, a function of our role in these complex interconnections.[14] Our understanding of our connection to the larger biosphere comes through our relationships to some animals or pieces of nature we do know. We develop a rich, complex, and deep sense of connection and commitment to the rest of the biosphere through this process of knowing.[15] How we frame that relationship, through our relationship to nature, either leads us in the direction of deepening our knowing or in the direction of limiting the scope of our knowing. Likewise, we learn to care for strangers by first developing strong attachments to particular others.[16] Commitment, attachment, "knowing" a place is the route to a moral point of view, not an impediment to rational decision-making. The direction of decision-making is not a fixed end point of universal truth such as "efficiency," but a vision of wholeness.[17]

The problems of community and land are very clearly ones that are played out daily in the lives of all of us. We continually engage in choices that entail responsibilities to land and community. Daily life perpetually presents us with issues of personal praxis. Our culture too often looks to big government, to technocratic science, or to other large-scaled solutions to problems generated by its very way of life. Our culture needs its individual members to examine and alter their own daily lives, in conjunction with others who share their place and communities. We need to follow plant geneticist and visionary Wes Jackson's prescription:

> What if we employed our rivers and creeks in some ritual atonement? Their sediment load is largely the result of agricultural practices based upon arrogance, tied in turn to an economic system based upon arrogance . . . but perhaps we need an annual formal observance in the spring—when the rivers are particularly muddy—a kind of ecological rite of atonement, in which we would "gather at the river." Maybe we should ally ourselves by virtue of a common watershed . . . for a watershed can and often does cut through more than one bioregion. There would be nothing abstract about a common covenant among people of a common watershed.[18]

Notes

1. Wendell Berry, *A Timbered Choir: The Sabbath Poems 1979-1997* (Washington, D.C.: Counterpoint, 1998), 216.

2. Joan Tronto, *Moral Boundaries: A Political Argument for an Ethic of Care* (New York: Routledge, 1994), 27.

3. Nel Noddings, *Caring: A Feminine Approach to Ethics and Moral Education* (Berkeley: University of California Press, 1984), 25.

4. Noddings, *Caring,* 26.

5. E. H. Schreur, "The Swine Crisis and the Church," *Perspectives* 15 (2000): 3.

6. Noddings, *Caring,* 96.

7. Patricia Hill Collins, *Fighting Words: Black Women and the Search for Justice,* Contradictions of Modernity, vol. 7 (Minneapolis: University of Minnesota Press, 1998), 188.

8. Collins, *Fighting Words,*189.

9. Collins, *Fighting Words,*190.

10. Noddings, *Caring,* 79-80.

11. Noddings, *Caring,* 80.

12. Rita Manning, *Speaking from the Heart: A Feminist Perspective on Ethics.* (Lanham, Md: Rowman & Littlefield, 1992), 66.

13. J. E. Ikerd, "Sustainable Agriculture, Rural Economic Development, and Large-Scale Swine Production," in *Pigs, Profits, and Rural Communities*, eds. K. M. Thu and E. P. Durrenberger (Albany: State University of New York Press, 1998), 157-69, 158.

14. Manning, *Speaking from the Heart,* 84.

15. Manning, *Speaking from the Heart,* 129.

16. Manning, *Speaking from the Heart,* 149.

17. Virginia Held, *Feminist Morality: Transforming Culture, Society, and Politics* (Chicago: The University of Chicago Press, 1993), 210.

18. Wes Jackson, *Altars of Unhewn Stone: Science and the Earth* (New York: North Point Press, 1987), 155.

INDEX

245

ABOUT THE AUTHORS

JANEL M. CURRY is dean for research and scholarship and professor of geography and environmental studies at Calvin College, Grand Rapids, Michigan. She has published in major geography and resource management journals in her areas of interest—rural geography and natural resource management. She is in the process of learning more about fisheries management, which will take her to Great Barrier Island, New Zealand, for a good part of 2002.

STEVEN MCGUIRE teaches peacemaking, cultural anthropology, and other courses in the Department of Sociology and Anthropology at Muskingum College in Ohio. He publications include several on the philosophy of science and on teaching that emphasizes active learning and creativity. He is presently working on the anthropology of peaceful societies and on environmental law. He serves as the president of the Association of Humanist Sociology.